UNDERSTANDING PEER INFLUENCE
IN CHILDREN AND ADOLESCENTS

Duke Series in Child Development and Public Policy

Kenneth A. Dodge and Martha Putallaz, *Editors*

Understanding Peer Influence in Children and Adolescents

Edited by
MITCHELL J. PRINSTEIN
KENNETH A. DODGE

THE GUILFORD PRESS
NEW YORK   LONDON

© 2008 The Guilford Press
A Division of Guilford Publications, Inc.
72 Spring Street, New York, NY 10012
www.guilford.com

Printed in the United States of America

This book is printed on acid-free paper.

Last digit is print number: 9   8   7   6   5   4   3   2

Library of Congress Cataloging-in-Publication Data

Understanding peer influence in children and adolescents / edited by Mitchell J.
Prinstein, Kenneth A. Dodge.
  p. cm.
  Includes bibliographical references and index.
  ISBN: 978-1-59385-397-6 (hardcover)
  1. Interpersonal relations in children. 2. Peer pressure in children. 3. Interpersonal
relations in adolescence. 4. Peer pressure in adolescence. I. Prinstein, Mitchell J.,
1970–   II. Dodge, Kenneth A.
  BF723.I646U53 2008
  303.3′27083—dc22

                                                                        2007043136

About the Editors

Mitchell J. Prinstein, PhD, is Associate Professor and Director of Clinical Psychology at the University of North Carolina at Chapel Hill. His research examines interpersonal models of internalizing symptoms and health-risk behaviors among adolescents, with a focus on the unique role of peer relationships in the developmental psychopathology of depression, self-injury, and suicidality. Currently an Associate Editor of the *Journal of Consulting and Clinical Psychology* and a member of the National Institutes of Health's Study Section on Psychosocial Development, Risk, and Prevention, Dr. Prinstein is a recipient of the Blau Early Career Award from the Society of Clinical Psychology of the American Psychological Association (APA). He is a Fellow of the APA Society of Clinical Child and Adolescent Psychology.

Kenneth A. Dodge, PhD, is the William McDougall Professor of Public Policy and Professor of Psychology and Neuroscience at Duke University, and Director of the Duke Center for Child and Family Policy. He is interested in how problem behaviors such as chronic violence, school failure, drug use, and child abuse develop across the lifespan; how they can be prevented; and how communities can implement policies to prevent these outcomes and promote children's optimal development. Dr. Dodge has been honored with the Distinguished Scientific Contribution Award from the APA; the Boyd McCandless Award from APA Division 7, Developmental Psychology; and the Senior Scientist Award from the National Institutes of Health.

Contributors

Joseph P. Allen, PhD, Department of Psychology, University of Virginia, Charlottesville, Virginia

Suzanne W. Ameringer, PhD, RN, School of Nursing, Virginia Commonwealth University, Richmond, Virginia

Jill Antonishak, PhD, U.S. Congress, Washington, DC

Jeremy P. Bakken, MS, Department of Educational Psychology, University of Wisconsin–Madison, Madison, Wisconsin

Jonah Berger, PhD, Department of Marketing, The Wharton School, University of Pennsylvania, Philadelphia, Pennsylvania

Hart Blanton, PhD, Department of Psychology, Texas A&M University, College Station, Texas

Mara Brendgen, PhD, Department of Psychology, University of Quebec, Montreal, Quebec, Canada

B. Bradford Brown, PhD, Department of Educational Psychology, University of Wisconsin–Madison, Madison, Wisconsin

William M. Bukowski, PhD, Department of Psychology and Centre for Research in Human Development, Concordia University, Montreal, Quebec, Canada

Melissa Burkley, PhD, Department of Psychology, Oklahoma State University, Stillwater, Oklahoma

Thomas J. Dishion, PhD, Child and Family Center and Departments of Psychology and School Psychology, University of Oregon, Eugene, Oregon

Kenneth A. Dodge, PhD, Center for Child and Family Policy, Duke University, Durham, North Carolina

Wyndol Furman, PhD, Department of Psychology, University of
Denver, Denver, Colorado

Adriana Galván, PhD, Department of Psychology, University of
California, Los Angeles, California

Meg Gerrard, PhD, Department of Psychology, Iowa State University,
Ames, Iowa

Frederick X. Gibbons, PhD, Department of Psychology, Iowa State
University, Ames, Iowa

Jaana Juvonen, PhD, Department of Psychology, University of
California, Los Angeles, California

Shelly D. Mahon, MS, Department of Human Development and
Family Studies, University of Wisconsin–Madison, Madison,
Wisconsin

Michael W. Myers, MS, Child and Family Center and Department of
Psychology, University of Oregon, Eugene, Oregon

Timothy F. Piehler, MS, Child and Family Center and Department of
Psychology, University of Oregon, Eugene, Oregon

Elizabeth A. Pomery, MS, Department of Psychology, Iowa State
University, Ames, Iowa

Deborah A. Prentice, PhD, Department of Psychology, Princeton
University, Princeton, New Jersey

Mitchell J. Prinstein, PhD, Department of Psychology, University of
North Carolina at Chapel Hill, Chapel Hill, North Carolina

Valerie A. Simon, PhD, Merrill Palmer Skillman Institute and
Department of Psychology, Wayne State University, Detroit,
Michigan

Ana Maria Velasquez, MA, Department of Psychology and Centre for
Research in Human Development, Concordia University,
Montreal, Quebec, Canada

Series Editors' Note

The Duke Series in Child Development and Public Policy aims to cross the chasms in our field. The goal of the series is to bring cutting-edge research and theory in the vibrant field of child development to bear on problems facing children and families in contemporary society. Although this kind of translational effort has become popular recently, it often falls short of its aspirations, because either the science is lacking or the policy world is not poised to utilize new findings. The success of the series depends on identifying important problems in public policy toward children and families at the time that researchers in child development have accumulated sufficient knowledge to contribute to a solution and policymakers are ready to utilize scientific information. The current volume, *Understanding Peer Influence in Children and Adolescents*, is well timed to have chasm-crossing impact.

This volume addresses a basic fact of life that has vexed parents, teachers, and authorities for centuries but which has become particularly salient in the 21st century: During adolescence, parents *lose* influence over their sons and daughters while peers *gain* influence. In a contemporary world filled with easy access to drugs, sex, and violence, the thought that peers might sway vulnerable minds and hearts frightens adults. Recent news that one in four American adolescent girls has a sexually transmitted disease and over half of American adolescents have tried illicit drugs brings home the realities that the current generation of youths faces in growing up. School teachers, community leaders, and parents are searching for ways to "protect" their children from the evil influences of . . . other parents' children.

This volume brings rigorous scientific analysis to the pervasiveness and process of peer influence. Some old myths are destroyed, and new insights are offered. Contributing authors report that peer influence is not always bad: Sometimes, peers influence youths toward positive life-course outcomes. And other authors report that influence is not uniform: Some youths are more vulnerable to influence by peers than are other youths, and some contexts elicit more influence than other contexts. And still other authors report what influence is all about: developing identity and one's place in the world.

The findings reported in this volume highlight what is still unknown and where further scientific inquiry is needed. The findings will also be helpful to psychologists and to policymakers who are charged with creating after-school programs and community organizations that will attract youth. They are important for school officials who need to decide whether to increase, or decrease, the number of middle school students who are retained in grade and placed with younger peers.

Each volume in the series has grown out of a national conference held at the Center for Child and Family Policy at Duke University. The conference held for this volume was a lively occasion, with contributions of cutting-edge syntheses of empirical research, challenges by public policymakers and practitioners, and vigorous debate by audience members. Participants across conferences have included nationally renowned scholars from multiple disciplines, officials in public service who are charged with improving the lives of families and children, and students who are learning how to integrate scholarship with service.

Reflecting the goal of intersecting basic psychological science with public policy, the series is a partnership between the Duke University Department of Psychology and Neuroscience and the Center for Child and Family Policy, with Series Editors Martha Putallaz and Kenneth Dodge anchoring these two groups, respectively. Each volume in the series also follows the model of an editorial partnership between a scholar at Duke University and a scholar at another university. This volume benefited enormously from the wisdom of Dr. Mitchell Prinstein, a psychologist at the University of North Carolina at Chapel Hill, who collaborated with one of the series editors from Duke, Kenneth Dodge.

This volume is the sixth in the series. The highly successful first volume addressed the growing problem of aggressive and delinquent behavior in girls. Although violent behavior rates have remained stable over the past decade, violence by girls has increased, to the dismay of public officials who are at a loss as to how as to prevent these problems or respond through placement and treatment. The second volume examined emerging interventions and policies to promote secure attachment relationships between parents and infants. Developmental neuroscience, clinical therapies, and ecological analysis of family life all point toward the first several years of life as a crucial time for intervention to promote secure relationships between an infant and his or her parents. The third volume addressed the state of African American families in the 21st century. A portrait of these families finds many strengths to celebrate but also challenges, ranging from the wealth gap to cultural uniqueness in parenting styles. The fourth volume assembled findings regarding the possibility that well-intentioned interventions and policies for deviant youth may actually bring harm by aggregating these youth in settings where they may push each other toward greater deviance. The fifth volume took a turn toward the concerns of families immigrating to this country by addressing the question, Why do some groups of foreign-born families experience better outcomes than others?

Like previous volumes, the current volume has benefited from financial support provided by the Duke Provost's Initiative in the Social Sciences. We are grateful to Duke Provost Peter Lange, PhD, and Duke Vice Provost Susan Roth, PhD. Conference organizer Erika Layko, Center for Child and Family Policy Associate Director Barbara Pollock, and staff manager extraordinaire Lynda Harrison made it happen.

KENNETH A. DODGE, PHD
MARTHA PUTALLAZ, PHD

Contents

PART I

INTRODUCTION

CHAPTER I

Current Issues in Peer Influence Research

Mitchell J. Prinstein *and* Kenneth A. Dodge

Perhaps one of the most consistent findings revealed in the social science literature pertains to the remarkably potent effects of peer influence. Indeed, developmental psychopathologists interested in identifying the developmental precursors to adolescents' health risk or aggressive behaviors, social psychologists aimed toward understanding the sources of influence on individuals' attitudes and behaviors, sociologists exploring whether individuals' attitudes may be nested within the attitudes of a larger group, and marketing researchers examining how popular ideas or behavioral practices enter the cultural zeitgeist of youth all have arrived upon a similar, and deceptively simple finding: There is a remarkably strong association between youths' behaviors and the behaviors of their peers.

This volume examines current theoretical and empirical evidence to understand the breadth of peer influence effects, as well as the mechanisms and moderators that may be targeted by prevention efforts to reduce susceptibility to peer influence. In this Introduction, we offer a brief summary of several pressing issues that has attracted recent attention of investigators in the field.

HOMOPHILY

Studies of peer influence effects, or of social processes that may facilitate them, have been ongoing for quite some time. A half-century ago, sociologists noted that social contact occurs at a higher rate among similar individuals than among dissimilar individuals, a phenomenon known as "homophily" (Lazarsfeld & Merton, 1954). A similar phenomenon has been identified by psychologists studying the behavior of adolescents in groups called "cliques" (Cairns, Cairns, Neckerman, Gest, & Gariepy, 1988; Dishion, Andrews, & Crosby, 1995). Desehields and Kara (2000), in their studies of peer influence in marketing, noted that the study of homophily in sociology paralleled the study of homogamy (similarity in marriage) in classical anthropology.

The two most prominent explanations for homophily are selection and socialization. *Selection effects* refer to the tendency of youth to affiliate with peers who exhibit similar attitudes or behaviors as themselves. This explanation has been heralded by Kandel (1978). It does not presume that individuals influence each other; rather, similar individuals are simply attracted to each other, an idea captured by the saying, "Birds of a feather flock together." Long ago, Plato (1968) wrote in his work *Phaedrus* that "similarity begets friendship" (p. 837). *Socialization effects* refer to the process by which youths' behavior may be affected by their affiliation with other peers. This explanation posits that initial dissimilarity among affiliates will grow into similarity over time through peer influence.

Since homophily theories were introduced, several hundred empirical investigations have examined processes of selection and/or socialization among different populations of youth, with respect to a wide variety of attitudes and behaviors. Although some equivocal findings have emerged, there now is fairly consistent evidence supporting selection and socialization effects for a wide variety of behaviors, including delinquency (Thornberry & Krohn, 1997); violence (Elliott & Menard, 1996); covert antisocial behavior (Keenan, Loeber, Zhang, Stouthamer-Loeber, & Van Kammen, 1995); early and high-risk sexual behavior (Dishion, 2000); substance use behaviors, including use of alcohol (Bosari & Carey, 2001), marijuana and "hard" drugs (Andrews, Tildesley, Hops, & Li, 2002; Dishion & Skaggs, 2000); weight-related behaviors (Christakis & Fowler, 2007; Paxton, Schutz, Wertheim, & Muir, 1999), self-injurious and suicidal behavior (Brent et al., 1993; Prinstein, Boergers, & Spirito, 2001), as well as internalizing symptoms, such as depression (Prinstein, 2007; Stevens & Prinstein, 2005). Recent evidence also has suggested similar selection and/or socialization effects for prosocial behaviors (e.g., volunteer work, academic activities, altruism), as well as health-promotive behaviors, such as exercise and fitness-related behaviors (Barry & Wentzel, 2006; Rancourt & Prinstein, 2006).

Over the past decade, studies have emerged to indicate that socialization effects reflecting peer influence also operate in intervention groups that bring together similar deviant youth for the purpose of treatment (Dishion, McCord, & Poulin, 1999). Harmful effects of being placed with deviant peers have been shown in juvenile justice (Lipsey, 2006), mental health (Dodge & Sherrill, 2006), education (Reinke & Walker, 2006), and after-school (Lansford, 2006) settings. These studies are methodologically powerful in demonstrating peer influence because of the random assignment of youth to peer groups. Furthermore, these studies highlight the fact that placement of a deviant youth with other deviant youth is the most common intervention in public policy toward these youth (Dodge, Lansford, & Dishion, 2006), costing more than $10 billion annually in the United States alone. The questions of whether peer influences operate to enhance social competence or exacerbate deviance, how homophily emerges, and the processes that catalyze selection and socialization effects are crucial ones for social science theory, clinical practice, and public policy.

GAPS IN KNOWLEDGE

Past work has offered a tremendous contribution by demonstrating the wide impact of peer influence effects on a variety of outcomes. Still, substantial work is required to understand selection and socialization phenomena more fully. For example, remarkably little is known regarding basic descriptive aspects of peer influence effects, including the behaviors that may be most salient for friendship selection, or most susceptible to socialization effects. More work is needed regarding developmental issues that may predispose youth to peer influence or the extent to which socialization effects endure over time. The bidirectional nature, or reciprocity, of peer influence effects between youth and their peers also has remained relatively underexplored, despite general acknowledgement that selection and socialization effects are due to sophisticated transactions between youth and multiple contextual factors.

Some gaps in prior work may be due, in part, to the lack of a consistent methodology in studies of peer influence. Perhaps most frequently noted within the literature is an overreliance on cross-sectional designs that severely limit the ability to distinguish selection and socialization effects. In addition, prior research has varied considerably, particularly across social science disciplines, in the manner in which "peers" are operationalized. In much research, *peers* refer to youths' best and closest friends. Typically, studies have examined a single dyadic relationship, or occasionally, multiple close friends identified by youth themselves. However, in other work, "peers" include interaction-based cliques of youth based on reciprocal nominations, members of the broader peer context who do not share a dyadic relationship with the target adolescent, members of reputation-based peer crowds (e.g., athletically oriented "jocks"; academically oriented "brains"; deviant "burnouts," etc.), or an undefined reference group of "peers" (i.e., others).

When examining selection or socialization effects, past research also has differed meaningfully in the assessment of youths' and their peers' behavior. In some work, youth are asked to report their own behavior as well as the behavior of their peers. This approach captures youths' perceptions of their peers' behavior, and shared method variance should be considered when interpreting the magnitude of selection or socialization effects. In other work, separate informants (e.g., youth and peers themselves) are asked to report their frequency of a relevant behavior, and associations between these independent reports are used as evidence of peer influence.

Information regarding the descriptive characteristics of peer influence, and methodological uniformity in the study of peer influence effects, will offer needed contributions from a basic science perspective. Ultimately, this information will prove useful for the development of prevention and intervention programs designed to mitigate the effects of peer influence on maladaptive behavior, or possibly to promote peer effects on healthful behavior. To date, an obvious strategy to reduce deleterious effects of peer influence has involved attempts to discourage potentially harmful friendship affiliations or to disaggregate groups of deviant peers. In the gang prevention domain, such attempts have been extremely difficult, with little evidence of positive effects based on an overall review (Klein, 2006) and occasional evidence that attempts to disrupt gang influence can actually amplify crime (Klein, 1995). Indeed, adolescents in particular may be sharply resistant toward attempts to modify their peer preferences and friendship choices, and attempts to do so can sometimes strengthen ties with their original choices.

FILLING THE GAPS

Fortunately, rigorous research on peer influence from diverse disciplines has proliferated in the past decade. This volume is organized around three research questions addressing the processes and mechanisms that apparently drive selection and socialization effects, factors that moderate, buffer, or exacerbate peer influences, and contexts in which the possibility of homophily effects has been underexplored. These are themes that may provide directions for more efficacious prevention and intervention strategies.

Peer Influence Mechanisms

The first section of this volume specifically examines mechanisms of peer influence. Multiple theories have been offered in the past to understand how and why youth emulate the behavior of their peers. For example, past research has suggested that youths may emulate the deviant behaviors of their closest friends following friends' verbal or nonverbal reinforcement of deviant utterances, a process known as deviancy training (Dishion, Poulin, & Burraston, 2001). Other theories suggest that conformity may be due to youths' interpretations of social norms. Conformity thus is due to a specific desire to be aligned with an admired group of peers, to help distance one's identity away from undesired peers, to adhere to presumed frequencies of behavior within a relevant reference group, or may be subsequent to the adoption of beliefs that are presumed to underlie the observed behaviors of others. Still other theories have suggested that peer affiliation enhances labeling by the self and others, which leads to self-fulfilling prophecies in behavior (Dishion & Dodge, 2006).

It may be that intervention efforts can provide an alternate avenue for addressing the underlying functions of peer influence, thereby reducing the drive to conform to peers. For example, social norms or identity-based theories of peer influence suggest that identity enhancement interventions may obviate the need youth to conform to their peers.

In this volume, Brown, Bakken, Ameringer, and Mahon (Chapter 2) provide a succinct history of research on peer influence, from Asch's (1951) laboratory studies of conformity through recent field studies of influence in real-world settings (Deković, Wissink, & Meijer, 2004). They then propose a comprehensive transactional model of peer influence that emphasizes life events and contexts that trigger influence in adolescence.

Gibbons, Pomery, and Gerrard (Chapter 3) examine social-cognitive mediators of peer influence effects. These investigators' work on the prototype-willingness model suggests that individuals' beliefs of others' engagement in behaviors, and individuals' perceptions of the rewards that may be associated with these behaviors, can contribute to the motivation to conform (Bandura, 1973; Fishbein & Ajzen, 1975; Fisher & Fisher, 1992). Specifically, motivations to engage in risk behavior may be especially high if the norms in question are associated with high-status or popular groups (Gerrard et al., 2002; Gibbons & Gerrard, 1997; Gibbons, Gerrard, Blanton, & Russell, 1998). In other words, individuals are likely to emulate not behaviors that match any social norms but specifically those behaviors that are associated with a group that individuals wish to join because of its social prestige.

Dishion, Piehler, and Myers (Chapter 4) expand on deviancy training models by offering and testing three new social interactional hypotheses of possible mechanisms: social augmentation, arrested socialization, and intrasubjectivity. Social augmentation suggests that deviant peer affiliation is a normal response to atypical family and school experiences. The arrested socialization hypothesis suggests that deviant peer affiliation impedes the development of specific skills that might have increased resistance to peer influence. Interactions within a deviant peer context may offer intrinsic reinforcement of deviant attitudes, values, and engagement in behaviors (i.e., intrasubjectivity hypothesis).

Finally, Blanton and Burkley (Chapter 5) propose deviance regulation theory to explain the apparent reinforcing effect of deviant behavior on oneself and one's peers. These authors argue that adolescents in particular struggle to establish an identity that conforms to the values of peers, but simultaneously differentiates from peers enough to maintain uniqueness. The deviance regulation theory suggests that the desire to establish and maintain a positive self-image primarily will dictate individuals' decisions either to conform to, or create distance from, "normative" attitudes and behaviors. Moreover, social norms are most relevant for influencing behavior if they are created or evaluated by a salient reference group. Thus, if a salient reference group conveys social norms regarding behaviors that are important to that groups' (or its members') identity, then individuals may feel intrinsically and extrinsically motivated to conform to these norms.

Altering Peer Influence Effects: Moderators and Interventions

The second theme of this volume pertains to the examination of factors that may alter youths' susceptibility to peer selection and socialization effects. These chapters include reviews for basic science research investigating factors that are associated with differences in peer influence susceptibility, as well as reviews of applied work that have attempted to manipulate the mechanisms that are thought to underlie peer influence effects.

Basic science research examining moderators of peer influence remain relatively rare, yet extant work has suggested many possible factors that increase susceptibility/resistance to peer influence. For example, past research has suggested that specific characteristics of youth (e.g., demographics, psychological symptoms, peer status), characteristics of peer influence prototypes (i.e., influencers), or variables that characterize the nature of the relationship between target youth and prototypes all may be relevant for changing the potency of peer influence effects. In sum, past results have suggested that susceptibility to peer influence may be due to two central factors. First, youth who are most likely to conform to peers include those who have some uncertainty regarding their self-concept or social identity (sometimes manifested as social anxiety, low self-esteem, etc.—Cohen & Prinstein, 2006; Prinstein, 2007). Uncertainty may be heightened especially during times of transition, including school transitions or opportunities for behavioral experimentation (e.g., transitioning from an experimenter to regular user of substances). Second, peer conformity appears to be especially likely when youth are in the presence of another who is of higher perceived status. This may be because the presence of a higher status peer promotes uncertainty or dissatisfaction regarding one's own status, or perhaps due to the perceived social rewards that are thought to be associated with emulation and affiliation to high-status peers.

Bukowski, Velasquez, and Brendgen (Chapter 6) offer a theory of peer influence moderators that is framed in terms of disequilibrium or discrepancy with regard to the self. They propose moderators at each of multiple levels of a complex social system. At the individual level, the desire for friendship and low self-esteem enhance susceptibility to peer influence effects. At the social group level, reinforcement and support provided by specific types of peers enhance influence. Finally, they propose that the strength of peer influence might vary as a function of characteristics of the culture.

Several prevention and intervention avenues also have been explored in attempts to modify peer influence processes. Allen and Antonishak (Chapter 7) propose that under some circumstances peer influence, and the susceptibility to being influenced by peers, may not be such a bad thing after all, especially during adolescence. They tie peer influence to attachment theory and argue that being socialized means being ready to be influenced by others as one navigates the social world. Allen and Antonishak argue that the best way to modify peer influence effects may be to change the values that adolescents communicate with one another. A recent outreach program developed by these authors offers preliminary evidence to support this principle.

Prentice (Chapter 8) reviews social norm and pluralistic ignorance theories, and how applications of these theories have been used to modify alcohol usage, particularly on college campuses. This research has involved attempts to change peer norms, to benevolently exploit peer infuence processes; the use of individualized, personal feedback regarding relevant social norms; as well as strategies that attempt to correct false assumptions regarding the motives that underlie others' engagement in risk behaviors.

Berger (Chapter 9) casts influence in terms of identity signaling. His work suggests that individuals will conform to specific values, or engage in particular behaviors so long as the behavior is uniquely associated with an identity that they wish to project. As the behavior is adopted by other groups, it loses its meaning as a signal of a desired identity. If the behavior is later adopted by those with an undesirable image, it will quickly be abandoned by those who initiated the behavior.

Peer Contexts

The final section of this volume pertains to the multiple peer contexts in which peer influence has been observed to occur. Evidence from past research suggests that youth likely are exposed to multiple messages regarding potential engagement in adaptive or maladaptive behaviors. These messages, communicated by friends, school peers, neighborhood peers, or romantic partners, for example, may be concordant or perhaps conflicting. Research understanding which peer contexts are most influential in affecting youths' behavior, or the processes by which youth may resolve conflicting messages, may offer an important opportunity for interventions. It may be that prevention or intervention messages can be framed in an effective manner by replicating these natural decision-making processes.

Furman and Simon (Chapter 10) suggest that in addition to the friendship context, peer influence may occur among adolescent romantic partners. They also emphasize contextual factors that trigger influence, such as the role that a romantic partner plays in social support for an adolescent.

Juvonen and Galván (Chapter 11) examine peer influence in another context, that of bullying and victim relationships in youth. They propose that influence effects can be interpreted in terms of social structure, norms, and personal motives.

CONCLUSION

This volume offers a summary of research from leading investigators examining peer influence mechanisms, moderators, and contexts. We hope that this volume will help to encourage additional research on peer influence, multidisciplinary investigations, and an enhanced understanding of these powerful phenomena. The implications of this work are substantial and can have potentially wide-reaching effects of policy.

REFERENCES

Andrews, J. A., Tildesley, E., Hops, H., & Li, F. (2002). The influence of peers on young adult substance use. *Health Psychology, 21,* 349–357.

Asch, S. E. (1951). Effects of group pressure upon the modification and distortion of judgments. In H. Guetzkow (Ed.), *Groups, leadership, and men* (pp. 177–190). Oxford, UK: Carnegie Press.

Bandura, A. (1973). *Aggression: A social learning analysis.* Englewood Cliffs, NJ: Prentice Hall.

Barry, C. M., & Wentzel, K. R. (2006). Friend influence on prosocial behavior: The role of motivational factors and friend influence. *Developmental Psychology, 42,* 153–163.

Bosari, B., & Carey, K. B. (2001). Peer influences on college drinking: A review of the research. *Journal of Substance Abuse, 13,* 391–424.

Brent, D. A., Pepper, J. A., Moritz, G., Allman, C., Schweers, J., Roth, C., et al. (1993). Psychiatric sequelae to the loss of an adolescent peer to suicide. *Journal of the American Academy of Child and Adolescent Psychiatry, 32,* 509–517.

Cairns, R., Cairns, B., Neckerman, H., Gest, S., & Gariepy, J. (1988). Social networks and aggressive behavior: Peer support or peer rejection. *Developmental Psychology, 24,* 815–823.

Christakis, N. A., & Fowler, J. H. (2007). The spread of obesity in a large social network over 32 years. *New England Journal of Medicine, 357,* 370–379.

Cohen, G. L., & Prinstein, M. J. (2006). Peer contagion of aggression and health-risk behavior among adolescent males: An experimental investigation of effects on public conduct and private attitudes. *Child Development, 77,* 967–983.

Deković, M., Wissink, I. B., & Meijer, A. M. (2004). The role of family and peer relations in adolescent antisocial behavior: Comparison of four ethnic groups. *Journal of Adolescence, 27,* 497–514

DeShields, O. W., & Kara, A. (2000). Homphily effects in advertising communication moderated by spokesperson's credibility. *Sociometry, 37,* 315–325.

Dishion, T. (2000). Cross-setting consistency in early adolescent psychopathology: Deviant friendships and problem behavior sequelae. *Journal of Personality, 68,* 1109–1126.

Dishion, T., Andrews, D., & Crosby, L. (1995). Antisocial boys and their friends in early adolescence: Relationship characteristics, quality and interactional process. *Child Development, 66,* 139–151.

Dishion, T. J., & Dodge, K. A. (2006). Deviant peer contagion in interventions and programs: An ecological framework for understanding influence mechanisms. In K. A. Dodge, T. J. Dishion, & J. E. Lansford (Eds.), *Deviant peer influences in programs for youth: Problems and solutions* (pp. 14–43). New York: Guilford Press.

Dishion, T., McCord, J., & Poulin, F. (1999). When interventions harm: Peer groups and problem behavior. *American Psychologist, 54,* 755–764.

Dishion, T. J., Poulin, F., & Burraston, B. (2001). Peer group dynamics associated with iatrogenic effects in group interventions with high-risk young adolescents. In C. Erdley & D. W. Nangle (Eds.), *Damon's new directions in child development: The role of friendship in psychological adjustment* (pp. 79–92). San Francisco: Jossey-Bass.

Dishion, T., & Skaggs, N. (2000). An ecological analysis of monthly "bursts" in early adolescent substance use. *Applied Developmental Science, 4,* 89–97.

Dodge, K. A., & Sherrill, M. R. (2006). Deviant peer group effects in youth mental health interventions. In K. A. Dodge, T. J. Dishion, & J. E. Lansford (Eds.), *Deviant peer influences in programs for youth: Problems and solutions* (pp. 97–121). New York: Guilford Press.

Dodge, K. A., Lansford, J. E., & Dishion, T. J. (2006). The problem of deviant peer influences in intervention programs. In K. A. Dodge, T. J. Dishion, & J. E. Lansford

(Eds.), *Deviant peer influences in programs for youth: Problems and solutions* (pp. 3–13). New York: Guilford Press.

Elliott, D., & Menard, S. (1996). Delinquent friends and delinquent behavior: Temporal and developmental patterns. In J. D. Hawkins (Ed.), *Delinquency and crime: Current theories* (pp. 28–67). New York: Cambridge University Press.

Fishbein, M., & Azjen, I. (1975). *Belief, attitude, intention, and behavior: An introduction to theory and research.* Reading, MA: Addison-Wesley.

Fisher, J. D., & Fisher, W. A. (1992). Changing AIDS-risk behavior. *Psychological Bulletin, 111,* 455–474.

Gerrard, M., Gibbons, F. X., Reis-Bergan, M., Trudeau, L., Vande Lune, L. S., & Buunk, B. (2002). Inhibitory effects of drinker and nondrinker prototypes on adolescent alcohol consumption. *Health Psychology, 21,* 601–609.

Gibbons, F. X., & Gerrard, M. (1997). Predicting young adults' health risk behavior. *Journal of Personality and Social Psychology, 69,* 505–517.

Gibbons, F. X., Gerrard, M., Blanton, H., & Russell, D. W. (1998). Reasoned action and social reaction: Willingness and intention as independent predictors of health risk. *Journal of Personality and Social Psychology, 74,* 1164–1180.

Kandel, D. B. (1978). Homophily, selection and socialization in adolescent friendships. *American Journal of Sociology, 84,* 427–436.

Keenan, K., Loeber, R., Zhang, Q., Stouthamer-Loeber, M., & Van Kammen, W. (1995). The influence of deviant peers on the development of boys' disruptive and delinquent behavior: A temporal analysis. *Development and Psychopathology, 7,* 715–726.

Klein, M. W. (2006). Peer effects in naturally occurring groups: The case of street gangs. In K. A. Dodge, T. J. Dishion, & J. E. Lansford (Eds.), *Deviant peer influences in programs for youth: Problems and solutions* (pp. 234–250). New York: Guilford Press.

Klein, M. W. (1995). *The American street gang: Its nature, prevalence, and control.* New York: Oxford University Press.

Lansford, J. E. (2006). Peer effects in community programs. In K. A. Dodge, T. J. Dishion, & J. E. Lansford (Eds.), *Deviant peer influences in programs for youth: Problems and solutions* (pp. 215–233). New York: Guilford Press.

Lazarsfeld, P., & Merton, R. K. (1954). Friendship as a social process: A substantive and methodological analysis in freedom and control in modern society. In M. Berger, T. Abel, & C. H. Page (Eds.), *Freedom and control in modern society* (pp. 18–66). New York: Van Nostrand.

Lipsey, M. W. (2006). The effects of community-based group treatment for delinquency: A meta-analytic search for cross-study generalizations. In K. A. Dodge, T. J. Dishion, & J. E. Lansford (Eds.), *Deviant peer influences in programs for youth: Problems and solutions* (pp. 162–184). New York: Guilford Press.

Paxton, S. J., Schutz, H. K., Wertheim, E. H., & Muir, S. L. (1999). Friendship clique and peer influences on body image concerns, dietary restraint, extreme weight-loss behaviors, and binge eating in adolescent girls. *Journal of Abnormal Psychology, 108,* 255–266.

Plato. (1968). *Laws. Plato in twelve volumes* (Vol. 11). Cambridge, MA: Harvard University Press.

Prinstein, M. J. (2007). Moderators of peer contagion: A longitudinal examination of depression socialization between adolescents and their best friends. *Journal of Clinical Child and Adolescent Psychology, 36,* 159–170.

Prinstein, M. J., Boergers, J., & Spirito, A. (2001). Adolescents' and their friends' health-risk behavior: Factors that alter or add to peer influence. *Journal of Pediatric Psychology, 26,* 287–298.

Rancourt, D., & Prinstein, M. J. (2006, November). *Peer contagion of adolescent girls' body dissatisfaction and weight-related concerns.* Chicago: Association for Behavioral and Cognitive Therapies.

Reinke, W. M., & Walker, H. M. (2006). Deviant peer effects in education. In K. A. Dodge, T. J. Dishion, & J. E. Lansford (Eds.), *Deviant peer influences in programs for youth: Problems and solutions* (pp. 122–140). New York: Guilford Press.

Stevens, E. A., & Prinstein, M. J. (2005). Peer contagion of depressogenic attributional styles among adolescents: A longitudinal study. *Journal of Abnormal Child Psychology, 33,* 25–37.

Thornberry, T., & Krohn, M. (1997). Peers, drug use, and delinquency. In D. Stoff, J. Breiling, & J. Maser (Eds.), *Handbook of antisocial behavior* (pp. 218–233). New York: Wiley.

PART II

PEER INFLUENCE
MECHANISMS

CHAPTER 2

A Comprehensive Conceptualization of the Peer Influence Process in Adolescence

B. Bradford Brown, Jeremy P. Bakken,
Suzanne W. Ameringer, *and* Shelly D. Mahon

One of the most prominent concerns that American adults express about adolescence as a life stage is the power of peer influence. Journalists who have immersed themselves in the adolescent social world and practitioners working with troubled youth point to the preeminence of peer relations and the challenges they pose for mental health of male and female teenagers (Gurian, 1998; Hersch, 1998; Perlstein, 2003; Pipher, 1994). Researchers report that one of the strongest predictors of adolescent delinquency is the delinquency level of close friends (Elliott, Huizinga, & Ageton, 1985). Peers also seem to contribute to health-compromising behaviors such as drug use or risky sexual activity (Hawkins, Catalano, & Miller, 1992; Kandel, 1985; Rodgers & Rowe, 1993). Such findings have sparked considerable interest in prevention and intervention programs that can thwart the ability of peers to lead children and adolescents into problem behavior. To ward off the undesirable influences of peers, it seems imperative to know how these influences operate. Surprisingly few studies, however, have focused on the specific processes by which peers affect individual behavior in adolescence.

The failure to scrutinize the peer influence process has not deterred researchers or practitioners from making assumptions or assertions about how it works. *Peer pressure* is the most common term used to describe the mechanism of influence. Although operationalized in a variety of ways, the term carries a connotation of youth being cajoled or coerced into some behavior by peers. Careful examination of peer dynamics quickly reveals that such pressure is not the primary mode of peer influence (Michell & West, 1996; Urberg, Shyu, & Liang, 1990). More recently, *peer contagion* has emerged as a popular term among researchers (Dishion & Dodge, 2005). Meant to capture the more indirect form that peer influence often takes, it still carries a negative connotation, as if the influence were some sort of disease that one catches by being in close proximity to peers. Both terms reflect the inclination to regard peer influence as an undesirable and unhealthy feature of adolescent development and social interaction. Indeed, the vast majority of studies that address peer influence focus on delinquent, deviant, or health-compromising behavior.

More careful examination of studies related to peer influence reveals three important things. First, peer influence is multidirectional; it is capable of encouraging healthy as well as harmful behavior. Second, it is multidimensional; peer influence operates in a variety of ways that are not equally well documented. Third, peer influence is a complex process that, at present, is not well understood (Hartup, 2005)—partly because there has been more emphasis on the outcomes than the process of influence, but also because there has been too little effort to connect the vast and divergent literature. In this chapter we briefly review past efforts to assess adolescent peer influences, highlighting major shortcomings of previous research. Then, based on a set of principles that we believe underlies the peer influence process in adolescence, we present a new model of this process, illustrating its major components through references to current studies in the area. All model components have been mentioned by other investigators over the years, but no one has gathered them into a comprehensive portrait of the peer influence process. In the model we acknowledge the potential for peers to encourage positive as well as problematic behavior. We end by suggesting how the model could guide future research.

EARLY STUDIES OF PEER INFLUENCE

Several theories emerged in the middle of the 20th century that assigned peers a central and generally positive role in adolescent development. Theorists emphasized how peers helped a young person to co-construct a social cognitive understanding of the social world (Piaget, 1950; Youniss, 1980), explore identity (Erikson, 1968), or navigate a succession of relationships to prepare for adult heterosexual ties (Sullivan,

1953). The positive contributions of peers envisioned by these theorists are a surprising contrast to much of the contemporaneous empirical research on peer influence, which focused on the capacity of young people to be led astray by peers.

Empirical Approaches and Objectives

Over the past 50 years, scholars have employed a variety of research strategies to chart the magnitude of effects that peers have on young people or the conditions under which such effects are apparent. Much of this work can be collapsed into four basic approaches, each of which features different objectives and perspectives on peer influence or individual conformity.

Laboratory Studies of Conformity

In a series of experimental laboratory studies following a format laid out by Solomon Asch (1951), a number of investigators explored the tendency for various groups of respondents to follow the misjudgments of peers. The most classic of these studies involved judging the length of lines, but investigators used numerous stimuli varying in the degree to which the right answer was unambiguous. At issue was whether or not participants who had shown a capacity to make accurate judgments would nevertheless select an inaccurate response if it was consistently endorsed by peers (who had been recruited as confederates into the experiment). Situational and individual factors affected respondents' conformity. Individuals were more likely to follow the opinions of friends than acquaintances or unknown peers and were most easily persuaded when the correct answer was ambiguous and/or when it was clear that peers would know their responses (Deutsch & Gerard, 1955). Conformity also tended to be greater among first-born than later-born children (Becker, Lerner, & Carroll, 1966) and individuals who had weak self-images (Costanzo, 1970). Age differences were inconsistent across studies (see Costanzo & Shaw, 1966; Hoving, Hamm, & Galvin, 1969; Iscoe, Williams, & Harvey, 1963), but there appeared to be either a decrease in conformity from childhood through adolescence (especially when the stimuli were unambiguous) or a peak in conformity during early to midadolescence (especially when stimuli were ambiguous).

Cross-Pressure Studies

Complementing these laboratory studies of conformity behavior were investigations of conformity dispositions, based on individuals' responses to hypothetical dilemmas. Some of these involved situations in which the protagonist received conflicting advice from parents and peers; respondents were asked what advice the protagonist would or should follow (Brittain, 1963; Larson, 1974; Sebald & White, 1980). In some cases (e.g., Brittain, 1963) the investigators used clever devices to mask the focus on parent–peer cross-pressures, but all of these studies still reflected an assumption that parents and peers routinely offer young people opposing advice. To many people's surprise, adolescents were more inclined to make decisions about what the protagonist should do based on the content of alternative courses of action rather than on which reference group (parents or peers) had recommended that alternative. However, youth did appear to be more receptive to peers' opinions in dilemmas involving present-oriented, social issues; they paid more attention to parents in dilemmas with serious or long-range consequences. In other words, the strength of conformity dispositions, as well as the source of influence to which adolescents attended, varied by situation.

Assessments of Susceptibility to Peer Influence

Another set of studies dealing with conformity dispositions posed situations in which friends or other peers encouraged an activity in which respondents, hypothetically, were reluctant to engage. Respondents rated the likelihood that they would join peers in the activity; this was interpreted as an indicator of an individual's susceptibility to peer influence. The most widely cited of these studies (Berndt, 1979) contained separate scales for prosocial, antisocial, and "neutral" events (focusing on social activities with friends); the investigator also controlled for how wrong the respondent thought it would be to engage in each activity included in the antisocial scale.

A fairly consistent pattern of age and sex differences emerged across these studies, with investigators reporting an inverted U-shaped age trend in susceptibility, peaking in early adolescence and more pronounced for antisocial than neutral or prosocial peer pressures (Berndt, 1979; Bixenstine, DeCorte, & Bixenstine, 1976; Brown, Clasen, & Eicher, 1986). Susceptibility to antisocial peer influences usually was significantly higher among boys than girls. Some scholars examined antecedents of susceptibility, such as poor parental monitoring (Steinberg & Silverberg, 1986); others focused on its consequences, such as higher rates of antisocial behavior (Brown et al., 1986). These studies warned of the dangers of antisocial peer influences even though, in most cases, they failed to measure the type or magnitude of influence (but see Allen, Porter, & McFarland, 2006; Brown et al., 1986).

Inferred Influence Studies

The final set of studies considered the effects of peer influence in "real-life" situations. The most common approach to demonstrating influence has been to chart the strength of association between a measure of peer behavior and an indicator of the target individual's behavior. Simplistic examples of these reports feature correlations between a self-reported outcome and self's assessment of peers on the outcome, each measured at a single time point (e.g., Deković, Wissink, & Meijer, 2004; Pruitt, Kingery, & Mirzaee, 1991; see Bauman & Ennett, 1996, for a review of problems with such studies). More sophisticated studies involve multiple time points and independent measures of self- and peer behavior, so that investigators can calculate the degree to which an adolescent's "follow-up" score on a given behavior is predicted by the baseline peer score on the same or a related measure, controlling for the adolescent's baseline score on the behavior and any other possible confounding variables (e.g., Aseltine, 1995; Ennet & Bauman, 1994). Researchers inferred that the degree of association between self's and peer behavior was the result of peer influence. There is a reasonable basis for this inference in the more sophisticated studies, but they still provide no information about the means by which peers exerted influence.

Shortcomings

None of these sets of studies focused directly on the process of peer influences. In fact, the first three were oriented toward quite different issues—either the features of the influence situation or characteristics of the individual being influenced. Yet each set harbors implicit assumptions about the influence process that researchers have yet to adequately explore. In their laboratory experiments, Asch and his followers assumed that influence was exerted indirectly, by setting a consistent example for others to follow. Cross-pressure studies presumed a more direct mode of influence, namely, giving advice about how to respond in a specific situation. Investigations based on hypothetical scenarios tended to represent peer influence as even more overt pressure, directing an individual how to behave even if the person expressed an inclination against the behavior. Inferred influence studies concentrated more directly on influence per se, but without specifying the nature of peers' behavior. The fact that peers exerted influence was important to these investigators, but the ways in which influence was expressed was not important. Added to other distinctions among the studies, these fundamental differences in perspectives on processes of peer influence make it difficult to compare findings across the four sets of investigations.

The value of findings emanating from these studies is tempered by several other shortcomings. In most cases, investigators gathered data at only a single time point. This is particularly problematic for inferred influence studies because investigators cannot differentiate selection from socialization effects (Jaccard, Blanton, & Dodge, 2005; Kandel, 1978). They cannot determine how much of the similarity observed between an individual and his or her peers stems from the person seeking out like-minded peers, rather than changing to conform more closely to peers. Even in the laboratory studies, a single evaluation raises concerns about the reliability of conformity observations. Would the target display the same degree of conformity with a different set of peers, or on a different task?

Many of the inferred influence studies relied on respondents to report not only their own behavior but also that of their friends or peers. Such data yield overestimates of peer influence because young people are inclined to exaggerate the degree of similarity between self and others (Kandel, 1985; Urberg et al., 1990).

Within each of the different types of investigation there has been virtually no effort to vary the form in which peer influence is manifest. In susceptibility studies, for example, hypothetical dilemmas could vary in whether peers simply displayed a certain behavior, advised the protagonist to follow suit, or pressured the protagonist more directly. Laboratory-based conformity studies could vary the stimulus situation, such that confederates occasionally ridiculed a target for failing to endorse their answer, rather than consistently offering no response to the target's action. Systematic variation of the mode of influence would not only obviate the confound between type of investigation and the way that influence is portrayed but also allow investigators to assess the degree to which individuals' response to peer influence depends on the way it is manifested.

We suspect that many authors of inferred influence studies would argue that the mode of influence is a trivial issue. Ethnographic accounts of adolescent peer dynamics undermine this argument. Several investigators describe how peers shift strategies to alter an individual's behavior if early efforts at influence are unsuccessful (Adler & Adler, 1998; Dunphy, 1963; MacLeod, 1995). A careful reading of these accounts also suggests that adolescents employ different influence strategies—or apply a strategy with different intensity—when attempting to influence friends as opposed to acquaintances, disliked peers, or individuals attempting to enter their group (Adler & Adler, 1998; Eckert, 1989; Fine, 1987; Merten, 1996). These observations suggest that different modes of influence are not necessarily equivalent in their power or purpose. Some quantitative studies do examine the comparative effects of multiple modes of influence (e.g., Vincent & McCabe, 2000; Wood, Read, & Mitchell, 2004), but there is little systematic work on the strategies underlying adolescents' use of various modes.

BASIC PRINCIPLES OF PEER INFLUENCE

To achieve a clear understanding of the peer influence process, researchers will need to address these and other shortcomings of existing studies. In doing so, they should be more mindful of some basic principles of peer influence that, over the years, researchers have discovered or debated in their work. We list 12 basic principles that can guide the formulation of a more comprehensive conceptual model for future studies.

1. *Peer influence is purposive behavior.* Researchers have focused nearly all of their attention on features of the influence situation, characteristics of the target of influence, or consequences of influence for the target. Some have considered who is engaging in influence (e.g., whether it is a close friend or a group of acquaintances), but rarely have they asked why someone would do so. Motivations for generating or responding to influence constitute a largely neglected component of the peer influence process, but they may be central to understanding adolescents' behavior in these situations. From our review of the literature we perceive a variety of motives for influencing others. The most obvious involves "normative regulation" (see, especially, Deutsch & Gerard, 1955; Eder, 1995): defining, clarifying, and maintaining or enforcing the norms of a dyadic relationship or a group. Other motives include "relationship development," or an effort to enhance important features of a close relationship (Lightfoot, 1997), and "self-enhancement," trying to advance one's own status or position among peers. Adler and Adler (1998) and Wiseman (2002) describe how group leaders sometimes try to manipulate the attitudes or behavior of other group members to ward off threats to their dominant position in the group. "Other enhancement," or acting in the best interest of the person being influenced, constitutes another, less frequently acknowledged motive for influencing peers. Close friends may pressure an adolescent into trying out for an activity if they think the person has a gift for the activity, or they may encourage the adolescent to spend more time with someone whom they think would make a good romantic match.

Just as there are motives to initiate influence, there are motivations for acceding to or rejecting the effort at influence. We do not have the space to consider these in detail, but it is important to acknowledge that motivations of the initiator and target of influence do not necessarily correspond to each other. Someone may respond to group efforts at normative regulation to enhance her or his position in the group, rather than out of a concern for the maintenance of group norms. The mix and match of motivations may be a key factor in how the influence process unfolds over time.

2. *There are multiple modes of peer influence.* Although it is typically regarded as a singular entity, peer influence actually encompasses a constellation of distinct behaviors. The most widely recognized is "peer pressure," which involves direct attempts to effect certain attitudes or behaviors in another person or group. Although usually cast in a negative light and understood as an effort to impose undesired attitudes or behavior on someone, it can also refer to more constructive efforts such as encouragement or cheering someone on to healthy, self-enhancing activities.

Probably a more common form of peer influence is "behavioral display." It is a basic component of social learning theory, in which someone displays the attitude or behavior that is desired of other people, and these others model the behavior as a manifestation of peer influence (Bandura & Walters, 1963). Dunphy (1963) described how other-sex interactions of clique leaders served as an example for other clique members to follow, allowing cliques to evolve from single-sex to mixed-sex groups. In a study of Canadian immigrant youth, Zine (2001) found that older adolescents served as role models for younger peers, demonstrating how they could retain their Muslim cultural identity in the face of peer pressure to conform to dominant cultural norms.

"Antagonistic behaviors" constitute a third mode of influence. They range from playful teasing, which is especially useful in normative regulation (Eder, 1991), to ridicule (Lashbrook, 2000) to more aggressive behavior such as bullying, threatening, or relational aggression (Cillessen & Mayeux, 2004; Merten, 1996). In its more strident forms, antagonistic behavior seems to mimic peer pressure, but the belittlement or intimidation that is characteristic of this behavior is not accompanied by demands for or encouragement of specific attitudes or actions, as is the case for peer pressure.

Two less frequently acknowledged modes of peer influence are "behavioral reinforcement" and "structuring opportunities." The latter involves the creation of a situation that facilitates certain behavior without necessarily imposing or encouraging it. When a teenager invites peers to an unchaperoned party, for example, the young person may not consciously intend to encourage the peers to experiment with alcohol or sexual activity, but the party guests may find such activities easier to engage in than had they not been included on the party list. *Behavioral reinforcement* refers to efforts to encourage or reward activities in which a target is already engaging. Granic and Dishion (2003) found that conversations between friends about deviant activities were longer if one friend gave verbal or nonverbal cues of interest in and agreement with the other's statements. Moreover, duration of such conversations predicted participants' level of deviant activity 3 years later.

One challenging feature of peer influence is that the same peer behavior may constitute a different mode of influence for different individuals. Someone who is the target of bullying by a group of classmates will experience the episode as antagonistic behavior, whereas for an uninvolved bystander the bullying will serve as an instance of behavioral display. For some bystanders, witnessing how bullying is accomplished will encourage them to later model the behavior when they have an opportunity to antagonize a classmate. Other witnesses may focus on how bullying affects the victim and later take action to guard against becoming a victim. Merten (1996) describes these dynamics among a sample of middle school youth. After one boy antagonizes a member of the "mel" crowd, his cliquemates who observe the event later take their own turns teasing the mel, whereas other mels endeavor to avoid the clique and even avoid contact with their fellow mel who has been victimized, to avert becoming a target of the group's bullying.

Although researchers are aware of these varying forms of peer influence there has been little effort to catalog the circumstances under which each is used or to compare their effects (see Graham, Marks, & Hansen, 1991, for an exception). There may even be a hierarchy of strategies in which some modes are considered more forceful or intrusive than others (Michell & West, 1996). It is noteworthy that none of the modes seems inherently and exclusively oriented toward promoting undesirable, antisocial or desirable, socially acceptable behavior.

3. *Peer influence can be direct or diffuse, intentional or unintentional.* Given that peer influence is purposive behavior, one would expect that it would be consciously directed toward a specific target. Although this is often the case, it is not necessarily always the case. Eckert (1989) described the social system in one high school that featured two dominant groups embroiled in an oppositional relationship: norms that one group embraced, the other group eschewed. When a leader of the "jock" crowd in this school sported a new clothing style, many of her fellow jocks would rush out to buy similar clothing. At the same time, Eckert observed, this new look would immediately be dismissed and derided by the opposing group, the "burnouts." Whereas the leader probably expected to have a direct influence on her own clique of jocks, she may not have anticipated that her influence would extend more diffusely to burnouts, in general. Much of peer influence can be overlooked if researchers concentrate solely on direct and intentional efforts to affect an individual's attitudes or behavior.

4. *Multiple peer influences operate simultaneously or contemporaneously.* This is the first of two principles that make peer influence especially challenging to investigate. Research studies, understandably, portray peer influence as a singular, monolithic force. In experiments using some form of the Asch technique, all confederates endorse the same incorrect answer on experimental trials. All peers referred to in hypothetical dilemmas provide the same advice or urge participation in the same activity. Such consistency is vital to the integrity of experimental or statistical manipulations inherent in these studies. In real life, however, peers are unlikely to speak with such unanimity. Robin and Johnson (1996) found that, when given the opportunity, adolescents acknowledged pressure from peers toward and against use of various drugs. Pressure in each direction, alone and in combination, were significantly associated with use patterns, but to different degrees for various substances.

Contradictory peer influences are especially common among immigrant youth, whose home cultural norms differ sharply from those of the dominant group in their new society. Zine (2001), for example, described how Muslim immigrants in Canada confronted contradictory pressures from Muslim peers and the broader network of agemates in their schools. Of course, there are also cases in which adolescents experience multiple instances of peer influence, all of which offer the same message about how they should act. In fact, consistency of peer influence across multiple relationships is an important predictor of problem behavior such as tobacco or other drug use (Jaccard et al., 2005).

The challenge for adolescents is not simply to respond to each of these influences as it is encountered but to anticipate them and modulate them into a coordinated response. Likewise, the challenge for researchers is to derive a method for measuring the consistency of peer influence, then understanding how adolescents sort through multiple and often-contradictory influences in determining an appropriate course of action.

5. *Peer influence is a reciprocal, transactional process.* For the sake of research design and statistical analyses, investigators tend to establish one person as the target of peer influence and others as the source of influence. Thus, they portray peer influence as a linear process. Upon closer examination, however, one realizes that the response to peer influence, more often than not, is itself a peer influence. If one teenager says to a friend, "Hey, I bet you don't have the guts to take this corner at 65 MPH," and the friend retorts, "Hey, I bet you don't have the intelligence to actually *get* a drivers license!," who is actually influencing whom? When a group presses one of its members to conform to a group norm and the member refuses, that refusal can be seen as a member's effort to get the rest of the group to drop or change the norm. Thus, a proper analysis of peer influence should consider not only the effect of an initia-

tor of influence on a target but also the effect of the target's response on the initiator.

Currently, there are few effective methodological models for engaging in transactional analyses. Some investigators have used dynamic systems theory to chart the behavior of two or more individuals over time, examining whether or not their joint behavior is predictive of individual outcomes (e.g., Granic & Dishion, 2003). Typically, however, this approach is not well suited to differentiating relative levels of influence among individuals who are part of the group that serves as a unit of analysis. Sequential analyses of social interchanges would permit investigators to trace the "give and take" of influence between two individuals or between an adolescent and a group of peers. The foreboding challenges of these approaches have driven most researchers to rely on more linear models, despite their shortcomings in representing the reciprocal nature of peer influence.

6. *Peer influence is contingent on openness to influence.* A basic principle of social learning theory is that individuals cannot model an exemplar's behavior if they fail to attend to it (Bandura & Walters, 1963). Applied to peer influence, this serves as an important reminder that peer attitudes or behaviors are not automatically sources of influence on individuals (as is often presumed in inferred influence studies). There must be some evidence that an individual actually perceives the peer behavior and recognizes it as a source of influence. Sarcastic remarks from cliquemates won't affect an adolescent unless he or she actually hears them and recognizes the sarcastic tone and its underlying intent. Likewise, clique members in Dunphy's (1963) study could not benefit from the lessons in cross-sex interaction that their leaders tried to provide for them if the members failed to watch and listen to leaders when they interacted with the other sex.

Beyond basic attentional processes, openness to influence also concerns dispositions. The dispositional aspect of openness to influence constitutes the central construct in many research studies, typically referred to either as "conformity disposition" or "susceptibility" to peer pressure (Berndt, 1979; Brown et al., 1986; Sim & Koh, 2003; Steinberg & Silverberg, 1986). As already mentioned, most of these studies have focused either on factors associated with the level of susceptibility an individual displays or with the consequences of susceptibility for subsequent behavior. For example, several recent peer studies have identified youth with an unusually high openness to peer influence, often referred to as "extreme peer orientation" (Fuligni, Eccles, Barber, & Clements, 2001; Goldstein, Davis-Kean, & Eccles, 2005; Kiesner, Cadinu, Poulin, & Bucci, 2002). By definition, these youth are so focused on peers that they are willing to eschew adult-approved norms or endanger the quality of their relationships with adults to retain their standing among peers. Investigators have found that these youth are more likely to engage in health-compromising behaviors, presumably because of peer influence. However, it is not clear that these youth confront more influence from peers, accede to such influence more readily, or simply lack the balance between peer and adult influences that might lead to a less problematic pattern of behavior. More careful research is required to understand how openness to influence moderates associations between influence exposure and adolescent behavior.

7. *The impact of peer influence depends on the salience of those exerting influence.* Over the course of an average day, most adolescents encounter a variety of peers in a number of different settings. Each of these encounters has the potential of creating peer influence, but many of the interactions have no discernible impact on the individual, even if the person is cognizant of the peer behaviors and, by disposition, generally receptive to influence. One factor determining whether peer encounters will be transformed into influence episodes is the salience of peers to the target individual. In essence, the issue is whether or not particular peers are worthy of one's attention. One would expect adolescents to accede to peer influence emanating from admired associates whom they wish to emulate more often than from peers who don't really matter to them.

Investigators commonly assume that adolescents are more receptive to influence from close friends than from other associates. As a result, cross-pressure studies, research based on hypothetical dilemmas, and inferred influence investigations typically target close friends as the influencing agent. This focus on friends could lead to underestimates of influence if other highly salient groups are overlooked. For example, researchers give comparatively little attention to the effects of peers who are highly admired but not (yet) close friends, as well as peers who are actively disliked and avoided, despite some intriguing evidence of the salience of these groups. In her ethnographic study of youth in one high school, Eckert (1989) discovered that jocks and burnouts disliked and disparaged each other yet had a strong impact on one another's values and activities by virtue of their conscientious effort to avoid any appearance of affinity for the outgroup. In a recent experimental study, Cohen and Prinstein (2006) demonstrated that adolescents of moderate peer social status were likely to accede to the opinions of peers whom they thought were high in social status and distance themselves from peers who appeared to be low in status, even when none of these peers was a close friend.

8. *Relationship dynamics also affect the capacity of particular peers to influence an adolescent.* In addition to the salience of peer asso-

ciates, investigators of peer influence need to consider how the nature of the relationship that an adolescent has with peers will affect patterns of influence. Two issues that are particularly pertinent are the duration of the relationship and the power dynamics that characterize it. Scholars have debated whether adolescents are most receptive to influence from a significant other just before the relationship blossoms (when one is preoccupied with gaining the attention, affection, or affiliation of another), in the early stages of their affiliation (when companions are negotiating the norms of their relationship or when a person is striving to prove worthy of membership in a group), or after they have been associated for some time (when a bond of mutual trust and support has been formed). Intuitively, one might expect that long-standing relationship featuring close ties would offer the strongest source of influence, but this has not always been the case in studies that consider stage of relationship. Burton, Ray, and Mehta (2003) reported that best friends were less likely than acquaintances to inspire cheating in school. Nearly all of the adolescents whom Lightfoot (1997) interviewed acknowledged that a teenager would be persuaded more easily to smoke by acquaintances than friends. Existing evidence is scant and equivocal, primarily because researchers rarely consider relationship stage or duration as an important variable in their analyses.

Another factor to consider is the power differential between the individual or group exerting influence and the person receiving it. Although, by definition, "peer relationships" are regarded as associations among equals, close inspection of groups reveals clear differences in the relative status or authority of group members (Adler & Adler, 1998; Dunphy, 1963; MacLeod, 1995). The same dynamic is often (although not always) apparent in dyadic relationships. Being in a subordinate position in a group or dyad undermines the capacity of an individual to exert influence and may actually enhance openness to influence as a means of ensuring continuation of the relationship.

On the other hand, Crosnoe and Needham (2004) found that adolescents who were in positions of prominence within their friendship network were more likely to reflect the norms of that group (whether prosocial or antisocial) than more peripheral members. Although this could have been because central members were more likely to exemplify the group's primary characteristics, it is also conceivable that they felt stronger pressure to uphold group norms.

9. *Peer influence is contingent on an individual's opportunity and capacity to enact the behavior.* Much of the existing research is predicated on the assumption of an immediate connection between peer influence and consequent behavior. Laboratory conformity studies as well as research using hypothetical situations place respondents in a position re-

quiring an immediate response to peer influence. Inferred influence studies allow for a longer latency period between influence and response but
still assume a rather direct connection. In most cases this is sensible, but
it is important for investigators to bear in mind that there may be
circumstances that prevent the peer influence from being transformed
immediately—or perhaps ever—into responsive behavior. In giving or
selling a fake identification card (ID) to a teenager, peers may structure
an opportunity for the adolescent to engage in illegal drinking. If, however, the adolescent never has an occasion to use the fake ID or is prevented from attending a bar or nightclub by other means (e.g., parents'
close supervision), then there is no discernible evidence of peer influence
on the adolescent's behavior. Strong peer norms encouraging participation in sports may have no impact on an adolescent who is uncoordi-
nated or has physical disabilities that prevent her or him from qualifying
for an athletic team. Opportunity and capacity to enact a behavior are
qualifying factors of peers' ability to influence someone's activities. It is
rare for investigators to take these factors into account, and in many
cases the idiosyncracies of these factors may justify their being relegated
to the ranks of error variance. However, researchers should be careful
not to confuse the absence of opportunity or capacity to respond to peer
influences with the lack of exposure to or ability to resist such influences.

10. *Other individual differences can affect exposure or response to
peer influence.* In addition to the characteristics already specified (openness to influence, salience of influence agents, opportunity and capacity
to enact behaviors that are the subject of influence), a wide range of individual factors may qualify the effects of peer influence on individuals
and thereby qualify the peer influence process. Characteristics that researchers have considered are far too numerous to enumerate, but they
involve demographic background (including gender), personality traits
or dispositions, aspects of psychological well-being, activity patterns, relationships outside of the peer context (especially with family members),
and social and cognitive skills. An important issue in considering these
individual difference variables is whether they operate directly to modify
exposure to peer influence or the effects of peer influence on behavior, or
more indirectly through their impact on more proximal factors in the
peer process (openness to peer influence, relationship dynamics, etc.).

11. *Peer influence is situated behavior.* The manifestations and effects of peer influence depend on the context in which it occurs. Usually,
investigators retain a tight focus on specific features of peer influence, either neglecting or controlling for the fact that this influence operates
within the broader context of adolescents' lives. Some of the earliest
studies of peer influence serve as reminders of the value of keeping this

broader context in mind. Bronfenbrenner (1967), for example, found that Soviet and American early adolescents tended to shift their answers toward more adult-oriented norms on a cross-pressures type instrument when told that their responses would be shared with adults (parents or teachers). More surprising was that, when told that responses would be posted for classmates to see, American youth shifted their responses toward more of a peer orientation while Soviet students shifted again toward adult norms. Although peer influence was apparent in both comparison groups, the "antisocial" nature of this influence was apparent only for American youth. Similar cultural distinctions are apparent in more recent studies of immigrant youth (Umaña-Taylor & Bámaca-Gómez, 2003; Zine, 2001).

Not only do contextual factors shape the nature or direction of peer influence but they also may affect variables that moderate adolescents' responses to peer influence. Steinberg (1986) reported an inverse association between level of parental monitoring and early adolescents' susceptibility to antisocial peer pressures (openness to influence).

These findings raise concerns about how much can be gleaned from studies that remove the peer influence process from its naturally occurring context. Investigators have questioned the dynamics being tested in Asch experiments involving judgments about ambiguous stimuli. Are respondents acting in response to perceived peer group norms or simply attempting to give the best answer about an informational issue (e.g., which line is the same length as a criterion line) (Becker et al., 1966; Deutsch & Gerard, 1955)? Different age trajectories of conformity occur when the stimulus involves group norms, which are inherently ambiguous, as opposed to an informational item that has clearly right and wrong answers. Moreover, how closely would a respondent's behavior in the arbitrarily arranged peer group of a laboratory correspond to responses when confronted with an actual situation occurring in his or her own peer group? Similar questions can be raised about responses to hypothetical scenarios, many of which would be unlikely to ever occur within the respondent's actual group of friends (see Michell & West, 1996). As a general rule, the more closely investigators can approximate "real-life" circumstances in laboratory studies or investigations involving forced-choice self-report instruments, the more credible their findings will be. Recent investigations offer promising examples of ways to inject more reality into these settings (e.g., Cohen & Prinstein, 2006; Gardner & Steinberg, 2005).

12. *Peer influence is a temporal process, existing in several dimensions of time.* One of the greatest challenges for those interested in understanding the peer influence process is to establish the appropriate timetable for studying its dynamics. Laboratory studies typically focus

on immediate responses to instances of potential influence, but it may take more than one exposure to an influence for adolescents to be persuaded to accede to it (Walker-Barnes & Mason, 2001). Inferred influence studies, when well designed, allow for some latency period, but the length of this period is highly variable, from several months to a year or more. Significant events can occur in this interim that dilute the effects of the initial influence and lead to a misspecification of its effects: others may offer counterinfluences that figure into a respondent's behavior at follow-up measurement, or the friendships on which initial measures of influence were based can be terminated and replaced by associates with different values or behavior patterns.

Because peer influence is a rather constant but unpredictable set of events in the lives of most young people, it may be most prudent to conceptualize it as a collection of experiences occurring over time. The frequency and consistency of these experiences, along with their emotional or psychological impact, may be better metrics than the actual timing of exposure to influence. One can imagine, for example, a young person quickly crossing the street or the school courtyard or playground to avoid contact with a peer who is perceived to be heading the person's way. Although the peer has done nothing at that moment to affect the young person's behavior, events remembered in the past (a series of antagonistic interactions, for example) may inspire a current response from the person that clearly indicates peer influence. McIntosh, MacDonald, and McKeganey (2003) found that adolescents initiated drug use not in response to direct pressure from peers but out of fear of what their friends would say or do if they don't try the drug. Peers need not even be present to have an impact on young people's behavior. Shopping alone for clothing, adolescents may still be heavily influenced by peers through their anticipation of how peers would respond to a particular purchase, based on their recollection of previous encounters in which peers have commented on or responded to different dress and grooming styles.

THE CONCEPTUAL MODEL

With these 12 basic principles in mind we now present a comprehensive conceptual model of the peer influence process. The basic intent of this model is to provide a framework that investigators can use either to devise a coordinated set of studies of peer influence or to compare findings across a wide range of studies that address a variable assortment of model components. Although we have emphasized the transactional nature of peer influence, we downplay this basic principle in the model in deference to the overwhelming tendency of researchers to approach peer influence from a more linear perspective. As we present features of the model we refer in parentheses to the principle that each feature addresses— "(P2)," for example—to indicate that a feature focuses on the multiple modes of peer influence.

The model assumes that events in an adolescent's life trigger the peer influence process, and that when an adolescent encounters peer influence he or she will respond either by accepting or acceding to the influence, rejecting or ignoring it, or confronting it directly with a counter-influence. This response becomes an event in its own right, either constituting or leading to a new instance of peer influence that demands a response from the person to whom it is directed. This basic sequence of event, peer influence, and response, with the feedback loop, portrays the transactional nature of peer influence (P5), but with an emphasis on the steps in the sequence that allow for more linear analyses.

As presented in Figure 2.1, the event–influence–response sequence is the core of the model, along with the additional component of measurable outcome to the individual. Ultimately, most researchers and practitioners are concerned not with the existence of peer influence or a person's immediate response to it, but with its impact on a person's attitudes or behavior. These core components are presented in rectangular boxes, connected by bold-faced lines. Beyond these four core components, the model includes a number of other constructs or variables that qualify the sequence of events that transpire in the influence process, thus affecting the ultimate consequences of influence for the individual. We comment briefly on several features of the model.

Key Characteristics of Peer Influence

In characterizing the nature of influence, there are four features that researchers should consider, all based on the notion that such influence constitutes a constellation of experiences, rather than one specific act by peers. The first, which we label "timing," concerns whether the set of influences relevant to the triggering event are immediate and actual behaviors of peers, or peer behaviors that an individual anticipates based on previous experiences with agemates (P12). This feature acknowledges that adolescents may be influenced as much by peer reactions that might occur as by those that do occur, but that both of these are rooted at some point in actual experiences. In addition to timing, researchers should be aware of the mode or modes by which the influence is expressed (e.g., peer pressure versus structuring opportunities), especially if scholars demonstrate at some future point that modes vary systematically in their capacity to inspire compliance (P2). The intensity of peer influence (how strident peers are in pressing an adolescent to act or think in a certain

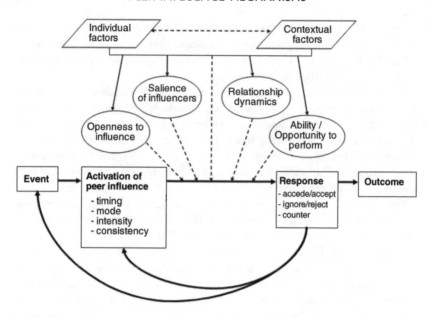

FIGURE 2.1. Conceptual model of the peer influence process.

way) and its consistency (the extent to which peers' actions all support a certain action or encourage a variety of actions) are also important features of peer influence to consider (P4). If all of these cannot be measured or controlled within a given study, then investigators need to be cautious about the conclusions they draw from their findings. Understandably, it is almost impossible for an investigator to identify the entire range of experiences with peers that may be brought to mind in the face of a specific instance of peer influence, but some effort to examine respondents' previous as well as present experience with peers is desirable.

Response Options

In most cases, investigators consider only two responses to peer influence: acceptance/accession or rejection/noncompliance. Those who wish to pursue the transactional nature of peer influence will be more concerned with the third option: efforts to deflect the peer action by generating counterinfluence (P5). Experimental laboratory studies and forced-choice questionnaire measures are rarely set up to allow for counterinfluences to be displayed and assessed, but the behaviors are readily apparent in observational and ethnographic research (Fordham & Ogbu, 1986; Granic & Dishion, 2003).

Modifying Variables

We emphasize four factors that can modify the effects of peer influence on individuals' response and ultimate behavior. These are represented in the model in the ovals, connected to the primary influence process by dashed lines. The first is how open individuals are to influence, in terms of attending to the peer behaviors that can constitute influence as well as having a general disposition of susceptibility to influence (P6). Even with the appropriate attention and disposition to be influenced, an individual may not be affected by peer behaviors if they are not generated by salient peers (P7), or if the individual's relationship with peers mediates against them being persuasive sources of influence (P8). Finally, the effectiveness of peer influence depends on the individual's opportunity and capacity to perform the behaviors that agemates are urging upon the person (P9).

The model treats the four major qualifiers as independent effects on the peer influence process, but that may not be accurate. The salience of various peers is probably not independent of the history of an adolescent's relationship with them. Young people may be more disposed to attend to the behavior of some peers rather than others. Studies that incorporate all of the qualifiers can examine the degree to which they operate independently, as opposed to in a more complex, interdependent fashion.

Individual and Contextual Factors

Two additional qualifiers are portrayed as having more complex associations with other elements of the conceptual model. Both are placed in rhombuses to set them apart from other moderating variables. The first comprises individual difference variables not highlighted in the four major qualifiers (P10). The two individual characteristics most likely to be incorporated into research studies are age and gender, but a wide variety of other variables would fit into this category, including characteristics whose effects may be confined to specific events or outcomes. Peer pressures involving sexual activity may be affected by individuals' attitudes toward sexuality or history of sexual and romantic relationships, whereas these variables could be expected to have negligible effects on pressures involving sports participation.

Contextual factors constitute the other qualifier, reflecting the basic principle that peer influence is situated behavior (P12). Through this factor the peer influence process is connected to contexts beyond the peer social system: school, family, neighborhood and community, religious institutions, ethnic and cultural background, and so on. This encourages investigators to avoid thinking of peer influences in monolithic terms, as somehow disconnected from the rest of young people's lives.

Although we have indicated that individual and contextual factors may directly modify the connection between influence and response or outcome, we also suggest that these factors may be connected indirectly to the process through their effects on other qualifiers. For example, gender and ethnic or cultural background seem to affect adolescents' openness to peer influence (Berndt, 1979; Giordano, Cernkovich, & DeMaris, 1993; Sim & Koh, 2003; Umaña-Taylor & Bámaca-Gómez, 2003). Similarly, one would expect that adolescents who value school success will look to high-achieving peers as more salient role models than peers who do poorly in school.

Developmental Considerations

Developmental or temporal considerations, which were the focus of our last basic principle (P12), may not be immediately apparent in this conceptual model, but they are encompassed in several of its components. Differences related to chronological age are incorporated in the individual factors qualifier. Relationship dynamics encompass temporal features of peer relationships that can moderate an individual's response to peer influence. The timing aspect of activation of peer influence addresses differences between the immediate experience of influence and anticipatory influence based on previous peer experiences. Finally, the event, activation, response, outcome sequence, with its potential transactional feedback loops, reflects the temporal order of actions that make up the peer influence process. Thus, developmental or historical time is manifest in each of the model's major features. Investigators are thereby urged to look beyond any specific developmental or temporal metric to consider the multiple ways in which time affects the peer influence process.

EXEMPLARY RECENT RESEARCH

To illustrate how the conceptual model can be used to connect findings from disparate research studies, we briefly review three recent investigations that address peer influence. The studies feature markedly different measures and methodological approaches, and they address distinct aspects of peer influence. By situating them within components of the conceptual model, one can begin to see how they converge to enhance our understanding of the peer influence process.

Allen and Colleagues: Effects of "Susceptibility"

Allen and colleagues (2006) examined how early adolescents' susceptibility to influence from a close friend was associated concurrently and
longitudinally with problem behaviors and negative affect (depression).
Their novel approach to measuring susceptibility, the number of times a
target adolescent yielded to a friend in a joint decision-making task, is
controversial because it could be argued that it actually measures response to peer influence, rather than susceptibility (openness to influence). If one treats the yielding measure as an indicator of openness to
influence, the study findings indicate that this disposition not only moderates another qualifier in our model (relationship history, in that higher
susceptibility was associated with lower rates of close friend stability)
but also seems to affect rates of peer influence: observed level of susceptibility was associated with friend's reports of how much he or she influenced the target adolescent in various domains. Openness also func-
tioned as predicted in our influence model, moderating associations
between peer reports of drug use and adolescents' self-reported drug use,
but this was only true for concurrent measures of drug use—not in assessments of adolescents' change over time. Moreover, openness was
associated with changes in an important individual factor: the target
adolescent's popularity among peers—reversing the direction of association between openness and individual factors as specified in our model
and suggesting more of a bidirectional association between these two
qualifiers.

If the yielding measure is treated as an indicator of response to peer
influence, then the data provide evidence to support the presumed association between yielding to peer influence and psychological well-being
(increased rates of depression over time), but not to changes in two behavioral measures (involvement in drug use and heterosexual inter-
course). The connection between yielding and increases over time in
friends' reports of influencing the respondent would be interpreted as evidence of the transactional nature of peer influence: Adolescents who
yield to peers are likely to be subjected to increased rates of influence
over time. These discrepant interpretations of findings underscore the
need for consensus on definitions of key constructs in the peer influence
process.

Granic and Dishion: Conversations between Friends

Like Allen and colleagues (2006), Granic and Dishion (2003) based their
analyses on observations of close friends in a contrived, laboratory situation. However, they focused on the collaborative nature of the friends'

conversation (how one's reactions built on the other's comments, recip-
rocally), rather than on the competition for dominance that was central
to the conversational task in Allen and colleagues' study. Although the
samples in both studies were about the same age (early adolescence),
Granic and Dishion dealt with high-risk youth. They focused on the pattern of "deviant talk" (antisocial commentary or reactions to the partner's commentary) over the course of a 30-minute conversation, assessing quite specifically the pair's tendency to return to deviant topics and
spend progressively more time on these topics as the conversation went
along. In model terms, at issue is whether a deviant comment (event)
was greeted by behavioral reinforcement (peer influence), which drew a
response of additional deviant comments (response and new event),
leading to a feedback loop of deviant comments (response/event) and reinforcement (peer influence) that grew into longer conversation segments over the course of their discussion.

Analyses indicated that the degree of this conversational style predicted future antisocial behavior on several measures (outcomes), even
after controlling for a number of potent predictors of deviance: gender,
initial level of deviance, association with deviant peers, and coercive
family interaction patterns. Some of the model modifiers (salience of
influencers and relationship dynamics) were controlled in this analysis
by confining the selection of interaction partner to close friend and using
the dyad, rather than its members, as the unit of analysis for determining
conversational style. Other modifiers (openness to influence, ability and
opportunity to perform) were not considered, but some attention was
given to individual factors (gender, history of delinquent behavior) and
contextual factors (family features). The study's key contribution lay in
its focus on core components of the peer influence model, demonstrating
how a particular pattern of influence contributed to deviant outcomes in
at-risk youth.

Cohen and Prinstein: Responses to High- and Low-Status Peers

In contrast to these analyses of conversation patterns, Cohen and
Prinstein (2006) devised an intriguing variation on Asch's (1951) controlled laboratory experiment to examine how the salience of influencers
modified middle adolescent boys' responses to a consistent behavioral
display (peer influence). The respondents, all of whom had moderate
levels of peer status, were joined in an electronic chatroom by peers (in
reality, confederates created by the experimenters) whom the respondents were led to believe were specific classmates who were all either
high or low in peer status. At issue was whether or not respondents

would alter their responses to hypothetical scenarios toward the more aggressive responses endorsed by their chatroom peers. As predicted, respondents gravitated toward more aggressive responses when (ostensibly) in the company of high-status peers but actually shied away from such responses when joined in the chatroom by low-status peers. These patterns emerged when respondents thought their chatroom peers could see their responses to the hypothetical scenarios as well as when they were led to believe that responses would remain private. When the investigators introduced an individual factor, social anxiety, as a possible moderator of this conformity pattern, they found that level of social anxiety did not affect respondents' responses to high-status peers, but those with high levels of social anxiety were more likely to conform to the aggressive responses of low-status peers than were respondents with low levels of social anxiety. In other words, respondents with high social anxiety were inclined to conform to peers regardless of their social standing, whereas those with low social anxiety were more discriminating in their response to peer influence.

Not only did Cohen and Prinstein (2006) derive a way to transform the face-to-face laboratory interactions of the original Asch experiments into the electronic social environment to which early-21st-century adolescents are accustomed, but they also incorporated a variety of specific responses to peer influence into the experimental design. They sampled public and private responses to peers, and they also embraced the transactional nature of peer influence by giving respondents an opportunity, at the end of the experiment, to vote someone out of the chatroom—an action that could be interpreted as a new event or peer influence that might trigger a response from other group members.

Commentary

The findings of these three studies do not converge into a single message about peer influence. Although they all deal with antisocial outcomes, the investigations vary too much in the type of relationship existing between initiator and target of influence, the type of pressure exhibited, and the specific modifiers of influence examined to allow for a direct comparison of findings. However, by translating each study into components of the comprehensive model, one can identify points of convergence that help to suggest possible next steps in each investigator's research agenda. Is the conversational style recorded by Granic and Dishion (2003) altered when interacting pairs vary in susceptibility to influence, and how does that susceptibility affect the impact of deviant conversation styles on each partner's future delinquency? Would either susceptibility to peer influence or social anxiety modify that chatroom behavior of respondents in Cohen and Prinstein's (2006) experiment if they were made to believe that their chatroom partners were close friends rather than acquaintances of higher or lower status? The more that scholars keep the "big picture" of the peer influence process in mind, the easier it will be to design studies that do connect to other research in the area.

FINAL THOUGHTS

Some may question the wisdom of proposing a comprehensive general conceptual model of peer influence such as the one presented in this chapter. One could argue that the peer influence process is specific to various populations or types of behavior. The influence mechanisms and moderators are so different when it comes to one behavior (e.g., school achievement) than another (e.g., initiation into sexual activity or drug use) that it is more sensible to craft distinct conceptual models for each behavioral domain. Our careful review of the literature leads us to reject this argument because we found the same basic components being referred to across a diverse array of studies. Moreover, although investigators can easily focus on a particular source of influence or a specific behavior, adolescents do not encounter peer influence in such an isolated fashion. They move quickly from one peer social context to another, and within each context the focal topic is constantly shifting. If adolescents can learn to modulate this succession of types, targets, and topics of influence, scholars should be willing to work with a conceptual framework that can follow young people's efforts to negotiate this complicated social environment.

The three studies that we selected to illustrate our conceptual model exemplify the clever and novel ways in which scholars have isolated particular variables for study while engaging adolescents in tasks that closely approximate their actual experiences with peers. Combining self-report data, peer ratings, and/or reports of close associates with data from observations or controlled laboratory experiments is central to the success of these investigations. A challenge for future work is to coordinate these techniques of gathering information with ethnographic and other qualitative methodologies that provide data from the natural settings and naturally occurring interactions in which peer influence is manifest. In a society such as the United States whose dominant cultural group celebrates autonomy and demeans dependence on others, one must be especially conscious of social desirability response sets that may skew self-report data about peer influence processes (Carter, Bennetts, & Carter, 2003).

Over the past half-century, scholars have made remarkable progress in charting the nature and impact of peer influence on the lives of adolescents. Yet the dynamics of the peer influence process are just beginning to be well understood. The advent of more sophisticated and creative research designs allows scholars to build a better understanding of this influence process. We believe that a comprehensive conceptual model of peer influence can guide these efforts and lead to a more integrative view of this vital aspect of adolescent development and behavior.

ACKNOWLEDGMENTS

This chapter was prepared with the assistance of a grant to B. Bradford Brown from the Graduate School of the University of Wisconsin–Madison. We gratefully acknowledge the contributions of members of the Advanced Seminar in Adolescent Development: Conceptualizing and Measuring Peer Influence in Adolescence (autumn semester, 2004), Department of Educational Psychology, University of Wisconsin–Madison.

REFERENCES

Adler, P. A., & Adler, P. (1998). *Peer power: Preadolescent culture and identity.* New Brunswick, NJ: Rutgers University Press.

Allen, J. P., Porter, M. R., & McFarland, F. C. (2006). Leaders and followers in adolescent close friendships: Susceptibility to peer influence as a predictor of risky behavior, friendship instability, and depression. *Development and Psychopathology, 18,* 155–172.

Asch, S. E. (1951). Effects of group pressure upon the modification and distortion of judgments. In H. Guetzkow (Ed.), *Groups, leadership, and men* (pp. 177–190). Oxford, UK: Carnegie Press.

Aseltine, R. H., Jr. (1995). A reconsideration of parental and peer influences on adolescent deviance. *Journal of Health and Social Behavior, 36,* 103–121.

Bandura, A., & Walters, R. H. (1963). *Social learning and personality development.* New York: Holt, Rinehart and Winston.

Bauman, K. E., & Ennett, S. T. (1996). On the importance of peer influence for adolescent drug use: Commonly neglected considerations. *Addiction, 91,* 185–198.

Becker, S. W., Lerner, M. J., & Carroll, J. (1966). Conformity as a function of birth order and type of group pressure: A verification. *Journal of Personality and Social Psychology, 3,* 242–244.

Berndt, T. J. (1979). Developmental changes in conformity to peers and parents. *Developmental Psychology, 15,* 608–616.

Bixenstine, V. E., DeCorte, M. S., & Bixenstine, B. A. (1976). Conformity to peer-sponsored misconduct at four grade levels. *Developmental Psychology, 12*(3), 226–236.

Brittain, C. V. (1963). Adolescent choices and parent-peer cross pressures. *American Sociological Review, 28,* 385–391.

Bronfenbrenner, U. (1967). Response to pressure from peers versus adults among Soviet and American school children. *International Journal of Psychology, 2,* 199–207.

Brown, B. B., Clasen, D. R., & Eicher, S. A. (1986). Perceptions of peer pressure, peer conformity dispositions, and self-reported behavior among adolescents. *Developmental Psychology, 22,* 521–530.

Burton, B. A., Ray, G. E., & Mehta, S. (2003). Children's evaluations of peer influence: The role of relationship type and social situation. *Child Study Journal, 33,* 235–255.

Carter, D. S. G., Bennetts, C., & Carter, S. M. (2003). "We're not sheep": Illuminating the nature of the adolescent peer group in effecting lifestyle choice. *British Journal of Sociology of Education, 24,* 225–241.

Cillessen, A. H. N., & Mayeux, L. (2004). From censure to reinforcement: Developmental changes in the association between aggression and social status. *Child Development, 75,* 147–163.

Cohen, G. L., & Prinstein, M. J. (2006). Peer contagion of aggression and health risk behavior among adolescent males: An experimental investigation of effects on public conduct and private attitudes. *Child Development, 77,* 967–983.

Costanzo, P. (1970). Conformity development as a function of self-blame. *Journal of Personality and Social Psychology, 14*(4), 366–374.

Costanzo, P. R., & Shaw, M. E. (1966). Conformity as a function of age level. *Child Development, 37,* 967–975.

Crosnoe, R., & Needham, B. (2004). Holism, contextual variability, and the study of friendships in adolescent development. *Child Development, 75,* 264–279.

Deković, M., Wissink, I. B., & Meijer, A. M. (2004). The role of family and peer relations in adolescent antisocial behavior: Comparison of four ethnic groups. *Journal of Adolescence, 27,* 497–514

Deutsch, M., & Gerard, H. B. (1955). A study of normative and informational social influences upon individual judgment. *Journal of Abnormal and Social Psychology, 51,* 629–636.

Dishion, T. J., & Dodge, K. A. (2005). Peer contagion in interventions for children and adolescents: Moving towards an understanding of the ecology and dynamics of change. *Journal of Abnormal Child Psychology, 33,* 395–400.

Dunphy, D. C. (1963). The social structure of urban adolescent peer groups. *Sociometry, 26,* 230–246.

Eckert, P. (1989). *Jocks and burnouts: Social categories and identity in the high school.* New York: Teachers College Press.

Eder, D. (1991). The role of teasing in adolescent peer group culture. *Sociological Studies of Child Development, 4,* 181–197.

Eder, D. (1995). *School talk: Gender and adolescent culture.* New Brunswick, NJ: Rutgers University Press.

Elliott, D. S., Huizinga, D., & Ageton, S. S. (1985). *Explaining delinquency and drug use.* Beverly Hills, CA: Sage.

Ennett, S. T., & Bauman, K. E. (1994). The contribution of influence and selection to adolescent peer group homogeneity: The case of adolescent cigarette smoking. *Journal of Personality and Social Psychology, 67,* 653–663.

Erikson, E. H. (1968). *Identity, youth and crisis.* New York: Norton.

Fine, G. A. (1987). *With the boys: Little League baseball and preadolescent culture.* Chicago: University of Chicago Press.

Fordham, S., & Ogbu, J. U. (1986). Black students' school success: Coping with the "burden of acting white." *Urban Review, 18,* 176–206.

Fuligni, A. J., Eccles, J. S., Barber, B. L., & Clements, P. (2001). Early adolescent peer orientation and adjustment during high school. *Developmental Psychology, 37,* 28–36.

Gardner, M., & Steinberg, L. (2005). Peer influence on risk taking, risk preference, and risky decision making in adolescence and adulthood: An experimental study. *Developmental Psychology, 41,* 625–635.

Giordano, P. C., Cernkovich, S. A., & DeMaris, A. (1993). The family and peer relations of black adolescents. *Journal of Marriage and the Family, 55,* 277–287.

Goldstein, S., Davis-Kean, P., & Eccles, J. (2005). Parents, peers, and problem behavior: A longitudinal investigation of the impact of relationship perceptions and characteristics on the development of adolescent problem behavior. *Developmental Psychology, 41,* 401–413.

Graham, J. W., Marks, G., & Hansen, D. (1991). Social influence processes affecting adolescent substance use. *Journal of Applied Psychology 76,* 291–298.

Granic, I., & Dishion, T. J. (2003). Deviant talk in adolescent friendships: A step toward measuring a pathogenic attractor process. *Social Development, 12,* 314–334.

Gurian, M. (1998). *A fine young man: What parents, mentors, and educators can do to shape adolescent boys into exceptional men.* New York: Tarcher/Putnam.

Hartup, W. W. (2005). Peer interaction: What causes what? *Journal of Abnormal Child Psychology, 33,* 387–394.

Hawkins, J. D., Catalano, R., & Miller, J. (1992). Risk and protective factors for alcohol and other drug problems in adolescence and early adulthood: Implications for substance abuse prevention. *Psychological Bulletin, 112,* 64–105.

Hersch, P. (1998). *A tribe apart: A journey into the heart of American adolescence.* New York: Ballantine.

Hoving, K. L., Hamm, N., & Galvin, P. (1969). Social influence as a function of stimulus ambiguity at three age levels. *Developmental Psychology, 1,* 631–636.

Iscoe, I., Williams, M., & Harvey, J. (1963). Modification of children's judgments by a simulated group technique: A normative developmental study. *Child Development, 34,* 963–978.

Jaccard, J., Blanton, H., & Dodge, T. (2005). Peer influences on risk behavior: An analysis of the effects of a close friend. *Developmental Psychology, 41,* 135–147.

Kandel, D. B. (1978). Homophily, selection, and socialization in adolescent friendships. *American Journal of Sociology, 84,* 427–436.

Kandel, D. B. (1985). On processes of peer influences in adolescent drug use: A developmental perspective. *Advances in Alcohol and Substance Abuse, 4,* 139–163.

Kiesner, J., Cadinu, M., Poulin, F., & Bucci, M. (2002). Group identification in early adolescence: Its relation with peer adjustment and its moderator effect on peer influence. *Child Development, 73,* 196–208.

Larson, L. E. (1974). An examination of the salience hierarchy during adolescence: The influence of the family. *Adolescence, 9,* 317–332.

Lashbrook, J. T. (2000). Fitting in: Exploring the emotional dimension of adolescent peer pressure. *Adolescence, 35,* 747–757.

Lightfoot, C. (1997). *The culture of adolescent risk-taking.* New York: Guilford Press.

MacLeod, J. (1995). *Ain't no makin' it: Aspirations and attainment in a low-income neighborhood.* Boulder, CO: Westview Press.

McIntosh, J., MacDonald, F., & McKeganey, N. (2003). The initial use of drugs in a sample of pre-teenage schoolchildren: The role of choice, pressure and influence. *Drugs: Education, Prevention and Policy, 10,* 147–158.

Merten, D. E. (1996). Visibility and vulnerability: Responses to rejection by nonaggressive junior high school boys. *Journal of Early Adolescence, 16,* 5–26.

Michell, L., & West, P. (1996). Peer pressure to smoke: The meaning depends on the method. *Health Education Research 11,* 39–49.

Perlstein, L. (2003). *Not much just chillin': The hidden lives of middle schoolers.* New York: Ballantine Books.

Piaget, J. (1950). *La construction du réel chez l'enfant, 2ème éd [The construction of reality according to the child, 2nd ed.*), Neuchatel, France: Delachaux et Niestlé.

Pipher, M. (1994). *Reviving Ophelia: Saving the selves of adolescent girls.* New York: Ballantine Books.

Pruitt, B. E., Kingery, P. M., & Mirzaee, E. (1991). Peer influence and drug use among adolescents in rural areas. *Journal of Drug Education, 21,* 1–11.

Robin, S. S., & Johnson, E. O. (1996). Attitude and peer cross pressure: Adolescent drug and alcohol use. *Journal of Drug Education, 26,* 69–99.

Rodgers, J., & Rowe, D. (1993). Social contagion and adolescent sexual behavior: A developmental EMOSA model. *Psychological Review, 100,* 479–510.

Sebald, H., & White, B. (1980). Teenagers' divided reference groups: Uneven alignment with parents and peers. *Adolescence, 15,* 979–984.

Sim, T. N., & Koh, S. F. (2003). Domain conceptualization of adolescent susceptibility to peer pressure. *Journal of Research on Adolescence, 13,* 58–80.

Steinberg, L. (1986). Latchkey children and susceptibility to peer pressure: An ecological analysis. *Developmental Psychology, 22,* 433–439.

Steinberg, L., & Silverberg, S. B. (1986). The vicissitudes of autonomy in early adolescence. *Child Development, 57,* 841–851.

Sullivan, H. S. (1953). *The interpersonal theory of psychiatry.* New York: Norton.

Umaña-Taylor, A. J., & Bámaca-Gómez, M. Y. (2003). Generational differences in resistance to peer pressure among Mexican-origin adolescents. *Youth and Society, 35,* 183–203.

Urberg, K. A., Shyu, S., & Liang, J. (1990). Peer influence in adolescent cigarette smoking. *Addictive Behaviors, 15,* 247–255.

Vincent, M. A., & McCabe, M. P. (2000). Gender differences among adolescents in family, and peer influences on body dissatisfaction, weight loss, and binge eating behaviors. *Journal of Youth and Adolescence, 29,* 205–221.

Walker-Barnes, C. J., & Mason, C. A. (2001). Perceptions of risk factors for female gang involvement among African American and Hispanic women. *Youth and Society, 32,* 303–336.

Wiseman, P. (2002). *Queen bees and wannabes.* New York: Three Rivers Press.

Wood, M. D., Read, J. P., & Mitchell, R. E. (2004). Do parents still matter?: Parent and peer influences on alcohol involvement among recent high school graduates. *Psychology of Addictive Behaviors, 18,* 19–30.

Youniss, J. (1980). *Parents and peers in social development: A Sullivan–Piaget perspective.* Chicago: University of Chicago Press.

Zine, J. (2001). Muslim youth in Canadian schools: Education and the politics of religious identity. *Anthropology and Education Quarterly, 32,* 399–423.

CHAPTER 3

Cognitive Social Influence

Moderation, Mediation, Modification, and ... the Media

Frederick X. Gibbons, Elizabeth A. Pomery,
and Meg Gerrard

Social influence has an important impact on behavior throughout the lifespan. It is a dominant force during adolescence, however, especially for behaviors that are risky and/or health relevant, such as substance use (Fuemmeler et al., 2002; Prinstein & Wang, 2005). There are two primary sources of social influence for adolescents when it comes to substance use: their peers—friends and others they come in contact with— and their family, mostly their parents, but also, in some instances, their siblings. Researchers have identified four ways in which this influence can occur, three of which involve direct influence, the fourth, indirect influence. The simplest of the four is "provision": Whether intentional or incidental, parents and peers can and do make substances available to adolescents. A second avenue of influence is "modeling." Besides actually learning how to use the substance, observing others using affects the expectancies, positive and negative, that young people develop with regard to the effects that the substances are likely to have. Adolescents may learn at a very young age, for example, that marijuana or beer can liven up a party (Zucker, Kincaid, Fitzgerald, & Bingham, 1995). Related to modeling is the third type of influence, which is "encouragement." This is, of course, much more likely to come from peers than from parents; in fact, the extent to which "peer pressure" affects adolescent use is a focal issue in the influence literature. Finally, peers and family members (e.g., older siblings) can influence the substance use of adolescents by shaping the attitudes and other cognitions that they develop about substances and substance use (Brody, Ge, Katz, & Arias, 2000).

If application (intervention) is an indication, one could argue that the third means of influence, peer pressure, is the most important. Many interventions and preventive interventions have focused on bolstering resistance efficacy as a means of reducing use. Using the most popular program (at least in terms of funding; Brown, 2001) as an example, the D.A.R.E. approach is based on an assumption that empowering young people to resist offers of drugs or alcohol should go a long way toward solving the drug problem. Although elegant in its simplicity, evaluations of these programs suggest less-than-impressive results, in spite of their popularity (Hansen & McNeal, 1997; Lynam et al., 1999). There are undoubtedly many reasons why these (and other) programs struggle, but one of the more interesting ones is discussed in reviews by Donaldson and his colleagues (Donaldson et al., 1996), who found that this approach oftentimes doesn't work and sometimes produces iatrogenic effects: increases in use. They speculate that one incidental effect of the publicity and attention given to the programs is that some adolescents conclude that the problem—substance use—is more common among their peers than they had originally thought. And, as many studies have documented, high (peer) prevalence estimates are associated with increased use (Callas, Flynn, & Worden, 2004). In short, the explicit or direct message (don't use) may conflict with the implicit, or cognitive message (many of your peers are using), and the implicit message may result in unwanted behavior change.

Our research has focused on this latter type of influence—the fourth type mentioned above—and that is the role that attitudes or cognitions, and changes in these cognitions, play in determining use and nonuse among young people. It is our contention that these cognitions—what adolescents take with them when they mature and leave the home—are ultimately going to have the most impact on their substance use. In this chapter, we review some of our own research and relevant work by others that has examined factors that affect these cognitions and their relations with substance use. We will also review the results of efforts by ourselves and others to alter these cognitions and, in the process, delay or reduce substance use.

PATHWAYS OF INFLUENCE

Adolescents' earliest exposure to substances is likely to occur in the home (National Institute on Drug Abuse [NIDA], 2003; White, Bates, &

Johnson, 1991), mostly through observation of parents' use. Their earliest "experiences" with substances, however, usually occur outside the home and the purview of their parents. Thus, much of parents' influence is likely to be indirect, through the impact they have on their children's attitudes about use and users and on their choice of friends (Engels, Vitaro, Blokland, de Kemp, & Scholte, 2004; Kandel, 1996). Studies examining parents' impact on the attitudes of their children toward substances generally suggest a positive relation: Children of parents who drink or smoke are likely to have more favorable attitudes toward these substances than are children whose parents don't engage in these behaviors, but the correlations are modest (Casswell, Brasch, Gilmore, & Silva, 1985). Relations between peer use and adolescent attitudes are typically stronger, but these relations include an additional cognitive element when the adolescents report on their friends' use (a common procedure): The adolescents may attribute or project some of their own attitudes and behavior on to their friends and peers (Bauman & Ennett, 1996). This inflates the relation, of course, but, at the same time, it also highlights the importance of the role of cognitions.

Clearly, the influence of peers and parents are important. Our research suggests, however, that the process by which peer versus parent influence works is different in some important ways. Children growing up in homes where one or both parents drink alcohol will have opportunities, perhaps on a daily basis, to observe the behavior and its consequences. By the time they reach late adolescence, when drinking has become a realistic possibility for them, they may very well have had years to think about whether they want to drink or not. They have some sense of the costs and benefits associated with the behavior and presumably have taken these into account when deciding how to behave. This type of decision making fits well within the expectancy value perspective in social psychology that is at the core of many influential attitude—behavior theories, most prominent among them being the theories of reasoned action (Fishbein & Ajzen, 1975) and planned behavior (Ajzen, 1985). This perspective maintains that all human behavior is intentional. Thus, behavioral intentions (BI) are the only proximal antecedents to action; in other words, people don't do things that they hadn't planned on doing. Intentions, in turn, are the result of a decision-making process that is deliberate and includes consideration and evaluation of the action and its likely consequences. Although that resulting action may not be rational, it is, by definition, reasoned. The teenage child, then, may decide that the social and perhaps the physiological effects of drinking are worth the costs, whatever they might be, and so a decision to drink is made. Of course, the opposite decision is a possibility as well; in either case, the action or inaction is premeditated.

Although there is considerable evidence suggesting that much adolescent behavior does follow this kind of deliberative process, there is reason to believe that there is a different kind of decision making involved in adolescent-health risk behavior (cf. Reyna & Farley, 2006). We have argued that much of this behavior, especially among younger adolescents, is not intentional or planned, or even reasoned. Instead, it is a reaction to circumstances. This assumption forms the basis of a model of adolescent-health risk behavior that we have developed in an effort to improve the predictive validity of existing attitude—behavior theories, specifically as they apply to different types of adolescent-health risk behaviors. The model is named after its two focal constructs: prototypes and behavioral willingness. The prototype/willingness (prototype) model focuses on the cognitions that mediate the links between environmental factors, such as peers and peer influence, and health behaviors. The model has been described in detail elsewhere (Gibbons, Gerrard, & Lane, 2003; Gibbons, Gerrard, Reimer, & Pomery, 2006); a brief description of its focal constructs is relevant to the current discussion, however.

A SOCIAL REACTION MODEL OF ADOLESCENT HEALTH BEHAVIOR

Reasoned Action versus Social Reaction

The prototype model maintains that there are two pathways to adolescent health behavior. The first, the reasoned path, comes directly from the expectancy value perspective, specifically, the theory of reasoned action. This path begins with the adolescents' subjective norms—what he or she thinks others (e.g., peers) are doing and would want him or her to do—as well as his or her attitudes toward the behavior and its anticipated outcomes (akin to expectancies). The path proceeds to behavior through BI, which is the only proximal antecedent recognized by this perspective. The second path, called the "social reaction path," also begins with subjective norms and attitudes; however, it proceeds to behavior through an additional proximal antecedent, which is behavioral willingness (BW).

Behavioral Willingness

BW is defined as an openness to risk opportunity—what an adolescent or adult would be willing to do under certain circumstances—for example, an encounter with an interested (but unfamiliar) potential sex partner, a party in which drugs are available. The assumption here is that adolescents will from time to time find themselves in social situations that they had not sought out or anticipated in which substances (and/or partners) are available. Their actions in these types of risk-conducive situations are less likely to be reasoned or planned ahead of time. Instead, they are a response to the risk opportunity presented by the situation—hence the term *social reaction*.

To assess BW, a risk-conducive situation is first described to adolescents, along with a statement that no presumptions are being made as to whether they would ever be in that situation (or that they would seek out such an opportunity). They are then asked to think about the situation and what they would be willing to do if they were in it. A series of increasingly risky behavioral options is presented to them, and they are asked how willing they would be to do each one. The intent is to encourage the adolescents to focus more on the situation (and the "opportunity") and less on the self. As a result, attributions tend to be more externally focused, which means the adolescents are more likely to acknowledge the possibility of risky behavior; in contrast, typical BI questions are more likely to focus attention on the self: "What do you intend to do?" A number of studies have demonstrated the predictive validity of the BW construct, as well as its discriminant validity vis-à-vis BI, even though, as one would expect, the two are usually highly correlated. Moreover, longitudinal studies have indicated that BW is a better predictor than BI among adolescents, mostly because many of them really do not intend or plan on engaging in risky behavior but realize under the right circumstances they might (Gerrard et al., 2008; Gibbons et al., 2004; Spijkerman, van den Eijnden, & Engels, 2005). That relative predictive superiority of BW continues until about age 17 or 18, at which time BI usually becomes dominant for more normative behaviors, such as smoking or drinking (Pomery, Gibbons, Reis-Bergan, & Gerrard, 2008), although less so for high-risk behaviors (e.g., meth use; Litchfield & White, 2006).

Antecedents to BW are similar to antecedents to BI in the theory of reasoned action. They include a version of subjective norms—proscriptive rather than injunctive (i.e., what the adolescent thinks others are doing, rather than what others want him or her to do, which often shows little variance)—and attitudes, specifically, the adolescents' perceived personal vulnerability to the negative outcomes he or she associates with the behavior (see discussion below). There is a third antecedent, which is unique to BW (it is not antecedent to BI) and unique to the model: This is the risk image or prototype that the adolescent associates with the behavior—the perception of the type of person their age who does it (e.g., the "typical smoker" or drug user).

Prototypes

The model maintains that these risk images are widely recognized by adolescents and therefore are "social consequences" of engaging in the behavior—if they smoke in front of their friends and peers, for example, they are likely to be seen as being a member of that group, or at least as having some of the attributes associated with the group (cf. Stone & Brown, 1998). The image is more characterological than visual; in other words, it is more a perception of what type of person does the behavior rather than what that person looks like. Generally, these images tend to be negative, which means they are usually more inhibitive than facilitative. The less favorable the image, the less willing the adolescent (or adult) is to engage in the behavior, given the opportunity. A number of studies have demonstrated a relation between risk prototypes and risk behavior, and those relations are usually mediated by BW (see Gibbons et al., 2003, for a review).

Type of Processing

The prototype model is a modified dual-processing model (see Chaiken & Trope, 1999, for a discussion of dual-processing models). The contention is that the two pathways to risk involve different types of processing. In the reasoned pathway, processing is more analytic or systematic, reflecting the deliberation that is associated with the expected utility assessment leading up to the intention. Behavioral options are considered, their possible outcomes assessed, and then a decision to engage or not engage in the behavior is made. This takes time. The social reaction pathway involves more heuristic or experiential processing. Images (risk prototypes, for example) are important, affect is more influential, and reasoning is usually more intuitive than deductive. More generally, there is less premeditation, especially with regard to the risks or negative outcomes associated with the behavior. Finally, the behavior is more impulsive.

PEERS AND PROTOTYPES

Although subjective norms are a very important component of reasoned action, the evidence suggests that for adolescents, peer (social) influence is more likely to follow the social reaction pathway to health risk behavior. One reason for this is developmental and has to do with risk images, which begin to form at a very early age. Several studies, for example, have shown that 10- or 11-year-olds have fairly clear images of the type of young person their age (or a little older) who uses substances (Gerrard, Gibbons, Stock, Vande Lune, & Cleveland, 2005; Gibbons et al., 2004; Wills, Gibbons, Gerrard, Murry, & Brody, 2003). Wills and colleagues (2007) reported that the 9-year-olds in their study had distinct images of marijuana, cigarette, and alcohol users, and these images were related to their willingness to use these substances. It may be the case, however, that the images develop even earlier than that. In a cohort-sequential study over five annual waves of children ages 6–10 at Wave 1 (W1), Andrews and Peterson (2006) found that the risk images of the 6-year-olds were not distinct (i.e., reliability of the adjective list used to assess them was low); however, those images were cohesive for the 7-year-olds, and in fact their images resembled those of the older children. The images stayed fairly consistent over time; and, as the prototype model would predict, they were related to the children's BW to use, not their BI (Andrews, Hampson, Barckley, Gerrard, & Gibbons, 2008). Self-reports indicated that very few of the children younger than the age of 10 were actually using (the same was true in Wills et al., 2006), and their reports of use by their peers (i.e., subjective norms) also indicated that they knew their friends and peers were not using. Thus, consistent with the prototype model, these children had developed fairly clear (and impactful) risk images well before they or their friends were using.

Image Origination

So, where do the images come from? We asked this question directly of a sample of almost 900 African American adolescents (mean age 10.5 at W1), and 300 of their older siblings (mean age 13.5 at W1). These adolescents were members of the panel in the Family and Community Health Study (FACHS), which is an ongoing study of factors that influence the mental and physical health of African American families (see Cutrona, Russell, Hessling, Brown, & Murry, 2000; Simons et al., 2002, for further description). For the younger and older siblings, the most commonly endorsed source was TV and movies. We have followed up on this finding by looking at the impact of alcohol portrayal in popular Hollywood movies on adolescents' initiation and escalation of both types of use across four waves (ages 10–14 at Time 1 [T1]; $N > 6,500$; Gibbons et al., 2008). This second study is part of an ongoing project with colleagues at Dartmouth–Hitchcock Medical Center that is looking at the impact of portrayal in popular movies of substances like cigarettes and alcohol on adolescents' substance use (see Sargent, Wills, Stoolmiller, Gibson, & Gibbons, 2006, for further description). Substance portrayal is determined not by asking the adolescents how much they have seen, but by timing the substance depiction in each of more than 600 top box-office movies, and then asking respondents which movies they had seen.[1] These analyses indicated that the more alcohol use these adolescents had seen in movies, the more favorable their drinker images were and the greater their likelihood of starting or escalating their alcohol use. As we discuss later, there were also interesting and important racial/ethnic differences in these effects.

Homophily

The relation between peer use and self-reported use is perhaps the strongest relation in the adolescent substance-use area. The temporal ordering of that relation, however, remains a topic of much debate (Jaccard, Blanton, & Dodge, 2005). The basic question is whether the influence is more proactive or reactive: Are young people more likely to seek out others whose substance use is similar to their own (i.e., selection), or more likely to adopt or model the use habits of those around them (socialization)? The early-adolescence prototype research speaks to this issue. As mentioned earlier, risk images, which clearly have an impact in the decision-making process (even if that process is brief), appear to be fairly well developed before the adolescents' friends are actually using. Thus, the adolescent with a favorable drinker image, for example, may find peers who drink to be more interesting than would an adolescent with a negative image. That does not necessarily mean that the child will actively seek out imbibing friends, but he or she may be more open to inclusion in a group that does engage. The influence process certainly does not stop there, however, and there is much evidence that the development of risk images is greatly affected by what peers are doing (Gerrard, Gibbons, Benthin, & Hessling, 1996; Gibbons & Gerrard, 1997). In short, for adolescents, the prototype/peer use (affiliation) relation, just like that between adolescent use and peer use, is best characterized as reciprocal. In sum, adolescents' risk images come from a variety of sources, the media being a primary one, and those images are fairly well developed before they start experimenting. The images are dynamic, however, at least through adolescence; they change as a function of who the child is affiliating with, and what those friends are doing and what they are like.

---

[1]Each adolescent was only asked about 50 movies, and then responses were aggregated across the total. With more than 6,500 adolescents responding, each of the 601 movies was presented to more than 500 adolescents.

FAMILY VERSUS PEERS

As we suggested earlier, children of parents who drink are likely to have had multiple opportunities to observe and think about whether they also want to drink. By the same token, the discussions that parents have with their children about risky behaviors are not likely to focus on issues of impulsivity, affect, or images. Rather, those discussions are likely to involve efforts by the parents to get their children to think ahead of time about the situations they are likely to encounter, perhaps in the process, establishing a plan of action—just say no, or leave the situation, or maybe switch attention to some other behavior. In short, we would expect that parents will appeal to reason and forethought in an attempt to get their children to follow the reasoned path to use or, preferably, nonuse. Peers' influence, on the other hand, will follow a different route. This basic assumption—that parents' influence is more likely to follow the reasoned path whereas peer influence proceeds through the social reaction path—was tested directly in a panel study and then a (related) intervention, discussed later.

Parents and Friends

Figure 3.1 presents the structural equation model (SEM) from Gibbons and colleagues (2004), indicating factors that influenced the substance use of the younger adolescents from the African American family panel (FACHS). As the model indicates, T1 parent use (reported by the parents) had a direct effect on T2 adolescent use, as well as an indirect effect, through T2 BI. Thus, children of parents who used substances showed an increase in their intentions to use at T2 ($p < .01$). Parents' use had no relation with their children's BW, however. In contrast, friends' use was significantly predicted by earlier BW ($p < .001$), and, although friends' use predicted changes (increases) in BI and BW, the latter effect was much stronger than the former (βs = .41 vs. .07; cf. Litchfield & White, 2006). Overall, the pattern was consistent with the assumption that parental influence would follow the reasoned path to nonuse, whereas peer influence would follow the social reaction path.

Contextual Moderation

There were also some additional relations involving context that are relevant to the social influence question. The parents' and the adolescents' reports of neighborhood risk, which included items on substance availability, were positively related to risk images and friends' use, as would be expected. In addition, however, contextual risk also moderated the re-

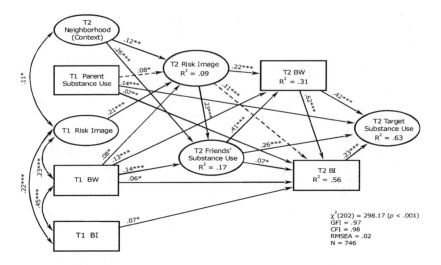

FIGURE 3.1. A structural equation model of cognitive mediation of social and environmental influences on the substance use behavior of a sample of African American adolescents. Solid lines reflect hypothesized paths from the prototype model. Dashed lines indicate paths suggested by the modification indices. *$p < .05$; **$p < .01$; ***$p < .001$. From Gibbons et al. (2004). Copyright 2004 by the American Psychological Association. Reprinted by permission.

lation of BW to use: The b was .19 in the low-risk neighborhoods, but .50 in the high-risk environments. Thus, BW translated into use at a much higher rate for those adolescents who more often encountered "risk opportunities." In fact, the rate of use among the high BW children living in high-risk environments was more than 10 times that of the rest of the sample. Interestingly, the path from BI to use, though generally weaker than the BW/use relation, was essentially the same in the high- and low-risk neighborhoods. In other words, for those (relatively few) adolescents who were intending to use, availability was much less of an issue than it was for those who were willing but not intending.

Siblings

Parents aren't the only family members who influence adolescents' attitudes and behaviors. Pomery and colleagues (2005) looked at the impact of peers vis-à-vis parents and older siblings on the FACHS adolescents' substance use, again using SEM. There was a direct path from T1 parent use to change in adolescent use, as expected. However, the path from the older siblings' T1 BW to the adolescents' T2 use was stronger than the path from the siblings' actual (T1) use. In other words, the siblings' cognitions were more important than what they were doing—perhaps because they had not yet started using, or were not actually using in front of their younger siblings. Further evidence of the importance of this intra-familial transmission of attitudes can be seen in the fact that the older siblings' BW moderated the impact of peers' use (as reported by the adolescents) on the adolescents' use. If the older sibling was willing to use, the path from peer use to adolescent use was strong (b = .31, p < .001), as it usually is; however, if the older sibling was not willing, peer use was not related to adolescent use at all (b = .00). This buffering occurred even though there was no difference in the amount of friends' use reported by adolescents whose siblings were high versus low in their BW.

RISK COGNITIONS AND SOCIAL INFLUENCE

Conditional Vulnerability

Other cognitions in the prototype model also have significant peer influence components. The attitude construct in the model consists of a perceived risk measure: personal, conditional vulnerability, assessed with items such as: "If *you were* to . . . [engage in *XXX*], what do you think the chances are that you would . . . ?" These measures differ from standard perceived risk items (e.g., "How dangerous is . . . ?") because they link risk with performance, and because, like the BW construct, they are hypothetical. They are also more likely to provide evidence of optimistic bias, which is a belief that for some reason (often not entirely logical and frequently hard to articulate), one is less likely than others to experience negative outcomes (see Weinstein, 1980). In other words, like many other cognitive biases, it involves a heuristic type of processing and so is part of the social reactive path. That means it is linked with BW: for example, the more an adolescent thinks he or she can engage in unprotected sex without contracting a sexually transmitted disease (STD) or drive after heavy drinking without having an accident, the more willing he or she is to do it.

These conditional measures also have a social influence component. In Gibbons, Lane, Gerrard, Pomery, and Lautrup (2002), we asked a panel of 400 adolescents (age 17.7 at T1; T2 was a year later) about their conditional vulnerability to drunk driving ("If you were to have several drinks and then drive, what do you think the chances are that you would be involved in an accident?"). We also had two measures of norms: "How many of your [friends] [peers] do you think drive under the influence of alcohol at least occasionally?" Finally, we included an individual difference measure that has been shown to relate to social influence; that is the Iowa–Netherlands Comparison Orientation Measure (INCOM; Gibbons & Buunk, 1999), which assesses social comparison tendencies. Those high on this dimension are more socially oriented and generally more likely to pay attention to and be influenced by the behavior of others (Buunk & Gibbons, 2007).

Regression analyses predicting change in conditional vulnerability revealed the anticipated main effects of behavior and norms and a Comparison × Norms interaction. The main effects reflected the fact that the more the adolescents had engaged in the behavior themselves, the less conditional vulnerability they reported (i.e., the more they thought they could "get away with" the behavior), and the more they thought their friends and peers had engaged, the less vulnerability they reported, controlling for their own use. The interaction indicated that the social influence effect—friends' use → less perceived risk—was much more pronounced among those adolescents who were high in a tendency to socially compare. However, consistent with the prototype model, the interaction term was significant for the conditional measure (part of the social reaction path), but not the absolute danger measure. In other words, conditional vulnerability, which involves a more heuristic assessment, was more susceptible to the impact of social influence.

The next set of analyses related these changes in conditional risk perception to changes in behavior. In spite of fairly high stability in the behavior over the one-year time span, changes in perceived risk did predict changes in drunk driving behavior. Moreover, the significant relation between perceived norms and change in behavior was partially, but significantly ($p < .01$), mediated by the change in conditional vulnerability. In other words, the social influence effect, which was strong (i.e., the zero-order correlation between T1 subjective norms and behavior was $r = .43$ for T1 behavior and $r = .35$ for T2 behavior, both $ps < .001$), was partly attributable to the impact that perceived norms had on these adolescents' perceptions of the risks associated with the behavior—much more so if they were high in social comparison tendencies.

Social Comparison and "Absent-Exempt"

Similar results were reported in a study by Stock, Gibbons, and Gerrard (2008). They assessed students' BW to have risky sex before and after they heard about another (fictional) student who had engaged in unprotected sex only a few times but still had gotten an STD. The impact of this information varied as a function of the participants' own sexual behavior, but in a nonintuitive manner: Those who had not engaged in a lot of risky sex with multiple partners reduced their BW to engage in the future, much as expected; however, those who had already engaged in a lot of risky sex, and not yet contracted an STD, actually increased (marginally) their willingness to engage in this behavior after hearing about the afflicted peer. Stock and colleagues interpreted these findings as evidence of a perception that Weinstein (1982) labeled "absent-exempt"—a type of optimistic bias in which an individual who hasn't experienced any negative consequences from a risky behavior even though he or she has engaged in that behavior, decides he or she is somehow immune from those consequences (e.g., "I have had sex many times without a condom and nothing bad has happened, so I guess I can keep doing it"). Stock et al. showed that this belief is enhanced by social comparison, specifically, an opportunity to compare with someone who has done much less of the risky behavior but still suffered the associated adverse consequences. Moreover, this response tendency is significantly more pronounced among those who are high in social comparison tendencies (as measured by the INCOM), which provides further evidence that the process does involve self-other risk comparisons. Once again, this kind of optimistic bias is less than rational—and these high-risk individuals have difficulty explaining logically why they are so optimistic. This suggests that like other types of cognitive biases, absent-exempt involves a more heuristic type of processing and therefore belongs somewhere in the social reaction path to risk. Whether it is irrational or not, however, it is consequential: Belief in absent-exempt, like optimistic bias, does predict behavior.

MODERATION

Culture

Several factors, besides social comparison, have been suggested as potential moderators of social influence effects among adolescents. These moderators are informative because, like the mediators discussed above, they can provide some insight into the influence process. In several studies, we have looked at nationality as a moderator of social influence effects. As we had expected, the United States generally tended to win this social influence "competition," although the results varied as a function of type of behavior. First, Luszczynska, Gibbons, Piko, and Tekozel (2004) looked at the correlation between adolescents' self-reports and their reports of what their friends were doing for physical activity and healthy eating. The relations were essentially the same for the United States, Hungary, Turkey, and Poland. However, these self- and other reports differed across country when it came to risky behavior: the self-other correlations were much higher for the Americans on sex and substance use (Piko, Gibbons, Luszczynska, & Tekozel, 2005). Taking smoking as an example, the correlation within the U.S. sample was $r = .60$, whereas the range within the other three countries was .41 to .44 (all $Ns > 530$). Of some interest as well, the correlations for reckless driving were .54 in the United States, and they ranged from .25 to .40 (mean = .32) in the other countries, which suggests that risky driving is more of a social phenomenon (as well as more prevalent) in the United States than it is in Europe. More generally, the pattern across countries and behaviors is reminiscent of earlier social influence work contrasting the false consensus and false uniqueness effects. "False consensus" is a tendency for those who are engaging in an unwise behavior to normalize their actions by overestimating the extent to which their peers are engaging in it (Prinstein & Wang, 2005; Ross, Greene, & House, 1977). "False uniqueness," on the other hand, is a tendency to underestimate peer participation; it is much more likely when the behavior is positive (Iedema & Poppe, 1999). In either case, the adolescent looks better vis-à-vis his or her peers, suggesting that the distortions are motivated by self-enhancement.

We found some evidence in support of this motivational explanation in an earlier study that compared Danish and American adolescents' reports of their own and their peers' sexual and smoking behaviors and attitudes (Gibbons, Helweg-Larsen, & Gerrard, 1995). The relation between the adolescents' self-reports of both behaviors and their estimates of their friends' behavior and their friends' reactions to their own behavior (i.e., subjective norms) were significantly higher for the Americans. The high correlation between reports of their own and their friends' behavior reflected the fact that the Americans who were engaging in the behavior also overestimated prevalence more (i.e., more false consensus). More generally, the Americans differed from the Danes in two important ways: (1) There was a very direct social influence question that the U.S. sample endorsed more—they were much more likely to say their behavior would be influenced by what their friends thought (cf. Unger, 2003); and (2) the U.S. sample reported more of a tendency to engage in social comparison (the same was true for the United States vis-à-vis the European countries in Piko et al., 2005, and also in Guimond et al., 2006).

The fact that the U.S. sample was higher in social comparison tendencies and self-enhancement tendencies suggests these differences may underlie the differences we observed in social influence. In fact, we concluded there is a type of cultural paradox here. On the one hand, these data are consistent with the data and observations of others regarding the highly individualistic nature of American society relative to almost all others (Hofstede, 1980, 2003). Americans want to go it alone and be distinctive. On the other hand, ironically, this individualism appears to involve, maybe necessitate, increased awareness of and orientation toward others. Thus, strong tendencies toward competitiveness and an equally strong social comparison orientation are reflections of a desire to distinguish oneself from others. Triandis, Bontempo, and Villareal (1988) made a similar point more generally with regard to the interdependence of individualistic relative to collectivist cultures.

Racial/Ethnic Differences

If one uses the correlation between adolescents' reports of their own behavior and that of their friends and peers as an indicator of social influence (as many researchers do), then there is a substantial amount of evidence suggesting that minorities, and especially African Americans, are less susceptible to this type of influence than are European Americans (Headen, Bauman, Deane, & Koch, 1991; Newcomb, Huba, & Bentler, 1983; Robinson et al., 2006; see Hoffman, Monge, Chou, & Valente, 2007, for a review), and also less likely to seek out friends based on their substance use (Hamm, 2000). Perhaps the most extreme example of this racial difference can be seen in work by Landrine, Richardson, Klonoff, and Flay (1994) who reported that perceived peer smoking explained 23.5% of the variance in smoking for the white adolescents in their sample, but it didn't explain any variance for the blacks. Similarly, Robinson and colleagues (2006) reported that perceived peer prevalence was not even a predictor of smoking among black adolescents (as it was among whites). These moderation effects have led some to suggest that because peer pressure is more of a risk factor for whites than blacks (Griesler & Kandel, 1998), resistance efficacy interventions may be less useful for blacks (Unger et al., 2001).

We looked at black–white differences in social influence for alcohol consumption within the Dartmouth–Hitchcock movie project mentioned earlier (Gibbons et al., 2007). This work has shown that part of the strong effect that movies have on adolescents' smoking and drinking is due to social influence—the impact that exposure to substances in movies has on adolescents' reports of the extent to which their friends smoke or drink (Wills et al., 2007). Cross-lag analyses have suggested this effect is more a reflection of movies' impact on affiliation than vice versa (i.e., affiliation with users does not appear to influence movie selection). Moreover, as mentioned earlier, this effect is mediated by the impact that movies have on alcohol prototype favorability (smoking images were not assessed); thus, exposure leads to more favorable risk images; and this, in turn, leads to more association with peers who are using. However, there were important differences between the black and white adolescents. In general, the strength of the movie influence effects (i.e., their impact on alcohol prototypes and willingness) followed a pattern of whites > Hispanics > blacks. This pattern occurs in spite of the fact that black adolescents (a) view more R-rated movies than the other groups and therefore see more substance use onscreen (Sargent, Wills, Stoolmiller, Gibson, & Gibbons, 2006); and (b) are exposed to more alcohol and tobacco advertising (Schooler, Feighery, & Flora, 1996), perhaps, as some have suggested, because they are targeted by the tobacco and alcohol industry (Chen, Cruz, Schuster, Unger, & Johnson, 2002; Luke, Esmundo, & Bloom, 2000; Muggli, Pollay, Lew, & Joseph, 2002; Stoddard, Johnson, Sussman, Dent, & Cruz, 1998).

Movie exposure did have an effect on the black adolescents, but that effect was much weaker than it was for whites. The difference appears to occur because the social influence "component" is not operative for the black adolescents. Some of the results from Gibbons and colleagues (2008) are presented in Figure 3.2. As can be seen in the figure, among blacks, exposure led to more favorable images and more reports of friends' use (i.e., affiliation), however, effects are much weaker than they are for whites. For the whites, exposure predicted affiliation (with users) 8 months later, and then change (an increase) in affiliation 16 months later. These indirect paths through affiliation contributed a lot to the overall movie effects for whites. It is not clear to what extent this effect is due to selection—movies encouraging young people to seek out friends who are using—or perhaps just that friends tend to see the same movies together and therefore are simultaneously influenced. We will have more information on this issue (see discussion below) when the next (5th) wave of this study is collected.

In an attempt to explore this racial difference in movie-based social influence further, we conducted similar mediational analyses (also reported in Gibbons et al., 2008) with adolescents in the African American family panel study (FACHS). There were two measures of exposure: amount of movie and TV watching, and how much violence is included in the media that you watch (controlling for amount of watching increases confidence that it is actually the violence in the media that is responsible for the effects and not total exposure). A measure of resistance efficacy, which included items on the extent to which the adolescents thought they could resist peer pressure to engage in risky behaviors, like substance use, was collected as well. Multigroup models, stacking on a median split of this resistance measure, showed that among the high-resistance group, there were virtually no movie effects on risk images. In addition, risk images were only weakly related to risk BW, suggesting that the movies and the images were social influence sources that these high-resistance adolescents were not responding to (as much). Resistance

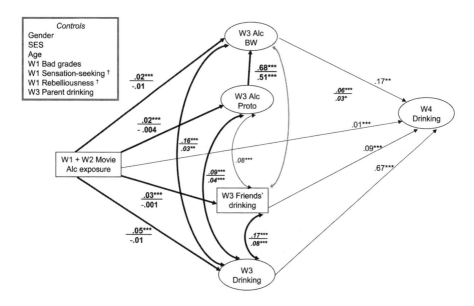

FIGURE 3.2. A multigroup structural equation model comparing factors that mediate the effects of exposure to alcohol in movies in European Americans versus African American adolescents. *Note.* Whites are above the line (n = 4036); blacks are below the line (n = 704). Significantly different paths and path coefficients are shown in bold. Correlations are in italics. Alc, alcohol; BW, behavioral willingness; Proto, prototype. $*p < .05$; $**p < .01$; $***p < .001$; † latent control variables.

efficacy was only weakly related to image favorability, BW, and use, so it was not a case of differential variance. Instead, the effects reflected the fact that high-resistance adolescents were not reacting cognitively or socially to the movies in the same way that the low-resistance group was. Our interpretation, then, was that the movie effects are largely a type of social influence—if a young person is good at resisting peer pressure, then that person is also likely to resist the pressure that comes with favorable image portrayals in the media that he or she sees.

Why the Difference?

As we stated earlier, other studies have found evidence suggesting that African Americans are less likely to be influenced by their peers than are European Americans, and some researchers have offered speculation as to why that is the case. A common perception is that peer influence may be replaced to some extent by parental and family influence among black children (Griesler & Kandel, 1998; Wallace & Muroff, 2002), though the evidence on this point appears to be mixed (Griesler, Kandel, & Davies, 2002). Others have focused more on the experience that black adolescents have growing up in environments that are often not accommodating and may be openly hostile. Flay and colleagues (1994) suggested that minorities may have a general mistrust of outsiders—others who might be telling them what to do. An interesting take on this perspective, with regard to substance use, can be seen in work examining racial/ethnic differences in response to tobacco advertising. Chen and colleagues (2002) reported that minorities, especially blacks, are less receptive to prosmoking advertising. More recently, Yerger, Daniel, and Malone (2005) suggested that black adolescents may be more inclined to view the efforts of tobacco companies to get them to smoke as coercive. Indeed, some have suggested that preventive interventions should use ethnic identity and ethnic pride as a means of bolstering resistance efficacy. The first step in this approach would be to point out to black children that they are being targeted by "big tobacco" in an effort to promote their product at the expense of the black community (Yerger et al., 2005). We did not find that either ethnic identity or racial socialization moderated the TV and movie effects in our FACHS sample. However, the resistance efficacy measure was significantly correlated with a measure of black pride (Smith & Brookins, 1997). The possibility that resistance efficacy could be boosted through ethnic pride campaigns is definitely worthy of future consideration.

Conclusion

There are meaningful and perhaps multiple individual differences in what we are calling "social influenceability." Culture and racial/ethnic background are two factors that we have explored, but others have considered additional factors, as well, including gender, age, and self-esteem, to mention a few. Our research has focused on cognitive mediation of influence effects—in essence, mediated moderation. Reviewing this work and that of others leads us to the conclusion that an individual difference factor that underlies most of these various effects is social comparison. Those who are high in comparison tendencies are also more other oriented and more image conscious. Thus, the path from risk image to BW is stronger for them (in fact, this is a basic assumption of the prototype model), and, more generally, they are more likely to pay attention to and respond to the behavior of others. Although there are no data to support this, it has been suggested that African American adolescents engage in different types of social comparison than do European Americans (Unger et al., 2001), and our data indicate that comparison is more common among Americans than Europeans, so there is reason to believe this may be an important factor.

INTERVENTION IMPLICATIONS

Recognizing the importance of peer influence in determining adolescent risk behavior, a number of interventions and preventive interventions have been developed that target adolescents' perceptions of what their friends and peers are doing. These "social norm" programs are based on a body of literature, mentioned earlier, indicating that adolescents tend to overestimate the prevalence of use among their peers (i.e., either false uniqueness or consensus, depending on whether the adolescents are doing the behavior themselves), and this overestimation, in turn, encourages their own use. Disabusing them of this misperception should, therefore, reduce the impact of (perceived) social influence, and several studies have suggested that it does (Donaldson, Graham, & Hansen, 1994; Fearnow-Kenney, Hansen, & McNeal, 2002).

Parenting

We used similar logic, along with the results of Gibbons and colleagues (2004), in a preventive intervention that was developed by Brody, Murry, Wills, and us (FG and MG). The Strong African American Families (SAAF) program was designed to slow onset and escalation of alcohol use among African American adolescents. SAAF is a family-based, dual-arm preventive intervention that targets both pathways to adolescent health risk, as outlined by the prototype model. One component of the intervention is based on previous work with families by Brody and his colleagues (Brody, Flor, Hollet-Wright, & McCoy, 1998; Brody & Stoneman, 1992). It is administered to the parents and concerns their communications with their children, as well as their rule setting and establishment of family norms. The focus here is on parents' attempts to encourage some forethought in their children—getting them to think ahead of time about the types of situations they are likely to be in and how they should respond, and how they (the parents) would want them to respond. In other words, this arm targets the reasoned pathway to (non)use.

Prototypes

The second component was based on the prototype model and was administered directly to the children. It focused on the social reaction pathway and its two primary elements. First, in group sessions, the children discussed their own risk images, as well as their perceptions of the images they thought their peers maintained (cf. Andrews et al., 2008). As in the social norm approach, they fairly quickly came to realize that their peers' risk images were as negative as their own, and much less favorable than they had originally thought. In addition, the concepts of social influence and peer pressure were discussed, but in terms of the distinction between BW and BI. In other words, the children discussed the fact that they had some curiosity and some interest in the behaviors—independent of what their peers were doing (or trying to get them to do). Thus, they acknowledged that, under the right circumstances, they might be willing to engage in some behaviors that they had no plans or intentions of engaging in.

The intervention had the desired effect on both members of the family (Gerrard, Gibbons, et al., 2006). As can be seen in Figure 3.3, parents' reports of their parenting effectiveness, including monitoring and communication, increased, and this effect was associated with less of an increase (relative to the control group) in the children's BI to drink. This change in BI, in turn, was related (marginally, $p < .07$) to less of an increase in reported consumption at the 24-month follow-up. Independent of this effect, the intervention also slowed the normal increase in risk image favorability that occurs during this developmental period (Andrews & Peterson, 2006), and this effect was associated with significantly less of an increase in BW, and then significantly less use at the follow-up. Moreover, comparisons of the dual-path model with models in which either the social reaction or the reasoned path was constrained (set to zero) indicated that the dual-path model provided a significantly better fit. In short, the results of the intervention offered support for the dual-path postulate of the prototype model, and in so doing, provide some evidence of an effective means of reducing adolescent alcohol consumption.

Conclusion

The family-based (dual-focus) approach to interventions is very popular (Kumpfer & Alvarado, 2003). The Gerrard and colleagues (2006) study provides some additional insight as to the cognitive changes that may underlie the effectiveness of these programs. The prototype model maintains that there are two pathways to risky behavior—some adolescents are planning to use and many others are willing but not intending to use. Inducing some forethought or consideration of the behavior, as well as its consequences and the situations in which it is likely to occur, will steer more adolescents onto the reasoned path, and

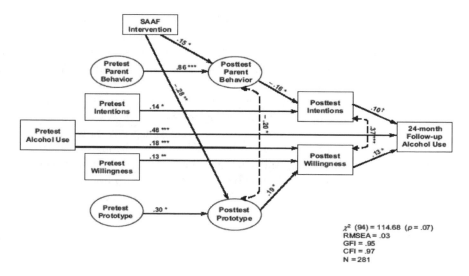

FIGURE 3.3. A structural equation model of mediation of the effects of a theory-based, dual-focus intervention to slow down escalation of alcohol use among African American preadolescents. SAAF, Strong African American Families Program; RMSEA, root-mean-square error of approximation; GFI, goodness-of-fit index; CFI, comparative fit index. † $p \leq .10$; *$p \leq .05$; **$p \leq .01$; ***$p \leq .001$. From Gerrard et al. (2006). Copyright 2006 by the American Psychological Association. Reprinted by permission.

that is likely to reduce their use. At the same time, focusing only on this path, perhaps by encouraging resistance to peer pressure, ignores many of the factors or motives that a number of studies have shown are influential, such as willingness to experiment, and perceptions of the attitudes and images associated with the behavior. At least through age 17 (Pomery et al., 2008), this dual-path approach is likely to be most effective in slowing down the escalation that inevitably occurs during adolescence.

GENERAL CONCLUSION

We began this chapter by suggesting that there are four ways that peers can influence the substance use behavior of adolescents and that three of them are direct: provision, modeling, and encouragement. Generally speaking, adolescents who hang out with others who are using substances are going to start using substances earlier, and they will use them more often. The same effects will hold for adolescents whose family members are using. Relatively speaking, however, those direct effects are likely to have more of an impact early on in the development of substance use habits, in other words, initiation more than escalation. As the adolescent ages and acquires more experience with substance use (and any other behavior) he or she is more capable of finding the substances, of using them, and of agreeing (or refusing) to use them when others suggest they should. The more enduring effects that peers, parents, and other family members are likely to have will operate through their impact on the adolescents' attitudes toward the substance, including their expectancies, such as the risks involved, their estimates of how common and acceptable the behavior is, and their perceptions of the type of person who uses. Examining how these indirect or mediated effects work will facilitate the understanding of this (sometimes) very irrational behavior and also the development of effective ways to change or at least slow it down.

REFERENCES

Andrews, J. A., Hampson, S., Barckley, M., Gerrard, M., & Gibbons, F. X. (2008). The effect of early cognitions on cigarette and alcohol use during adolescence. *Psychology of Addictive Behaviors, 22*, 96–106.

Andrews, J. A., & Peterson, M. (2006). The development of social images of substance users in children: A Guttman unidimensional scaling approach. *Journal of Substance Use, 11*, 305–321.

Ajzen, I. (1985). From intentions to actions: A theory of planned behavior. In J. Kuhl & J. Beckman (Eds.), *Action control from cognition to behavior* (pp. 11–39). Heidelberg, Germany: Springer.

Bauman, K. E., & Ennett, S. T. (1996). On the importance of peer influence for adolescent drug use: Commonly neglected considerations. *Addiction, 91*(2), 185–198.

Brody, G. H., Flor, D. L., Hollett-Wright, N., & McCoy, J. K. (1998). Children's development of alcohol use norms: Contributions of parent and sibling norms, children's temperaments, and parent-child discussions. *Journal of Family Psychology, 12*, 209–219.

Brody, G. H., Ge, X., Katz, J., & Arias, I. (2000). A longitudinal analysis of internalization of parental alcohol-use norms and adolescent alcohol use. *Applied Developmental Science, 4*, 71–79.

Brody, G. H., & Stoneman, Z. (1992). Child competence and developmental goals among rural black families: Investigating the links. In I. E. Sigel, A. V. McGillicuddy-DeLisi, & J. J. Goodnow (Eds.), *Parental belief systems: The psychological consequences for children* (2nd ed., pp. 415–431). Hillsdale, NJ: Erlbaum.

Brown, J. H. (2001). Youth, drugs, and resilience education. *Journal of Drug Education, 31*, 83–122.

Buunk, B. P., & Gibbons, F. X. (2007). Social comparison: The end of a theory and the emergence of a field. *Organizational Behavior and Human Decision Processes,* *102,* 3–21.

Callas, P. W., Flynn, B. S., & Worden, J. K. (2004). Potentially modifiable psychosocial factors associated with alcohol use during early adolescence. *Addictive Behaviors,* *29,* 1503–1515.

Casswell, S., Brasch, P., Gilmore, L., & Silva, P. (1985). Children's attitudes to alcohol and awareness of alcohol-related problems. *Addiction, 80,* 191–194.

Chaiken, S., & Trope, Y. (1999). *Dual-process theories in social psychology.* New York: Guilford Press.

Chen, X., Cruz, T. B., Schuster, D. V., Unger, J. B., & Johnson, C. A. (2002). Receptivity to protobacco media and its impact on cigarette smoking among ethnic minority youth in California. *Journal of Health Communication, 7,* 95–111.

Cutrona, C. E., Russell, D. W., Hessling, R. M., Brown, P. A., & Murry, V. (2000). Direct and moderating effects of community context on the psychological well-being of African American women. *Journal of Personality and Social Psychology, 79,* 1088–1101.

Donaldson, S. I., Graham, J. W., & Hansen, W. B. (1994). Testing the generalizability of intervening mechanism theories: Understand the effects of adolescent drug use prevention interventions. *Journal of Behavioral Medicine, 17,* 195–216.

Donaldson, S. I., Sussman, S., MacKinnon, D. P., Severson, H. H., Glynn, T., Murray, D. M., et al. (1996). Drug abuse prevention programming: Do we know what content works? *American Behavioral Scientist, 39,* 868–883.

Engels, R. C., Vitaro, F., Blokland, E. D., de Kemp, R., & Scholte, R. H. (2004). Influence and selection processes in friendships and adolescent smoking behaviour: The role of parental smoking. *Journal of Adolescence, 27,* 531–544.

Fearnow-Kenney, M., Hansen, W. B., & McNeal, R. B., Jr. (2002). Comparison of psychosocial influences on substance use in adolescents: Implications for prevention programming. *Journal of Child and Adolescent Substance Abuse, 11,* 1–24.

Fishbein, M., & Ajzen, I. (1975). *Belief, attitude, intention, and behavior: An introduction to theory and research.* Reading, MA: Addison-Wesley.

Flay, B. R., Hu, F. B., Siddiqui, O., Day, L. E., Hedeker, D., Petraitis, J., et al. (1994). Differential influence of parental smoking and friends' smoking on adolescent initiation and escalation of smoking. *Journal of Health and Social Behavior, 35,* 248–265.

Fuemmeler, B. M., Taylor, L. A., Metz, A. E., Jr., & Brown, R. T. (2002). Risk-taking and smoking tendency among primarily African American school children: Moderating influences of peer susceptibility. *Journal of Clinical Psychology in Medical Settings, 9,* 323–330.

Gerrard, M., Gibbons, F. X., Benthin, A. C., & Hessling, R. M. (1996). A longitudinal study of the reciprocal nature of risk behaviors and cognitions in adolescence: What you do shapes what you think, and vice versa. *Health Psychology, 15,* 344–354.

Gerrard, M., Gibbons, F. X., Brody, G. H., Murry, V. M., Cleveland, M. J., & Wills, T. A. (2006). A theory-based dual focus alcohol intervention for pre-adolescents: The Strong African American Families Program. *Psychology of Addictive Behavior, 20,* 185–195.

Gerrard, M., Gibbons, F. X., Stock, M. L., Vande Lune, L., & Cleveland, M. J. (2005). Images of smokers and willingness to smoke among African American pre-adolescents: An application of the prototype/willingness model of adolescent health risk behavior to smoking initiation. *Journal of Pediatric Psychology, 30,* 305–318.

Gibbons, F. X., & Buunk, B. P. (1999). Individual differences in social comparison: Development and validation of a measure of social comparison orientation. *Journal of Personality and Social Psychology, 76,* 129–142.

Gibbons, F. X., & Gerrard, M. (1997). Health images and their effects on health behavior. In B. P. Buunk & F. X. Gibbons (Eds.), *Health, coping, and well-being: Perspectives from social comparison theory* (pp. 63–94). Hillsdale, NJ: Erlbaum.

Gibbons, F. X., Gerrard, M., & Lane, D. J. (2003). A social reaction model of adolescent health risk. In J. M. Suls & K. Wallston (Eds.), *Social psychological foundations of health and illness* (pp. 107–136). Oxford, UK: Blackwell.

Gibbons, F. X., Gerrard, M., Reimer, R. A., & Pomery, E. A. (2006). Unintentional behavior: A subrational approach to health risk. In D. de Ridder & J. de Wit (Eds.), *Self-regulation in health behavior* (pp. 45–70). West Sussex, UK: Wiley.

Gibbons, F. X., Gerrard, M., Vande Lune, L. S., Wills, T. A., Brody, G., & Conger, R. D. (2004). Context and cognition: Environmental risk, social influence, and adolescent substance use. *Personality and Social Psychology Bulletin, 30,* 1048–1061.

Gibbons, F. X., Helweg-Larsen, M., & Gerrard, M. (1995). Prevalence estimates and adolescent risk behavior: Cross-cultural differences in social influence. *Journal of Applied Psychology, 80,* 107–121.

Gibbons, F. X., Lane, D., Gerrard, M., Pomery, E. A., & Lautrup, C. (2002). Drinking and driving: A prospective assessment of the relation between risk cognitions and risk behavior. *Risk Decision and Policy, 7,* 267–283.

Gibbons, F. X., Pomery, E. A., Gerrard, M., Sargent, J. D., Weng, C.-Y., Wills, T. A., et al. (2008). *Media as social influence: Individual differences in the effects of media on adolescent alcohol cognitions and consumption.* Manuscript submitted for publication.

Griesler, P. C., & Kandel, D. B. (1998). Ethnic differences in correlates of adolescent cigarette smoking. *Journal of Adolescent Health, 23,* 167–180.

Griesler, P. C., Kandel, D. B., & Davies, M. (2002). Ethnic differences in predictors of initiation and persistence of adolescent cigarette smoking in the National Longitudinal Survey of Youth. *Nicotine and Tobacco Research, 4,* 79–93.

Guimond, S., Chatard, A., Branscombe, N. R., Brundt, S., Buunk, A. P., Conway, M. A. (2006). Social comparisons across cultures II: Change and stability in self-views—Experimental evidence. In S. Guimond (Ed.), *Social comparison and social psychology: Understanding cognition, intergroup relations, and culture* (pp. 318–344). New York: Cambridge University Press.

Hamm, J. V. (2000). Do birds of a feather flock together?: The variables bases for African American, Asian American, and European American adolescents' selection of similar friends. *Developmental Psychology, 36,* 209–219.

Hansen, W. B., & McNeal, R. B., Jr. (1997). How D.A.R.E. works: An examination of program effects on mediating variables. *Health Education and Behavior, 24,* 165–176.

Headen, S. W., Bauman, K. E., Deane, G. D., & Koch, G. G. (1991). Are the correlates of cigarette smoking initiation different for black and white adolescents? *American Journal of Public Health, 81,* 854–858.

Hoffman, B. R., Monge, P., Chou, C.-P., & Valente, T. W. (2007). The roles of perceived peer influence and peer selection on adolescent smoking: Path analysis comparison by gender and ethnicity. *Addictive Behaviors, 32* 1546–1554.

Hofstede, G. (1980). *Culture's consequences: International differences in work-related values.* Beverly Hills, CA: Sage.

Hofstede, G. (2003). *Culture's consequences: Comparing values, behaviors, institutions and organizations across nations* (2nd ed.). Thousand Oaks, CA: Sage.

Iedema, J., & Poppe, M. (1999). Expectations of others' social value orientations in specific and general populations. *Personality and Social Psychology Bulletin, 25,* 1443–1450.

Jaccard, J., Blanton, H., & Dodge, T. (2005). Peer influences on risk behavior: An analysis of the effects of a close friend. *Developmental Psychology, 41,* 135–147.

Kandel, D. B. (1996). The parental and peer contexts of adolescent deviance: An algebra of interpersonal influences. *Journal of Drug Issues, 26,* 289–315.

Kumpfer, K. L., & Alvarado, R. (2003). Family-strengthening approaches for the prevention of youth problem behaviors. *American Psychologist, 58,* 457–465.

Landrine, H., Richardson, J. L., Klonoff, E. A., & Flay, B. (1994). Cultural diversity in the predictors of adolescent cigarette smoking: The relative influence of peers. *Journal of Behavioral Medicine, 17,* 331–346.

Litchfield, R., & White, K. M. (2006). Young adults' willingness and intentions to use amphetamines: An application of the theory of reasoned action. *E-Journal of Applied Psychology: Clinical and Social Issues, 2,* 45–51.

Luke, D., Esmundo, E., & Bloom, Y. (2000). Smoke signs: Patterns of tobacco billboard advertising in a metropolitan region. *Tobacco Control, 9,* 16–32.

Luszczynska, A., Gibbons, F. X., Piko, B. F., & Tekozel, M. (2004). Self-regulatory cognitions, social comparison, and perceived peers' behaviors as predictors of nutrition and physical activity: A comparison among adolescents in Hungary, Poland, Turkey, and USA. *Psychology and Health, 19,* 577–593.

Lynam, D. R., Milich, R., Zimmerman, R., Novak, S. P., Logan, T. K., Martin C., et al. (1999). Project DARE: No effects at 10-year follow-up. *Journal of Consulting and Clinical Psychology, 67,* 590–593.

Muggli, M. E., Pollay, R. W., Lew, R., & Joseph, A. M. (2002). Targeting of Asian Americans and Pacific Islanders by the tobacco industry: Results from the Minnesota Tobacco Depository. *Tobacco Control, 11,* 201–209.

Newcomb, M. D., Huba, G. J., & Bentler, P. M. (1983). Mothers' influence on the drug use of their children: Confirmatory tests of direct modeling and mediational theories. *Developmental Psychology, 19,* 714–726.

National Institute on Drug Abuse. (2003). *Preventing drug use among children and adolescents: A research-based guide for parents, educators, and community leaders* (2nd ed.; NIH Publication No. 04-4212B). Bethesda, MD: National Institute on Drug Abuse, National Institutes of Health.

Piko, B. F., Gibbons, F. X., Luszczynska, A., & Tekozel, M. (2005). Adolescents' health behavior from a cross-cultural perspective: Does a coherent lifestyle exist? *European Journal of Public Health, 15,* 393–398.

Pomery, E. A., Gibbons, F. X., Gerrard, M., Cleveland, M. J., Brody, G. H., & Wills, T. A. (2005). Families and risk: Prospective analyses of familial and social influences on adolescent substance use. *Journal of Family Psychology, 19,* 560–570.

Pomery, E. A., Gibbons, F. X., Reis-Bergan , M., & Gerrard, M. (2008). *From willingness to intention: Experience moderates the shift from reactive to reasoned behavior.* Manuscript submitted for publication.

Prinstein, M. J., & Wang, S. S. (2005). False consensus and adolescent peer contagion: Examining discrepancies between perceptions and actual reported levels of friends' deviant and health risk behavior. *Journal of Abnormal Child Psychology, 33*(3), 293–306.

Reyna, V. F., & Farley, F. (2006). Risk and rationality in adolescent decision making: Implications for theory, practice, and public policy. *Psychological Science in the Public Interest, 7,* 1–44.

Robinson, L. A., Murray, D. M., Alfano, C. M., Zbikowski, S. M., Blitstein, J. L., & Klesges, R. C. (2006). Ethnic differences in predictors of adolescent onset and escalation: A longitudinal study from 7th to 12th grade. *Nicotine and Tobacco Research, 8,* 297–307.

Ross, L., Greene, D., & House, P. (1977). The false consensus effect: An egocentric bias in social perception and attribution processes. *Journal of Experimental Social Psychology, 13,* 279–301.

Sargent, J. D., Wills, T. A., Stoolmiller, M., Gibson, J., & Gibbons, F. X. (2006). Alcohol use in motion pictures and its relation with early-onset teen drinking. *Journal of Studies on Alcohol, 67,* 54–65.

Schooler, C., Feighery, E., & Flora, J. A. (1996). Seventh graders' self-reported exposure to cigarette marketing and its relationship to their smoking behavior. *American Journal of Public Health, 86,* 1216–1221.

Simons, R. L., Murry, V., McLoyd, V., Hsiu, L. K., Cutrona, C., & Conger, R. D. (2002). Discrimination, crime, ethnic identity, and parenting as correlates of depressive symptoms among African American children: A multilevel analysis. *Development and Psychopathology, 14,* 371–393.

Smith, E. P., & Brookins, C. C. (1997). Toward the development of an ethnic identity measure for African American youth. *Journal of Black Psychology, 23,* 358–377.

Spijkerman, R., van den Eijnden, R. J., & Engels, R. C. (2005). Self-comparison processes, prototypes, and smoking onset among early adolescents. *Preventive Medicine, 40,* 785–794.

Stock, M. L., Gibbons, F. X., & Gerrard, M. (2008). *Absent-exempt bias: The downside of escaping the negative consequences of risky behavior.* Manuscript in preparation.

Stoddard, J. L., Johnson, C. A., Sussman, S., Dent, C., & Cruz, T. B. (1998). Tailoring tobacco advertising to minorities in Los Angeles County. *Journal of Health Communication, 3,* 137–146.

Stone, M. R., & Brown, B. B. (1998). In the eye of the beholder: Adolescents' perceptions of peer crowd stereotypes. In R. E. Muuss & H. D. Porton (Eds.), *Adolescent behavior and society: A book of readings* (5th ed., pp. 158–169). New York: McGraw-Hill.

Triandis, H. C., Bontempo, R., & Villareal, M. J. (1988). Individualism and collectivism: Cross-cultural perspectives on self-ingroup relationships. *Journal of Personality and Social Psychology, 54,* 323–338.

Unger, J. B. (2003). Peers, family, media, and adolescent smoking: Ethnic variation in risk factors in a national sample. *Adolescent and Family Health, 3,* 65–70.

Unger, J. B., Rohrbach, L. A., Cruz, T. B., Baezconde-Garbanati, L., Howard, K. A., Palmer, P. H., et al. (2001). Ethnic variation in peer influences on adolescent smoking. *Nicotine and Tobacco Research, 3,* 167–176.

Wallace, J. M., & Muroff, J. R. (2002). Preventing substance abuse among African American children and youth: Race differences in risk factor exposure and vulnerability. *Journal of Primary Prevention, 22,* 235–261.

Weinstein, N. D. (1980). Unrealistic optimism about future life events. *Journal of Personality and Social Psychology, 39*(5), 806–820.

Weinstein, N. (1982). Unrealistic optimism about susceptibility to health problems. *Journal of Behavioral Medicine, 5,* 441–460.

White, H. R., Bates, M. E., & Johnson, V. (1991). Learning to drink: Familial, peer and media influences. In D. Pittman & H. R. White (Eds.), *Society, culture and drinking patterns reexamined* (pp. 177–197). New Brunswick, NJ: Rutgers Center of Alcohol Studies.

Wills, T. A., Ainette, M. G., Mendoza, D., Walker, C., Gibbons, F. X., Gerrard, M., et al. (2007). Self-control, symptomatology, and substance use precursors: Test of a theoretical model in a community sample of 9-year old children. *Psychology of Addictive Behaviors, 21,* 205–215.

Wills, T. A., Gibbons, F. X., Gerrard, M., Murry, V. M., & Brody, G. H. (2003). Family communication and religiosity related to substance use and sexual behavior in early adolescence: A test for pathways through self-control and prototype perceptions. *Psychology of Addictive Behaviors, 17,* 312–323.

Wills, T. A., Sargent, J. D., Stoolmiller, M., Gibbons, F. X., Worth, K. A., & Dal Cin, S. (2007). Movie exposure to smoking cues and adolescent smoking onset: A test for mediation through peer affiliations. *Health Psychology, 26,* 769–776.

Yerger, V. B., Daniel, M. R., & Malone, R. E. (2005). Taking it to the streets: Responses of African American young adults to internal tobacco industry documents. *Nicotine and Tobacco Research, 7,* 163–172.

Zucker, R. A., Kincaid, S. B., Fitzgerald, H. E., & Bingham, C. R. (1995). Alcohol schema acquisition in preschoolers: Differences between children of alcoholics and children of nonalcoholics. *Alcoholism: Clinical and Experimental Research, 19,* 1011–1017.

CHAPTER 4

Dynamics and Ecology
of Adolescent Peer Influence

Thomas J. Dishion, Timothy F. Piehler,
and Michael W. Myers

OVERVIEW

There is ample evidence that peer influence can undermine children's and adolescents' emotional adjustment as well as the effectiveness of mental health interventions (for a review, see Dodge, Dishion, & Lansford, 2006). Research on peer factors associated with problem behavior has traditionally fallen within the purview of sociology and criminology. The focus on understanding the dynamics of peer influence, however, is fairly recent to developmental psychology. The study of the peer dynamics of influence has been useful, in that we are beginning to understand the developmental origins of peer influence as well as the dynamics under which the influence of peers are amplified.

This chapter proposes a developmental perspective of peer influence from childhood through adolescence, and is organized around testing the following three hypotheses:

1. *The social augmentation hypothesis:* Involvement with a network of friendships that encourage deviant behavior is a developmental adaptation that emerges from the school and family contexts.
2. *Arrested socialization hypothesis:* From a developmental perspective, chronic involvement in problem behavior precludes the

development of critical social and emotional competencies such as self-regulation and, therefore, renders youth more vulnerable to the influence of peers later in development.

3. *Intrasubjectivity hypothesis:* The key mechanism underlying peer influence is the intrinsic reinforcement resulting from the sharing of deviant values (thoughts, perceptions, experiences) within an interpersonal context of endorsement and agreement.

The empirical support for these three hypotheses is summarized below. Data from an ongoing prevention trial is presented as illustrative; in addition, future research is suggested that would more rigorously address each hypothesis.

SOCIAL AUGMENTATION HYPOTHESIS

The social augmentation hypothesis attempts to account for why some children become involved in friendships that, on face value, appear to be relatively undesirable, low quality, and promotive of antisocial values. This hypothesis purports that youth enter into these friendships because they are actually functionally adaptive within their immediate environments. The general idea of social augmentation is based on two principles. The first is that interpersonal attraction as early as childhood is based on similarities in attitude and behavior (Cairns, 1979; Dinges & Oetting, 1993; Gest, 2006; Kandel, 1986). In general, individuals will seek interaction with others like themselves. Furthermore, the characteristics that one uses to identify similar others change with development. For example, a tendency toward aggression may be the salient feature for organizing friendships in early to middle childhood (e.g., Snyder & Brown, 1983), whereas substance use may be the salient feature that organizes friendships in adolescence (Dinges & Oetting, 1993; Kandel, 1986). Clique and friendship formation, therefore, are influenced by the dynamics of attraction of individuals with similar behaviors and values.

The second principle is that marginalization (or peer rejection) amplifies the role of deviant values and behavior in the formation of cliques and friendships. *Marginalization* refers to the relative likelihood of reinforcement being lower for some individuals compared with others within a social context. For example, youth with poor social skills or high levels of aggressive behavior may experience very few positive interactions with their peers on a daily basis, whereas more socially skilled youth are likely to experience many more rewarding and reinforcing peer experiences. The typical index of marginalization in peer relations research is peer rejection (Coie, Dodge, & Coppotelli, 1982; Coie & Kuppersmidt, 1983; Dodge,

1983). Peer rejection in the school environment appears to be a developmentally salient experience. Children who are rejected by peers are likely to coalesce into groups of other rejected youth who support deviant behaviors and values (Bagwell, Newcomb, & Bukowski, 1998; Cairns, Cairns, Neckerman, Gest, & Gariepy, 1988; Dishion, Patterson, Stoolmiller, & Skinner, 1991; Laird, Jordan, Dodge, Pettit, & Bates, 2001; Miller-Johnson, Coie, Maumary-Gremaud, Bierman, & The Conduct Problems Prevention Research Group, 2002). Most research has examined the effect of peer rejection on subsequent social and emotional development during the developmental time span between childhood and adolescence. However, recent evidence suggests that for males, peer rejection at school in childhood predicts young adult social–emotional adjustment even after controlling for robust measures of antisocial behavior and academic skills in childhood and adolescence (Nelson & Dishion, 2004).

The confluence model of deviant peer aggregation and influence was originally introduced in the 1990s (Dishion, Patterson, & Griesler, 1994). The confluence model is summarized in Figure 4.1. In general, it suggests that antisocial behavior in childhood elicits peer rejection and interferes with academic success in the school context. Peer rejection and academic failure alone predict aggregation of children into deviant peer cliques. Although the precise manner in which this occurs has not been thoroughly studied, it is clear that academic tracking may be part of the problem (Kellam, 1990). The current strategy is to place children who do poorly in academic subjects in classes with curricula that meet their needs. This process in and of itself often places children with behavior problems in close proximity to other children with similar behavior problems, allowing friendships to develop.

Furthermore, it is assumed that marginalization vis-à-vis peer rejection over time augments the value of any peer interaction (even with other rejected and deviant youths) for high-risk children. Augmentation is a reinforcement concept that describes the increasing reinforcing value of a stimulus as a function of antecedent conditions such as deprivation.

FIGURE 4.1. The confluence model for deviant peer aggregation.

With regard to academic tracking, it would seem likely that these children and adolescents (coming from a context that was nonreinforcing and rejecting) will be less discriminating when selecting peer interactants in a new school context, and instead focus on the most salient feature—other children's problem behavior. This process that describes the movement of children experiencing academic difficulties and peer rejection in schools with movement into deviant peer cliques has also been described as "shopping" (Patterson, Reid, & Dishion, 1992) or niche finding (Scarr & McCartney, 1983).

We have conducted research on the social augmentation hypothesis in early adolescence with a sample of youth involved in the Project Alliance prevention trial (Dishion & Kavanagh, 2003). Project Alliance is an ongoing longitudinal trial of 998 multiethnic adolescents and their families in a large Pacific Northwest city. It was designed to prevent early onset of adolescent problem behaviors by supporting middle-school families living in high-risk neighborhoods. Participants were surveyed annually beginning in the sixth grade (ages 11–12), primarily in their schools, using a variety of instruments that assess problem behaviors and other indices of socioemotional adjustment and functioning, and they completed additional videotaped observation tasks at a research institute. We examined the grade 6 (ages 11–12) predictors of grade 8 gang involvement (ages 13–14) (Dishion, Nelson, & Yasui, 2005). We included only European American and African American children in the sample. We looked at these two cultural groups primarily because one reason gangs develop in multicultural contexts that involve minority youth is that peer rejection and stigmatization go hand in hand in such settings. Therefore, one would predict higher deviant peer–clique involvement and peer influence in contexts where children are partially rejected because of their racial and/or cultural background. As expected, we found higher levels of gang involvement for African American compared with European American children. However, when controlling for the process variables (i.e., peer rejection, academic failure, etc.), ethnic differences were minimal. Note that we predicted early adolescent gang involvement from grade 6 (age 11) antisocial behavior, peer nominations of rejection, peer nominations of peer acceptance, and academic grades. Gang involvement in grade 8 (age 13) was measured using an intensive composite based on peer nominations, counselor nomination, teacher ratings, and self-report. We examined these models for potential gender differences as well. The resulting multivariate models are summarized in Figures 4.2 and 4.3 for males and females. For girls, a history of antisocial behavior, peer rejection, and low academic grades combined to predict gang involvement at ages 13–14. For boys, the same predictors in addition to peer acceptance predicted gang involvement.

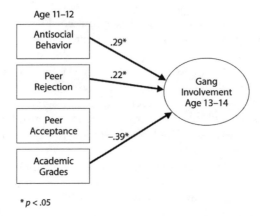

FIGURE 4.2. Predicting female gang involvement from sixth-grade adjustment.

These data do suggest that marginalization is a factor in describing the aggregation of peers into groups such as gangs. Gang involvement is particularly relevant to the issue of peer influence in that considerable research has shown that gang involvement leads to amplification of problem behavior for adolescents (e.g., Thornberry, 1998). The findings suggesting that peer nominations of liking and disliking contributed positively to deviant clique membership fits well with some of the work of Rodkin and colleagues (e.g., Rodkin, Farmer, Pearl, & Van Acker, 2000) on the heterogeneity of clique distribution of popular boys. Consistent

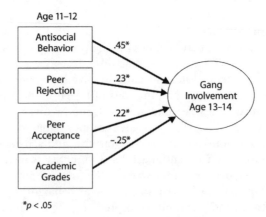

FIGURE 4.3. Predicting male gang involvement from sixth-grade adjustment.

with previous research, we also found that early adolescent problem behavior in high-risk contexts was associated with peer acceptance (Stormshak et al., 1999). Consistent with the social augmentation hypothesis, it was peer liking and rejection that predicted later gang involvement. Thus, in summary, we suggest that marginalization in the school predicts children's movement into high-risk, deviant peer contexts.

ARRESTED SOCIALIZATION HYPOTHESIS

The concept of arrested socialization first occurred in the volume on coercive family process by Patterson (1982). At one point in research on antisocial behavior, distinctions were made between unsocialized and socialized aggression (e.g., Quay, 1983; Shapiro, Quay, Hogan, & Schwartz, 1988). Dodge and Coie (1987) also used the terms to describe the distinction between reactive and proactive aggression. Children and adolescents who are arrested in development are those who lack myriad self-regulatory skills inherent in interpersonal relationships. There is some consensus in the literature that early onset of problem behavior is associated with arrested socialization (Moffitt, 1993; Patterson, 1993; Robins, 1966). There is support for this hypothesis when comparing basic social skills of early-onset delinquents versus nondelinquents (Dishion, Loeber, Stouthamer-Loeber, & Patterson, 1984), quality of the friendship (Poulin, Dishion, & Haas, 1999), and social-cognitive accuracy in the friendships of antisocial versus well-adjusted boys (Brendgen, Vitaro, & Bukowski, 2000). We propose that self-regulation is a unifying concept in the vast skill-deficit literature, in that control over one's own emotion, attention, and behavior is fundamental to skill development in childhood and adolescence. We futher propose that a lack of self-regulation renders youth more vulnerable to social influences toward deviance in friendships (Dishion & Patterson, 2006).

We examined this hypothesis with subgroups of the original Project Alliance sample. We created three developmental trajectory groups post hoc from the longitudinal data in the Project Alliance sample. The groups were defined to consist of an equal number of males and females. Thus, 40 youth were represented in each group, half of whom were male. One hundred twenty youth were selected reflecting the following three trajectories:

1. *Early-onset and persisting:* These were youth with high self-reported problem behavior (above the median) at ages 11, 12, 13, 14, and 16. Youth in this group reported high levels of prob-

lem behavior on self-reported surveys administered in the school context.

2. *Adolescent-onset:* These were youth with low to average levels of self-reported problem behavior at every age but high levels at age 16–17.

3. *Successful:* These were youth with low to average levels of self-reported problem behavior at all ages and average or better than average academic grades.

First, we conducted an analysis of the validity of the three groups with respect to involvement in high-risk deviant contexts. As expected, the early-onset and persistent youth had much higher scores on the composite measure of gang involvement at age 13–14 compared with adolescent onset and successful youth. The differences among the three groups were statistically reliable, $F(2, 97) = 32.30$, $p < .001$.

Second, we examined the levels of self-regulation of the three groups. In the conceptualization and measurement of self-regulation, we rely on the work of Rothbart and Posner (Rothbart, Ellis, & Posner, 2004; Rothbart, Ellis, Rueda, & Posner, 2003), which posits a correlation between temperamental effortful control and the emergence of self-regulation in childhood and adolescence. Effortful control from this perspective rests in attention management as it pertains to inhibiting or activating behavior, and for managing distracting information (such as in a Stroop task). To examine the three groups for differences in self-regulatory ability, we created a composite self-regulation score at age 16–17 from parent and self-reported ratings of inhibitory control, attention regulation, and activation control by using the Rothbart scales of effortful control. In addition, we used a teacher rating of self-regulation in the school context, focusing on a similar set of abilities measured with the Rothbart scale. Consistent with the arrested socialization hypothesis, early-starting youth demonstrated poorer self-regulation when compared with adolescent-onset and successful youth, $F(2, 117) = 20.30$, $p < .001$ (See Figure 4.4).

Self-regulation has been the focus of our recent research examining specifically how arrested socialization may affect the extent of peer influence. Looking at the same multireporter construct of self-regulation described earlier in the Project Alliance sample, we found that poor self-regulation was associated with a greater impact of association with a deviant peer group on growth in antisocial behavior (Gardner, Dishion, & Connell, 2007). Looking at tobacco use, those youth with poor self-regulation were more affected by associating with tobacco-using peers. Poorly regulated youth with tobacco-using peers were much more likely to demonstrate growth in tobacco use, even while controlling for patterns of past use (Piehler & Dishion, 2007). Self-regulatory ability seems

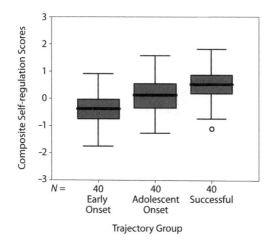

FIGURE 4.4. A composite measure of self-regulation as a function of developmental onset of problem behavior.

to be important in resisting the pull of joining in peers' problem behavior. It appears that more highly regulated youth have been better socialized to inhibit such prepotent responses that may be more immediately reinforcing (i.e., yielding to peer norms and influence) in favor of longer term goals. Broadly, the outcomes of arrested socialization appear to be profound, with poor self-regulatory abilities corresponding to maladjusted friendships, a heightened vulnerability to deviant peer influence, and a persistence of problem behaviors.

One critical aspect of self-regulation is establishing mutual, satisfying relationships with peers. Dyadic mutuality has typically been operationalized through ratings of responsiveness, reciprocity, and cooperation and has been demonstrated to be correlated with positive developmental outcomes in children in parent–child dyads (Deater-Deckard & Petrill, 2004; Kochanska, 1997; Kochanska & Murray, 2000). Piehler and Dishion (2007) developed a macro rating scale of dyadic mutuality that includes ratings of self-centeredness and other-mindedness, as well as conflict, shared understanding and shared attitudes, and values in our assessment of dyadic mutuality.

In examining differences in dyadic mutuality across the three groups, we found that early-onset and persistent youth demonstrated less mutuality in their interactions when compared with late-starting and successful adolescents $F(2, 117) = 6.37$, $p < .01$ (see Figure 4.5). That is, early starters' interactions were less responsive and reciprocal with their friends.

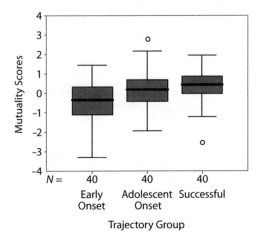

FIGURE 4.5. Dyadic mutuality as a function of developmental onset of problem behavior.

We return to the analysis of dyadic mutuality below, as it turns out the covariation between mutuality and deviant peer influence is not as it would seem from inspection of Figure 4.5 above (Piehler & Dishion, 2007). The concept of intrasubjectivity among friends is useful for further understanding influence over time.

INTRASUBJECTIVITY HYPOTHESIS

Intrasubjectivity refers to the concept of shared understanding. The concept arises from the vast contributions of Vygostky (1986) to the notion of children's cognitive development. Vygotsky proposed that cognitive development in children is best understood as a social process that involves scaffolding from the more competent adult world. Adults' efforts to promote cognitive development are optimized when they are made within their "zone of proximal development" (Wertsch, 1984). A shared cognitive understanding between the adult and child is necessary for working with a child within her or his zone of proximal development (Rogoff & Gardner, 1984). Initially the notion of intrasubjectivity was applied to research on effective adult strategies for promoting children's cognitive development in everyday life (e.g., creating shopping lists and the like). However, the concept of intrasubjectivity has also been applied to cultural learning in the context of peers (Rogoff, 1993; Tomasello, Kruger, & Ratner, 1993). We propose that intrasubjectivity is the cornerstone of an influence process that explains "deviance" as a culture within deviant peer groups.

During the past 15 years, we have been interested in identifying the interpersonal mechanism that underlies peer influence and the extent to which it predicts maintenance and amplification of problem behavior in children and adolescents. Not surprisingly, during that time our approach to understanding those mechanisms changed as we learned more. We start by describing the reinforcement approach (e.g., Skinner, 1954) that we used originally to frame this work. However, more recently we have conceptualized the mechanisms of peer influence in terms of a dynamic systems approach and discuss the key concepts and differences of this framework. Additionally, we provide examples of studies generated by this new framework.

The key idea of the reinforcement framework was that in close relationships, attention and positive reactions to verbal statements in deviant behavior to strengthen those response tendencies over time. In human learning, language plays a unique role. For example, statements that are value laden reflect a variety of potential response tendencies. Reinforcement for value-laden statements is often equivalent to reinforcement for those connected behaviors within that value network (Hayes & Berens, 2004; Hayes & Grundt, 1997). For example, descriptions of past actions such as "I locked the teacher in her classroom" accompanied by hysterical laughter from a friend functions to reinforce that behavior regardless of the true value of the statement. Finally, it is important to realize that it is the relative rate of reinforcement in a verbal interchange that is the salient factor for determining whether a set of values functions as a reinforcer. That is, if a friend responds almost exclusively to verbal statements of deviant behavior and ignores other types of verbal statements, the reinforcing value of deviant behavior and talk are augmented (Hernstein, 1970).

We have applied the reinforcement framework to verbal exchanges among friends and found it to be quite predictive of growth and amplification in problem behavior in middle adolescence (Dishion, Capaldi, Spracklen, & Li, 1995; Dishion, Eddy, Haas, Li, & Spracklen, 1997; Dishion & Patterson, 1996) and for growth in deviant behavior to young adulthood (Dishion, Nelson, & Bullock, 2004; Dishion et al., 2005; Patterson, Dishion, & Yoerger, 2000). More recently we have approached the friendship dyad as a dynamic system. The first effort to examine deviant talk as an "attractor" was to examine to what extent the length of the deviant discussions in some friendship dyads increased over the course of the observation period (Granic & Dishion, 2003). This increase in length in deviant talk episodes was most salient for adolescents who were characterized as experiencing internalizing and externalizing (i.e., comorbid) adjustment difficulties. Most recently, we examined the extent of order and predictability in the sequential transitions between an adolescent and his friend using the time-honored index of entropy. Entropy is a concept applicable to any dynamic system whether it be thermal dynamics or social behavior (Attneave, 1959). The index describes the predictability between two sets of events. The predictability of the peer's response given the target child's behavior is one example. Highly predictable systems are well-organized systems. In general, well-organized systems require energy, thus the term *entropy*. *Low entropy* refers to high predictability; *high entropy* refers to systems marked by disorganization and unpredictability.

In our analysis of friendships, we found a general tendency for the dynamic organization of the friendship interaction to become lower in entropy from early to late adolescence. This suggests that as adolescents mature, their interactions become more organized and predictable, as one would expect from a developmental framework. When comparing early-onset and persistent adolescents with typically developing adolescents, we found that, in general, the interactions of the antisocial youth were higher in entropy (i.e., less organized, predictable) than those of typically developing adolescents.

What is interesting, however, is that we found an interaction between the level of deviant talk and entropy. The interaction was such that the higher levels of deviant talk and the lower levels of entropy (more predictable, organized) predicted extreme growth in problem behavior from early adolescence to young adulthood (age 24). Thus, though the interactions of antisocial youth compared with those of typically developing youth were less predictable, when they were deviant and predictable, the influence seemed to be much greater. Of course, in a longitudinal analysis such as this, it is impossible to disentangle cause from effect in that more deviant youth could certainly select the most deviant friends; the better match would predict a more organized, fluid, and predictable interchange that in turn would mark a growth process.

These analyses of the friendship interactions, inspired by a dynamic systems approach (Granic & Dishion, 2003; Lewis, 2000), suggest a somewhat different interpersonal mechanism underlying peer influence. From a Skinnerian point of view, reinforcement would by definition require a reaction from the listener that is qualitatively different from the response of the speaker. The dynamic analysis of interactions, however, suggests that a shared understanding as indicated by reciprocating a topic may be as powerful in reinforcement terms as an effectively positive reaction. Indeed, perusal of the original observed data suggested that a majority of the reactions to verbal statements were either reciprocated topics or topic switches. Thus, we propose that the function of a value statement in maintaining the conversation, in general, can lead to maintaining of amplifying behavior consistent with those values.

We test this hypothesis using a second generation version of the Interpersonal Topic Code applied to the Project Alliance subsample described earlier (Piehler & Dishion, 2004). The revised Topic Code includes only five code categories: deviant talk, normative talk, moral talk, assent, and validate. These interactions were also coded using a Simple Affective Coding System (SACS) as described earlier, including the following five affect codes: negative affect, distressed affect, neutral affect, validating affect, and positive affect (Jabson & Dishion, 2004). We used the affective exchange as an indicator of the interpersonal dynamic between the youth and the best friend. Males and females were included in this analysis.

To understand the dynamic exchange between a youth and the friend, we used the state space grid approach developed by our colleagues (Granic & Lamy, 2002; Lewis, 1999, 2000). Figures 4.6a and 4.6b show two dyads mapped on the state space grid. Note that in Figure 4.6a, the interchange between the youth and his peer is somewhat chaotic; whereas in Figure 4.6b, the interchange between the youth and his friend is quite well organized and exclusively ranged between neutral, positive, and validating affect. Figure 4.6b reveals a low-entropy interchange, whereas Figure 4.6a reveals a high-entropy exchange. Using these dynamic grids as a guide, we defined conversation bouts as successive exchanges between neutral validating and positive affect between the youth and friend. The bouts could be described as either deviant or nondeviant based on the predominant topic during that interchange. Duration of the bout (either deviant or nondeviant) was used as an index of the intrasubjectivity in the friendship dyad with respect to normative and deviant behavior.

As expected, we found that early-onset persistent youth had on average longer deviant talk bouts than did either the adolescent-onset or successful youth. In fact, successful youth had very few deviant talk bouts of more than 1 or 2 seconds. In contrast, the average bout for a deviant youth was close to 10 seconds and the distribution was approximately normal. Figure 4.7 shows the box plots of deviant talk bouts for the three developmental groups in the Project Alliance subsample.

Similarly, the normative discussion bouts could also be compared for the three groups (see Figure 4.8). In contrast to the deviant talk bouts, the normative discussion bouts were normally distributed for all three developmental groups and were highest on average for successful youth, second for adolescent-onset, and third for early-onset. The differences among the three groups were statistically reliable on deviant and normative discussion bouts.

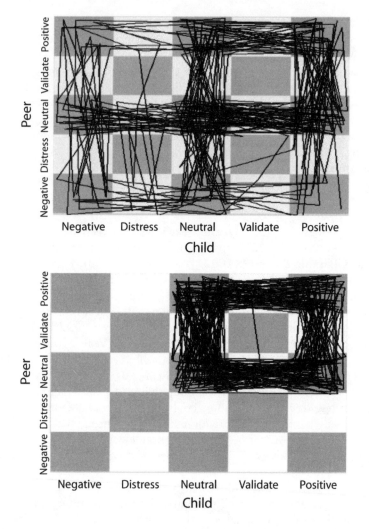

FIGURES 4.6a and 4.6b. Examples of state space grids describing friendship interactions.

We first looked at antecedents that predicted the length of deviant talk bouts. Table 4.1 shows the correlations between the youth's behavior in middle school and the length of their deviant talk bouts at age 16 and 17. The data are summarized for 60 males and 60 females collapsing across the three developmental groups. Perusal of Table 4.1 reveals that, as expected, teacher ratings of risk in sixth grade as well as peer nominations of rejection were positively correlated with the longer

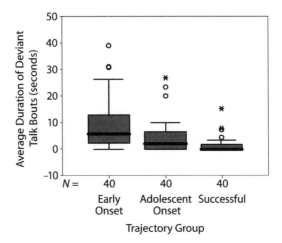

FIGURE 4.7. Average duration of deviant talk bouts as a function of developmental onset of problem behavior.

deviant talk bouts for males and females. Interestingly, the gang construct at eighth grade predicted most highly (correlation $r = .52$, $p < .001$) for only girls and not boys. This suggests, as we saw earlier, that involvement in gangs for males was less pathogenic and in fact, was positively correlated with liking nominations in middle school.

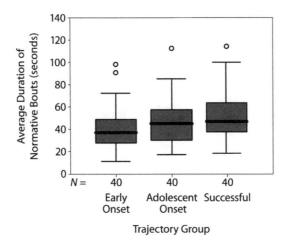

FIGURE 4.8. Average duration of normative talk bouts as a function of developmental onset of problem behavior.

TABLE 4.1. Predicting the Length of Deviant Talk Bouts

Antecedents	Males ($n = 60$)	Females ($n = 60$)
Teacher ratings, sixth-grade risk	.27**	.38**
Eighth-grade gang construct	.12	.52***
Sixth-grade peer nominations, rejection	.31**	.27**

Note. **$p < .01$; ***$p < .001$.

Table 4.2 reveals the outcomes associated with longer deviant talk bouts 2 years following the videotaped interaction tasks for males and females. Table 4.2 provides data on self-reported antisocial behavior, number of official police contacts, self-reported substance use, and self-reported sexual partners. As in previous research, the longer deviant talk bouts are associated with more self-reported antisocial behavior for males. Longer deviant talk bouts are also associated with antisocial behavior and drug use for females. It is also true that longer deviant talk bouts are associated with having more sexual partners by ages 18 and 19. In general, the length of the bout is correlated with higher levels of problem behavior for males and females and predictive validity is most consistent with adolescent females.

We considered the unique contribution of the duration of deviant talk bouts and dyadic mutuality to problem behavior at ages 16 and 17. A problem behavior composite was created from the cumulative number of arrests through adolescence and self-reported antisocial behavior at ages 16 and 17. We predicted the problem behavior composite from teacher ratings of problem behavior at age 11, average duration of deviant talk bouts, and dyadic mutuality. In addition, we added an interaction between dyadic mutuality and deviant talk bouts. This analysis is

TABLE 4.2. Outcomes Associated with Length of Deviant Talk Bouts

Outcomes (by age 18–19)	Males ($n = 60$)	Females ($n = 60$)
Self-report antisocial	.55***	.38**
Number of police offenses	.24†	.78***
Self-report alcohol use	.18	.28*
Self-report marijuana use	.31	.44***
Self-report polydrug use	.24†	.55***
Self-report number of sex partners	.40**	.61***

Note. *$p < .05$; **$p < .01$; ***$p < .001$; †$p < .10$.

described and summarized in detail by Piehler and Dishion (2007). In general, we find that the average duration of the deviant talk bout and dyadic mutuality predict problem behavior over and above the stability. Most interesting, we find an interaction between the deviant talk duration and the dyadic mutuality. As expected, the dyads that were more mutual with higher levels of deviant talk demonstrated the greatest levels of problem behavior. This finding is consistent with previous findings from another sample showing low-entropy and high-deviant talk predicting growth in deviant behavior over a 10-year time span.

SUMMARY AND IMPLICATIONS

Developmental Issues

These findings suggest that youth with attenuated peer relationships are more prone toward forming deviant cliques. Although we have suggested that academic failure and, in particular, peer rejection are critical for this process to unfold over time, we have not specifically tested the social augmentation hypothesis. Testing this hypothesis requires another level of analysis not available in the current data set. Network research showing shifts in network affiliations over time as dynamic processes that flow as a joint function of liking and disliking would be a more appropriate level of analysis to test the social augmentation hypothesis.

These findings also support the idea that children who start early and persist over time in their level of problem behavior tend to develop fewer prosocial interpersonal skills. We examined this hypothesis using observed indicators of friendship mutuality as well as self-reports on the quality of the friendship. Consistent with previous research (e.g., Brendgen et al., 2000; Poulin et al., 1999), we do find impoverished relationships tend to go hand in hand with the developmental trajectory of the youth. The findings were especially strong for females compared with males.

Although in general the youth involved in early antisocial behaviors show arrested development with respect to basic friendship skills, they are more advanced in their ability to hold and maintain deviant conversations. Indeed, the joint ability to hold a deviant conversation and to maintain a mutually satisfying friendship seems to be associated with growth in problem behavior from middle childhood to young adulthood. These findings are consistent with the idea that the ability to connect with others around themes of deviance is a mechanism in which peers mutually influence one another. Although positive affect is certainly embedded within these exchanges, we now think that the key reinforcing mechanism is intrasubjectivity. Skinner referred to this as *finding a verbal community.* Those of us who are able to find, select, and exchange similar value statements will at least maintain and perhaps amplify the behavior that corresponds with those value statements. This is an intrinsic quality of language learning (i.e., stimulus equivalence) and potentially powerful in the creation of normative as well as deviant cliques.

Intervention Implications

Among the implications of these findings is that several strategies are important for reducing the potential for peer influence in schools and communities. Efforts to improve school environments such as reductions in problem behavior at a school-wide level, support for positive student behavior at a school-wide level, and improved instructional practices would suggest reduced peer rejection and reduced academic failure. Changes such as these would presumably reduce the likelihood that deviant peer cliques will form. Interventions that would achieve these goals are school-wide discipline practices and positive behavior support (Crone, Horner, & Hawken, 2004).

Alternatively, it may be possible to design school environments so as to minimize peer network dynamics that influence the formation of gangs and deviant peer cliques. A dynamic indicator of an active peer network could provide adults in school settings information for engineering student learning groups that would promote positive adaptation and reduce maladaptation. In general, it is assumed that it is helpful in communities and schools for adults to actively attend and monitor emerging patterns of peer affiliation and behavior (Dishion et al., 2004; Dishion & McMahon, 1998). In fact, empirically supported interventions for problem behavior all involve some aspect of empowering adults with skills and motivation to be actively involved in children's social and peer activities (Dodge et al., 2006). Our own approach to intervening in adolescent problem behavior is referred to as "family centered" in that we provide feedback to parents regarding their child's peer network and provide suggestions and strategies for improved parental monitoring and behavior management strategies (Dishion & Kavanagh, 2003).

A pernicious problem in communities' efforts to improve the functioning of institutions like schools and to reduce problem behavior is the aggregation of youth into programs and juvenile justice settings. Although for some youth this aggregation strategy may lead to negative outcomes, one also has to weigh the benefit to the school or the community for moving very high-risk youth from those settings. The data suggest that not all programs that aggregate produce negative outcomes. Therefore, it is critical that we develop measures of peer influence and interventions in programs that aggregate that are dynamic indicators of the probable outcomes associated with those interventions. One potential measure of peer influence would be the extent to which the program allows peer interactions that share deviant stories or engage in discussions that have deviant content. Paradoxically, it may be that interventions that are designed to ameliorate problem behavior by having youth discuss their personal histories may actually increase these tendencies by creating the context of a verbal community with shared deviant values. From our own research (e.g., Dishion, Poulin, & Burraston, 2001), we found that even in conditions where groups were videotaped and supervised that subtle communications among group members indicating support and agreement around deviant values produced iatrogenic effects for some youth. Thus, training of mental health and juvenile justice workers to identify and disrupt iatrogenic dynamics is critical for programs and institutions designed to reduce problem behavior and promote youth development. In this way, further research is needed to link these developmental analyses with the optimal design of programs and interventions that minimize harm and support youth growth in prosocial skills.

REFERENCES

Attneave, F. (1959). *Application of information theory to psychology: A summary of basic concepts, methods, and results.* Oxford, UK: Henry Holt.

Bagwell, C. L., Newcomb, A. F., & Bukowski, W. M. (1998). Preadolescent friendship and peer rejection and predictors of adult adjustment. *Child Development, 69,* 140–153.

Brendgen, M., Vitaro, F., & Bukowski, W. M. (2000). Deviant friends and early adolescents' emotional and behavioral adjustment. *Journal of Research on Adolescence, 10,* 173–189.

Cairns, R. B. (1979). *Social development: The origins and plasticity of interchanges.* San Francisco: W. H. Freeman.

Cairns, R. B., Cairns, B. D., Neckerman, H. J., Gest, S. D., & Gariepy, J. (1988). Social networks and aggressive behavior: Peer support or peer rejection. *Developmental Psychology, 24,* 815–823.

Coie, J. D., Dodge, K. A., & Coppotelli, H. (1982). Dimensions and types of social status: A cross-age perspective. *Developmental Psychology, 18,* 557–570.

Coie, J. D., & Kupersmidt, J. B. (1983). A behavioral analysis of emerging social status in boys' groups. *Child Development, 54,* 1400–1416.

Crone, D. A., Horner, R. H., & Hawken, L. S. (2004). *Responding to problem behavior in schools: The behavior education program.* New York: Guilford Press.

Deater-Deckard, K., & Petrill, S. A. (2004). Parent–child dyadic mutuality and child behavior problems: An investigation of gene–environment processes. *Journal of Child Psychology and Psychiatry, 45,* 1171–1179.

Dinges, M. N., & Oetting, E. R. (1993). Similarity in drug use patterns between adolescents and their friends. *Adolescence, 28,* 253–266.

Dishion, T. J., Capaldi, D., Spracklen, K. M., & Li, F. (1995). Peer ecology of male adolescent drug use. *Development and Psychopathology, 7,* 803–824.

Dishion, T. J., Eddy, J. M., Haas, E., Li, F., & Spracklen, K. (1997). Friendships and violent behavior during adolescence. *Social Development, 6,* 207–223.

Dishion, T. J., & Kavanagh, K. (2003). *Intervening in adolescent problem behavior: A family-centered approach.* New York: Guilford Press.

Dishion, T. J., Loeber, R., Stouthamer-Loeber, M., & Patterson, G. R. (1984). Skill deficits and male adolescent delinquency. *Journal of Abnormal Child Psychology, 12,* 37–54.

Dishion, T. J., & McMahon, R. J. (1998). Parental monitoring and the prevention of child and adolescent problem behavior: A conceptual and empirical formulation. *Clinical Child and Family Psychology Review, 1,* 61–75.

Dishion, T. J., Nelson, S. E., & Bullock, B. M. (2004). Premature adolescent autonomy: Parent disengagement and deviant peer process in the amplification of problem behavior. *Journal of Adolescence, 27,* 515–530.

Dishion, T. J., Nelson, S. E., & Yasui, M. (2005). Predicting early adolescent gang involvement from middle school adaptation. *Journal of Clinical Child and Adolescent Psychology, 34,* 62–73.

Dishion, T. J., & Patterson, S. G. (1996). *Preventive parenting with love, encouragement, and limits: The preschool years.* Eugene, OR: Castalia.

Dishion, T. J., & Patterson, G. R. (2006). The development and ecology of antisocial behavior. In D. Cicchetti & D. J. Cohen (Eds.), *Developmental psychopathology, Vol. 3: Risk, disorder, and adaptation* (pp. 503–541). New York: Wiley.

Dishion, T. J., Patterson, G. R., & Griesler, P. C. (1994). Peer adaptation in the development of antisocial behavior: A confluence model. In L. R. Huesmann (Ed.), *Aggressive behavior: Current perspectives* (pp. 61–95). New York: Plenum Press.

Dishion, T. J., Patterson, G. R., Stoolmiller, M., & Skinner, M. S. (1991). Family, school, and behavioral antecedents to early adolescent involvement with antisocial peers. *Developmental Psychology, 27,* 172–180.

Dishion, T. J., Poulin, F., & Burraston, B. (2001). Peer group dynamics associated with iatrogenic effects in group interventions with high-risk young adolescents. In C. Erdley & D. W. Nangle (Eds.), *Damon's new directions in child development: The role of friendship in psychological adjustment* (pp. 79–92). San Francisco: Jossey-Bass.

Dodge, K. A. (1983). Behavioral antecedents: A peer social status. *Child Development, 54,* 1386–1399.

Dodge, K. A., & Coie, J. D. (1987). Social information-processing factors in reactive and proactive aggression in children's peer groups. *Journal of Personality and Social Psychology, 53,* 1146–1158.

Dodge, K. A., Dishion, T. J., & Lansford, J. E. (2006). Deviant peer influences in intervention and public policy for youth. *Social Policy Report, 20,* 3–19.

Gardner, T. W., Dishion, T. J., & Connell, A. (2008). Adolescent self-regulation as resilience: Resistance to antisocial behavior in the deviant peer context. *Journal of Abnormal Child Psychology, 36,* 273–284.

Gest, S. D. (2006). Teacher reports of children's friendships and social groups: Agreement with peer reports and implications for studying peer similarity. *Social Development, 15,* 248–259.

Granic, I., & Dishion, T. J. (2003). Deviant talk in adolescent friendships: A step toward measuring a pathogenic attractor process. *Social Development, 12,* 314–334.

Granic, I., & Lamey, A. V. (2002). Combining dynamic systems and multivariate analyses to compare the mother–child interactions of externalizing subtypes. *Journal of Abnormal Child Psychology, 30,* 265–283.

Hayes, S. C., & Berens, N. M. (2004). Why relational frame theory alters the relationship between basic and applied behavioral psychology. *International Journal of Psychology and Psychological Therapy, 4,* 341–353.

Hayes, S. C., & Grundt, A. M. (1997). Metaphor, meaning and relational frame theory. In C. Mendell & A. McCabe (Eds.), *The problem of meaning: Behavioral and cognitive perspectives* (pp. 117–146). Amsterdam: North-Holland/Elsevier Science.

Hernstein, R. J. (1970). Sexual activity and problem behaviors among black, urban adolescents. *Child Development, 41,* 2032–2046.

Jabson, J., & Dishion, T. J. (2004). *The Simple Affect Coding System: Unpublished observation coding manual.* Available from the Child and Family Center, University of Oregon, 195 West 12th Avenue, Eugene, OR 97401.

Kandel, D. B. (1986). Process of peer influence on adolescence. In R. K. Silbereisen (Ed.), *Development as action in context* (pp. 33–52). Berlin: Springer.

Kellam, S. G. (1990). Developmental epidemiological framework for family research on depression and aggression. In G. R. Patterson (Ed.), *Depression and aggression in family interaction: Advances in family research* (pp. 11–48). Hillsdale, NJ: Erlbaum.

Kochanska, G. (1997). Multiple pathways to conscience for children with different temperaments: From toddlerhood to age 5. *Developmental Psychology, 33,* 228–240.

Kochanska, G., & Murray, K. T. (2000). Mother–child mutually responsive orientation and conscience development: From toddler to early school age. *Child Development, 71,* 417–431.

Laird, R. D., Jordan, K. Y., Dodge, K. A., Pettit, G., & Bates, J. E. (2001). Peer rejection in childhood, involvement with antisocial peers in early adolescence, and the development of externalizing behavior problems. *Development and Psychopathology, 13,* 337–354.

Lewis, M. D. (1999). Emotional self-organization at three time scales. In M. D. Lewis & I. Granic (Eds.), *Emotion, development, and self-organization: Dynamic systems approaches to emotional development. Cambridge studies in social and emotional development* (pp. 37–69). New York: Cambridge University Press.

Lewis, M. D. (2000). The promise of dynamic systems approaches for an integrated account of human development. *Child Development, 71,* 36–43.

Miller-Johnson, S., Coie, J. D., Maumary-Gremaud, A., Bierman, K., & The Conduct Problems Prevention Research Group. (2002). Peer rejection and aggression and early starter models of conduct disorder. *Journal of Abnormal Child Psychology, 30,* 217–230.

Moffitt, T. E. (1993). Adolescence-limited and life course persistent antisocial behavior: Developmental taxonomy. *Psychological Review, 100,* 674–701.

Nelson, S. E., & Dishion, T. J. (2004). From boys to men: Predicting adult adaptation from middle childhood sociometric status. *Development and Psychopathology, 16,* 441–459.

Patterson, G. R. (1982). *Coercive family process.* Eugene, OR: Castalia.

Patterson, G. R. (1993). Orderly change in a stable world: The antisocial trait as a chimera. *Journal of Consulting and Clinical Psychology, 61,* 911–919.

Patterson, G. R., Dishion, T. J., & Yoerger, K. (2000). Adolescent growth in new forms of problem behavior: Macro- and micro-peer dynamics. *Prevention Science, 1,* 3–13.

Patterson, G. R., Reid, J. B., & Dishion, T. J. (1992). *Antisocial boys.* Eugene, OR: Castalia.

Piehler, T. F., & Dishion, T. J. (2004). *The Conversation Topic Code.* Unpublished coding manual available from the Child and Family Center, University of Oregon, 195 W. 12th Avenue, Eugene, OR 97401.

Piehler, T. F., & Dishion, T. J. (2007). Interpersonal dynamics within adolescent friendships: Dyadic mutuality, deviant talk, and the development of antisocial behavior. *Child Development, 78*(5), 1611–1624.

Piehler, T. F., & Dishion, T. J. (2007). *Self-regulation and progressions in adolescent substance use: Direct effects and the moderation of peer and parental influence.* Manuscript under review.

Poulin, F., Dishion, T. J., & Haas, E. (1999). The peer influence paradox: Relationship quality and deviancy training within male adolescent friendships. *Merrill–Palmer Quarterly, 45,* 42–61.

Quay, H. C. (1983). The behavioral reward and inhibition system in childhood behavior disorder. In L. M. Bloomingdale (Ed.), *Attention deficit disorder: New research in attention, treatment, and psychopharmacology* (pp. 176–186). New York: Pergamon.

Robins, L. N. (1966). *Deviant children grow up: A sociological and psychiatric study of sociopathic personality.* Baltimore: Williams & Wilkins.

Rodkin, P. C., Farmer, T. W., Pearl, R., & Van Acker, R. (2000). Heterogeneity of popular boys: Antisocial and prosocial configurations. *Development Psychology, 36,* 14–24.

Rogoff, B. (1993). Commentary on cultural learning. *Behavioral and Brain Sciences, 16,* 31–42.

Rogoff, B., & Gardner, W. (1984). Adult guidance of cognitive development. In B. Rogoff & J. Lave (Eds.), *Everyday cognition: Its development in social context* (pp. 95–116). Cambridge, MA: Harvard University Press.

Rothbart, M. K., Ellis, L. K., & Posner, M. I. (2004). Temperament and self-regulation. In R. F. Baumeister & K. D. Vohs (Eds.), *Handbook of self-regulation: Research, theory, and applications* (pp. 357–370). New York: Guilford Press.

Rothbart, M. K., Ellis, L. K., Rueda, M. R., & Posner, M. I. (2003). Developing mechanisms of temperamental effortful control. *Journal of Personality, 71*(6), 1113–1143.

Shapiro, S. K., Quay, H. C., Hogan, A. E., & Schwartz, K. P. (1988). Response perseveration and delayed responding in undersocialized aggressive conduct disorder. *Journal of Abnormal Child Psychology, 97,* 371–373.

Scarr, S., & McCartney, K. (1983). How people make their own environments: A theory of genotype rightwards-arrow environment effects. *Child Development, 54,* 424–435.

Shortt, J. W., Capaldi, D. M., Dishion, T. J., Bank, L., & Owen, L. D. (2003). The role of adolescent friends, romantic partners, and siblings in the emergence of the adult antisocial lifestyle. *Journal of Family Psychology, 17,* 521–533.

Skinner, B. (1954). The science of learning and the art of teaching. *Harvard Educational Review, 24,* 86–97.

Snyder, J., & Brown, K. (1983). Oppositional behavior and noncompliance in preschool children: Environmental correlates and skill deficits. *Behavioral Assessment, 5,* 333–348.

Stormshak, E. A., Bierman, K. L., Bruschi, C., Dodge, K. A., Coie, J. D., & The Conduct Problems Prevention Research Group. (1999). The relation between behavior problems and peer preference in different classroom contexts. *Child Development, 70,* 169–182.

Thornberry, T. P. (1998). Membership in youth gangs and involvement in serious and violent offending. In R. Loeber & D. P. Farrington (Eds.), *Serious and violent juvenile offenders: Risk factors and successful interventions* (pp. 147–166). Thousand Oaks, CA: Sage.

Tomasello, M., Kruger, A. C., & Ratner, H. H. (1993). Cultural learning. *Behavioral and Brain Sciences, 16,* 495–552.

Vygotsky, L. (1986). *Thought and language.* Cambridge, MA: MIT Press.

Wertsch, J. V. (1984). The zone of proximal development: Some conceptual issues. *New Directions for Child Development, 23,* 11–31.

CHAPTER 5

Deviance Regulation Theory

Applications to Adolescent Social Influence

Hart Blanton *and* Melissa Burkley

Enter the phrase "image is everything" on an Internet search engine, and you will encounter a large store of websites devoted to adolescents. If you continue on, you will encounter pages devoted to such topics as teen fashion, teen health, the evils of marketing to young people, and any number of commentaries on youth counter-culture. Implicit in many discussions are assumptions about the value of being different. Pages that focus on teen fashion, for instance, tend to assume that the driving identity concern for most teens is to be different, to find a unique identity. Interestingly, however, many of the other pages assume exactly the opposite. Pages that focus on adolescent health, for instance, tend to emphasize the pressures that teens feel to fit in, and these pages counsel teens with such slogans as, "it is okay to be different."

The seemingly contradictory messages about adolescent identity are not simply the result of sloppy scholarship on the Internet. To the contrary, these differing perspectives accurately reflect the (seemingly contradictory) messages that can be found in the psychological literature. In many scientific reports, adolescence is portrayed as a time when young people embark on a personal quest to find uniqueness, to stand out from the crowd. In other reports, however, adolescence is portrayed as a developmental stage where the driving concerns revolve around the need for a group, around "fitting in."

In this chapter, we examine these seemingly competing motives, and we situate them within a broader model of identity, which we term deviance regulation theory (DRT; Blanton & Christie, 2003). As we will show, the two opposing approaches to adolescent motivations arise from distinct research traditions. We first review these differing perspectives and past attempts to integrate them. We then offer a new viewpoint that provides the foundation for our work on DRT. We close by using this perspective to introduce many new (and sometimes yet to be tested) predictions about adolescent social influence, with particular emphasis in health communication.

DISTINCTIVENESS MOTIVES: FIT IN, STAND OUT, OR COMPROMISE?

Fitting In

The idea that people are driven to "fit in" was emphasized in the early psychological research on small groups, which dominated social psychology in the 1950s and 1960s (e.g., Asch, 1956; Deutsch & Gerard, 1955; Festinger, 1950, 1954; Schachter, 1951). In one way or another, these researchers emphasized individuals' desires to conform to the actions of others. A prime example is Solomon Asch's (1956) now-classic research demonstrating that college students (and members of the general population) often are willing to answer questions incorrectly to avoid the disapproval of their peers. The emphasis on conformity as a driving social motive can also be seen in the sociological traditions that paralleled these themes at the same time period (e.g., Becker, 1963; Hughes, 1945; Kitsuse, 1962). Although the small-groups tradition is no longer the driving force in social psychology that it once was, this perspective still forms the foundation for much of the contemporary work on social groups. As a general rule, the groups literature in social psychology focuses on internal group pressures toward uniformity (Crandall, 1988; Forsyth, 2000), ways in which social "deviants" are sanctioned by group members when they break from established norms (Bown & Abrams, 2003; Wellen & Neale, 2006), and it points to ways in which people shape actions to avoid rejection from others (Leary & Downs, 1995; Schroeder & Prentice, 1998).

Perhaps because peer acceptance is seen as particularly important to adolescents, there has been heavy emphasis on this conformity-striving view of human nature in the applied adolescent health literature. In particular, a great deal of recent attention has been given to social marketing techniques that are designed to alter perceptions of social norms for college drinking (Haines, 1996; Perkins, 1995; Perkins & Berkowitz, 1986; Perkins & Wechsler, 1996). Research indicates that college students' perceptions of alcohol are often biased or inaccurate, such that students typically overestimate the frequency of peers' college drinking, the amount consumed, and the favorability of attitudes toward heavy drinking (Baer, Stacy, & Larimer, 1991; Perkins & Berkowitz, 1986; Perkins & Wechsler, 1996; Prentice & Miller, 1993). Research also suggests that norm perceptions can influence students' attitudes and behaviors in ways that increase their tendency to drink heavily (e.g., Perkins & Berkowitz, 1986; Prentice & Miller, 1993). For this reason, many popular efforts to reduce college drinking have focused on "debiasing" social perceptions. The premise of these efforts is that college students want to conform to the norms in their schools, and so colleges can reduce alcohol abuse on campus simply by providing students with survey data that bring their perceptions more in line with reality (see Perkins, 2003). Numerous private groups have now emerged that can help college administrators implement social-norming campaigns, and many of our national campuses are applying this approach as a result. Unfortunately, a great deal of work needs to be done to know the full range of effects these media campaigns are having, how to implement them for maximum effect, and whether or not they are based on realistic models of adolescent social motives (see Prentice, Chapter 8, this volume).

Standing Out

Interestingly, at much the same time that conformity models dominated early social psychology and sociology, the models that were dominating personality psychology and some clinical models of identity emphasized the desire to stand out. The idea behind these models is that people are generally motivated to be unique, and that this motive is particularly strong during adolescence. This viewpoint was given strongest emphasis by the humanistic psychologists such as Erik Erikson (1950), Abraham Maslow (1968), and Carl Rogers (1961). These psychologists asserted that normal human development involves a pursuit of a distinct identity and argued that when an individual only lives up to the standards imposed by others (i.e., group norms), they are not fully functioning individuals. In this context, *healthy functioning* was generally synonymous with a person's ability to maintain a positive sense of self, one that is independent of the social environment. Therefore, humanistic principles assert that every person must realize his or her full potential by achieving a unique and authentic self that is not contingent on the approval of others.

Just as the conformity model of social motives has dominated some areas of adolescent social health, so has the uniqueness model. In particular, researchers have emphasized how adolescents are motivated to believe that they are likely to experience a uniquely positive future

(Weinstein, 1980). The desire to protect feelings of uniqueness have also been identified as a factor that can predict greater willingness to take health risks (e.g., Gerrard, Gibbons, & Reis-Bergan, 2000) and cause adolescents to resist health-promotion efforts designed to encourage healthier behaviors (Weinstein & Klein, 2002). Many have also suggested that adolescents who feel less socially embedded or who feel set apart from larger society are more likely to pursue risky behaviors (e.g., Hammersley, Lavelle, & Forsyth, 1992; Little & Steinberg, 2006; Shedler & Block, 1990).

The Compromise View

In summary, two literatures on identity concerns have gained traction in working models of adolescent identity and have found a foothold in the applied adolescent health literature. At times, adolescents are portrayed as "social lemmings" who will go along with their crowd at all costs; and, at other times, they are portrayed as dedicated individualists who will pursue uniqueness, seemingly at great cost as well.

In response to these apparent contradictory motivational systems, some have suggested that people seek a compromise between the opposing drives for similarity and difference. The first systematic presentation of this hypothesis was advanced in a series of studies organized by Snyder and Fromkin (1980). Their work tested a theory they termed "uniqueness theory." Although the title implies that it focused on the individual need for distinctiveness (and although it is often mischaracterized as arguing for this view), these theorists actually argued that people strive for a moderate degree of distinction between self and others. That is, people want to stick out and have some unique qualities that garner praise, but they do not want to be so different that others will reject them or view them as unsavory. In support of their model, Snyder, Fromkin, and their colleagues ran numerous studies suggesting that people resist feedback indicating they are "extremely similar" to others, just as they resist feedback indicating they are "extremely different" from others. The greatest comfort is found following feedback that indicates some middle degree of self-other similarity/dissimilarity (Fromkin, 1970, 1972; Snyder & Endelman, 1980; for a recent review, see Lynn & Snyder, 2002).

This "compromise view" continues to be force in contemporary approaches to identity. Most notably, Brewer and colleagues have applied this perspective to the study of group identification (Brewer, 1991, 1993; Brewer & Pickett, 1998). According to their (more appropriately named) optimal distinctiveness theory, there are two opposing motives behind the self-categorization process: assimilation (association with others) and differentiation (distinction from others). These two needs work in opposition, such that movement toward one need arouses a strong desire toward the other need. Thus, heightened awareness of the similarities between self and others (assimilation) will cause a person to seek out inclusion in small and distinct social groups (differentiation), whereas awareness of one's distinct personal qualities (differentiation) will cause the person to seek inclusion in large and amorphous groups (assimilation; Pickett, Silver, & Brewer, 2002).

One nice aspect of the compromise view is that it can account for a wide range of individual differences. At one end of the continuum are individuals who sacrifice degrees of difference for degrees of similarity. Thus, many young people might have greater preferences for peer-group similarity than older people (Snyder & Fromkin, 1980) and individuals from a Western culture might prefer greater self-other distinctions than individuals from an Eastern culture (Tafarodi & Swann, 1996). Regardless, however, old and young people from the East and West will seek some degree of compromise between extreme endpoints. It is because this system is in conflict, however, that psychologists can focus research attention on the desirable aspects of fitting in with one set of studies and then focus on the desirable aspects of standing out with another set of studies. If the literature on adolescent identity appears particularly contradictory in this regard, this is simply because adolescents have a greater investment in identity in pursuit in general, which would lead to stronger pulls in opposing directions for any population.

THE DEVIANCE REGULATION PERSPECTIVE: DEVIANCE IS INFORMATIVE

Deviance regulation theory differs from the previous models in that it does not focus on any inherent value in being different or being similar, nor does it concern itself with a need to compromise. This is not to say that the previous perspectives do not have merit. Certainly, people can feel at odds with the world when they fail to fit in, and most psychologists assume that there is some social value in having connections to others. However, the desires for affiliation and distinction are viewed as more distal concerns, concerns that influence emotions when people reflect on their global identity or the type of person they are becoming, in some broad sense (Ditto & Griffin, 1993). In the moment, however, when people are considering how a given act and might lead to a specific self-evaluation, DRT assumes that a more basic concern is driving decisions.

This more basic concern is the desire to have a positive identity. According to DRT, people do not choose actions so much out of a desire to feel more similar or more different, per se. Instead, they simply act out of a desire to have positive self-image. The implication of this model is that people will seek difference when difference generates a positive identity, and they will avoid difference when it generates a negative identity. Importantly, however, DRT does not assume that there is a valence inherent in either similarity or difference. Instead, it focuses attention on the potential that difference has to carry a valence. When an individual deviates from the typical actions of similar others, this act has more potential to influence his or her private self-concept and to alter his or her public image. A person should thus attend to the implications of being different from others. However, when an individual conforms to the typical acts of similar others, these actions will probably not inform his or her private self-concept or his or her public image. The implications of this model are examined below, but first, the features of this theory are spelled out in greater detail.

PRINCIPLES OF DEVIANCE REGULATION THEORY

At the heart of DRT are two basic principles of social behavior. The first principle states that certain behaviors are more informative than others. This principle highlights the fact that "deviant behaviors"—behaviors that cause one to stand out in relation to social norms—generate stronger reactions from observers than nondeviant behaviors. The second principle of DRT states that certain behaviors are more meaningful than others. This principle highlights the fact that behaviors become meaningful when they generate strong reactions from important reference others. Thus, the first principle explains when actions will be linked to a person's identity, and the second principle explains when these links will have motivational and emotional significance. We review each of these principles in turn.

The First Principle: Finding Information in Actions

Not all actions influence a person's private or public image. For instance, most people would not draw strong conclusions about an office worker from his decision to wear clothes to work or to remain emotionally stable during office meetings, but even a few instances of nudity and crying can generate more than passing interest from coworkers. Importantly, however, the powers that these latter two actions have to inform judgments about a person are not inherent to the actions themselves. They arise from the specific contexts in which these actions distinguish the actor from others who might encounter them. For instance, most observers would not draw strong conclusions about another office worker if they were to learn that he typically showers in the nude or that he recently cried at his mother's funeral. These two actions lose their "informational value" when they are placed in contexts in which they would be expected of many or most people.

The above example clearly illustrates the first principle of deviance regulation: An action becomes more informative the more it indicates that a person is deviating from social norms. This principle thus links the social information of a given action to the choices others would make. We expand upon our definition of a "social norm" in the next section but, for current purposes, think of it as a behavioral base rate or as the consensual way of responding to a specific situation. People's actions are thus viewed as informative (about who they are, who they think they are, who they appear to be, who they want to be or who they might want to become) when they distinguish the individual from similar other people.

This notion that difference is information has a long history in early attribution theories (Jones & Davis, 1965; Kelley, 1972). It also gains support from research on the self, which suggests that people think of themselves primarily in terms of their distinct (or rare) qualities (McGuire & McGuire, 1980; McGuire, McGuire, Child, & Fujioka, 1978; McGuire & Padawer-Singer, 1976; Mullen & Goethals, 1990). Both lines of work suggest that, in our own eyes and in others' eyes, we are that which makes us different.

Although it is not terribly provocative to say that observers draw inferences from distinctions, this first principle of deviance regulation points out a perceptual asymmetry that is thought to structure a great deal of social behavior. Specifically, it points out that difference is more informative than similarity; therefore judgments of how to act focus more on the consequences of deviating than on the consequences of conforming. Consider as an example an early adolescent who is thinking about smoking cigarettes. This individual knows few people who smoke and she knows that she would get more than a little attention from her peers if she were to initiate this action. DRT thus predicts that her decision to smoke will be based primarily on her assessment of smoking. If she thinks she will gain from smoking, then she will be oriented toward smoking. If she thinks she will lose from smoking, then she will be oriented toward not smoking. Importantly, however, this individual should give very little attention to the social consequences of not smoking. This is because not smoking is a "nonevent" in the life of this teenager.

Now consider an older adolescent who has dropped out of school to play in a band. All of his friends smoke and so do the patrons who come to the bars to see him play. For this individual, smoking is socially nondistinct—much like wearing clothes is nondistinct in this and other social contexts. This individual can still influence his image by the choices he makes, but he cannot do it by choosing to smoke. He can only do it by choosing not to smoke. Thus, this person should make his decisions not by attending to the consequences of smoking (a nonevent) but by attending to the consequences of not smoking. If this individual thinks he will gain from not smoking (in his own eyes or in the eyes of his peers), then he will be oriented toward not smoking. If he thinks he will lose from not smoking, then he will be oriented toward smoking. Importantly, however, this individual should give very little attention to the social consequences of not smoking.

The first principle of DRT thus predicts that, as the norms for a behavior become more common, social concerns regarding that action will exert less influence on behavioral decisions and social concerns toward the alternative to this action will exert greater influence. Blanton and Sanchez-Burks (2001) found support for this in a study of smoking behavior. They found that, among college students with few friends who smoke, the likelihood of smoking was best predicted by their attitudes toward smoking (and not their attitudes toward not smoking). In contrast, among college students with many friends who smoke, the likelihood of smoking was best predicted by their own attitudes toward not smoking (and not their attitudes toward smoking). In short, the attitude that best predicted behavior was the one that pertained to the action that would make participants stand out from their social environment—that caused them to deviate from the norms of their peer groups.

The Second Principle: Finding Meaning in Actions

Many times, an action will cause an individual to stand out from others, and so it can provide important information about that person, but this fact will have little or no consequences for the individual or for the decisions this person might make. Consider a high school student who is doing poorly in school. This student routinely skips out of school, she comes to class without her assignments completed and is at risk of being held back a year as a result. If most of this student's peers take school more seriously and expect to move up a grade, then her public image will probably be influenced by these actions and she will probably know that these actions help determine how others view her. However, it would be wrong to assume that this student is acting the way she is because she finds this image to be a desirable one or to assume that she will try to do better in school if she finds this image to be undesirable. Rather, it may be that this individual will give little thought or concern to her public image or to how her actions are causing her to deviate from established norms.

As this example illustrates, not all of the information we glean about actors, or that actors glean from themselves, carries much psychological meaning to the actor. If asked to reflect on all of the ways we differ from others, most of us could come up with large lists of subtle differences in speech patterns, energy levels, posture, and so on. But such differences probably do not influence our personal identities, because these differences carry little psychological importance. If asked, most of us could also come up with large lists of other people who would evaluate us unfavorably, but whose opinions carry little or no psychological relevance. As examples, most accountants would not care if a group of teenagers found them to be "boring," and most teenagers would not care if most accountants thought their lives seemed "unstable."

As these examples illustrate, not all of the information about the self is experienced as emotionally or psychologically meaningful. Much as William James (1890) professed little concern that he was "contented to wallow in the grossest ignorance of Greek," so too might most accountants and teenagers wallow in the disparaging evaluations each has of the other. This fact points to an observation that arose in early work on social comparison processes, that people care how they measure up in relation to some individuals and some norms more than others (Hyman, 1960; Hyman & Singer, 1968; Merton & Kitt, 1950; Sherif & Sherif, 1964; Singer, 1981). These researchers used the term *reference group* and *reference other* to define groups and individuals who hold special psychological significance for self-evaluation. Through socialization, where we come to value and internalize the opinions and views of some people more than others, reference groups give us a sense of what we should and should not be.

The importance of reference groups is incorporated into DRT's second principle: Reference groups determine when deviant acts will be seen as meaningful. In the example of the high school student, that individual was different than her peers, but she did not place any particular value on her standing relative to other high school students. Put in a different manner, she didn't view these students as important referent others. Consideration of the psychological importance of other people points to a need to expand upon the definition of "social norms" that was offered earlier. That tentative definition considered only the behavioral base rates exhibited by comparable others. It thus focused on "descriptive norms," which define what people are doing. These invoke comparisons between the self and the *behaviors* of other people. Consideration of reference groups encourages one to also consider evaluative norms, which define what people are thinking. These involve comparisons between the self and the opinions of important others. Consider again the high school student, above. It seems that this individual did not care if her actions generated approval or disapproval from her peers. These peers did not hold referent status, and so she did not shape her behaviors to increase the positivity of their evaluations.

Although descriptive norms and evaluative norms differ from one another, DRT assumes that the basic asymmetry between conformity and deviance applies for both types of norms. Thus, if another person holds reference group status, individuals will decide on courses of action by evaluating the consequences of deviating from evaluative norms (not conforming to them). Based on Higgins's (1987) self-discrepancy theory, DRT further differentiates between two types of evaluative norms: Ought norms and ideal norms. Both types reveal the opinions of referent others and can be internalized to provide a person with some internal standards of reference for evaluating his or her own behavior. They differ, however, in whether they focus attention on the consequences of deviating from norms in a bad way (ought norms) or of deviating from norms in a good way (ideal norms).

Ought Norms: Positive Norms, Negative Deviations

One way that a reference group influences the actions of its group members is to establish what behaviors it thinks others "ought" to perform or "should" perform. These norms identify the behaviors that are not just desired by a reference group but also required by them of all group members if they wish to be "members in good standing." Because most members of a reference group will try to live up to the requirements of their group, these norms functionally identify the "default" response that typical members will exhibit in most contexts.

The canonical examples of ought norms revolve around moral and ethical codes of conduct. Consider, as an example, a close-knit clique of high school girls. Many of the ways that they relate to one another will have an "optional quality" to them, in that some girls might choose to act one way and others might choose to act in different ways. There are no formal rules that dictate, for instance, how emotionally excited a member should be when she talks about a disliked teacher, and no member would fear rejection by members for "violation of contract" if she didn't notice that one of the members did particularly well on her homework assignment. But some behaviors do not bring with them the luxury of choice. Behaviors in this category are expected of all members, as they go to the heart of what it means to be in the group, to be friends with one another, and to be part of a shared community.

Consider actions that speak to the moral integrity of group members. Most teenage girls would expect for their friends to tell the truth to one another, to respect each other's secrets and not to steal from one another (whether they typically live up to these standards or not). Even if these expectations go unstated, they nonetheless can create a powerful expectancy structure that regulates how members will act toward one another (or how they will purport to act). Reference others communicate that they expect all group members to live up to the positive moral norms of the group, and they only take note when members choose to violate these norms.

The social expectations that surround these moralistic behaviors are typical for all "ought norms." In general, there is nothing provocative or interesting about one's decision to conform to ought norms. As a result, it is difficult for a reference group to confer a positive image on someone who personifies the positive qualities that are dictated by these ought norms. Members who do not steal from other members or who do not lie are not praised for their "honesty." Instead, the power of ought norms is that they clarify the negative actions that are worthy of criticism, derision, and rejection. They help delineate the actions that merit the label, "dishonest."

With ought norms, DRT therefore predicts that individuals will give greater weight to the perceived negative consequences of deviating from reference norms than they will the positive consequences of conforming to reference group norms (assuming they have internalized the views of important referent others). An implication of this is that, within a peer group, conformity pressure will typically take the form of a "negative incentive system." This system reminds members of the negative consequences of deviating, not the positive consequences of conforming.

The reason that conformity pressure typically is negative in form is that it typically will only arise for behaviors that reference others think one "ought" or "should" perform. If not for these views, the behavior would be optional and, perhaps, noteworthy. Recall, as an illustration, that the early literature on small groups emphasized the desire of individuals not to stand out or be different. DRT suggests that this finding occurred because past groups research typically studied behaviors for which conformity of opinion was obligated by the research situation. Researchers in these studies typically placed participants in working groups, where all members worked together toward common goals. Thus, uniformity of opinion and action were required for these groups to move forward toward a group solution (e.g., Festinger, Gerard, Hymovitch, Kelley, & Raven, 1952; Festinger & Thibaut, 1951; Schachter, 1951). In contexts such as these, a person who breaks from the pack is no longer a member in good standing, and so it made sense for the group to punish individuals such as these. It did not make sense, however, for the group to reward the majority of those who lived up to their group obligations, who met the normative expectations of the group.

A similar dynamic can evolve in adolescent peer groups. Recall that the social health literature often focuses attention on the pressure to engage in health-risk behaviors. At first glance, it does not seem that any group would "need" for all members to smoke cigarettes, to drink excessively, or to engage in any other health-risk behaviors. These behaviors are not mandated by formal moral or ethical codes, and the survival of the group is not dependent on these actions. However, these behaviors can be socially construed in moralistic terms by adolescents. As adolescents develop, and as they seek more "adult" behaviors, it often becomes important for them to show signs of their newfound maturity to the outside world. For many reference groups, this means taking on "adult-looking" risk behaviors. Although smoking and drinking ultimately are personal decisions, peers can feel implicated by the decisions of other group members. As a peer group becomes invested in promoting a mature image to the outside world, it may view it as imperative that all members take on these behaviors. In this type of environment, where there is conformity pressure on members to engage in risky behaviors, the power of the group is not its ability to reward those who go along with the norms of the group. The power of the group is in its ability to punish those who deviate.

Ideal Norms: Negative Norms, Positive Deviations

But groups are not all negative, all of the time. Although the literature on small groups has focused on the negative incentives systems that reinforce conformity, groups do much more than simply promote uniformity of behavior. Consider the many groups that might influence the later career choices that a young adolescent one day will make. Most young people who grow up to be lawyers, doctors, or social psychologists can point to any number of important referent others who initially sent them down their chosen paths. And, individuals would not take on the challenges of law school, medical school or risk their futures on the social-psychological job market if these pursuits did not confer some positive benefit to them. When people freely choose careers or other significant roles in society, they typically are choosing between positive alternatives, between different sources of pride. These outcomes could only be framed in this way if the actors have internalized the positive opinions of important referent others; others who have reinforced accomplishments in these domains.

Pursuits such as these differ from those that are reinforced by ought norms, in that they are not required by many reference groups. Few reference groups would require group members to have success in legal, medical, or social-psychological disciplines. These outcomes nevertheless can represent ideals that various referent groups will value and reinforce. In fact, many of the behaviors that reference groups reinforce have this quality. They are "optional" pursuits that are worthy of praise, if one chooses to take them on. Like the individual who challenges the "ought norms" of a group, the individual who achieves success at a high ideal is worthy of distinction. In this case, however, the individual is worthy of positive distinction, not negative. What teenager would not want to feel pride at becoming a social psychologist?

DRT thus predicts that social influences surrounding ideal norms will take the form of a "positive incentive system." This system reminds members of the positive consequences of deviating, not the negative consequences of conforming. Thus, whereas ought norms form around behaviors that are expected of everyone and define the deviations from the norm that are worthy of criticism, ideal norms form around behaviors that are optional and define deviations from the norm that are worthy of praise. Whereas ought norms promote conformity toward a shared way of acting, ideal norms promote diversity and a multitude of actions. Thus, two people who internalize the values of the same reference groups generally would share all of the same definitions of morality and conform in their moral actions, but they may differ considerably in the sorts of achievements they value or choose to pursue.

Formal Predictions of Deviance Regulation Theory

The key features of DRT are displayed in Table 5.1. When actions are required by a group, then groups promote "ought norms" that convey the behaviors that one should or ought to perform. If the group has reference status, individuals will internalize these norms as "ought self-guides" and use them to interpret events in their own lives. Because it is a "nonevent" to live up to behaviors mandated by a group, ought self-guides are motivating in that they drive a person to avoid negative deviations from the group (see Higgins, Shah, & Friedman, 1997; Shah, Higgins, & Friedman, 1998). The classic behaviors fitting this description are moralistic in nature, where positive actions (e.g., honesty) are given less attention than their negative counterparts (e.g., dishonesty; Skowronski & Carlston, 1989). Focusing on one's sense of obligation to important reference others should thus focus people more on conforming to the actions of others and instill a desire to not stand out from the group.

TABLE 5.1. Key Features of DRT

Required actions	Optional actions
• Reinforced through "ought norms" and a negative incentive system.	• Reinforced through "ideal norms" and a positive incentive system.
• Internalized as "ought self-guides" and avoidance motivation.	• Internalized as "ideal self-guides" and approach motivation.
• Normative act is socially desirable Example: Telling the truth	• Normative act is socially undesirable Example: Not winning science fair
• Informative act is socially undesirable Example: Telling a lie	• Informative act is socially desirable Example: Winning science fair
• Promotes conformity	• Promotes distinction

In contrast, when actions are desired by a group but not required, then groups promote "ideal norms" that convey the behaviors that one might perform to generate praise from others. If the group has reference status, individuals will internalize these norms as "ideal self-guides" and use them to interpret events in their own lives. Because it is a "nonevent" when people fail to achieve most ideals, ideal self-guides are motivating in that they drive a person to seek some small subset of positive deviations from the group. The classic behaviors fitting this description are ability based in nature, for which negative actions (e.g., average success in school) are given less attention than their positive counterparts (e.g., winning the science fair; Skowronski & Carlston, 1987). Focusing on the ideals of important reference others should thus focus people more on differentiating themselves from others and instill a desire to be distinct or unique.

Although this theory leads to too many predictions to be tested in a single study, the proposed link between reference group norms and distinctiveness goals was examined directly in a series of recent studies (Blanton, Hall, & Prentice, 2006). In one of these studies, participants wrote about their personal ideals (e.g., "the things I want to achieve in my life") or their personal oughts (e.g., "the moral codes that guide my actions"), or they wrote a control essay explaining to a stranger how one plays badminton. Participants then completed a measure of uniqueness striving by Snyder and Fromkin (1977). As predicted, those who had written about their ideals expressed a greater desire for uniqueness compared to the control participants, whereas those who had written about their oughts expressed less desire for uniqueness relative to the control participants. Follow-up studies revealed that these same procedures influenced behavioral tendencies toward similarity or difference.

In the most dramatic demonstration, participants again completed essays on their oughts or ideals and then went to a second room to complete a questionnaire. When they sat down in a cubicle, they noticed a series of pens in the cubicle that they could use to complete these questionnaires. As predicted, a strong majority of participants (88%) who had just completed an essay about their sense of moral obligation chose to complete the questionnaire using a common (normative) color of ink (black). In contrast, among those who completed an essay about essay about their personal ideals, only a slim majority (62%) chose to complete the questionnaire using this same pen color. The remaining 38% reached for pens that were less common in color (red or green).

We think these studies nicely demonstrate the way that ideals orient people toward the pursuit of difference and oughts orient people toward the pursuit of similarity. However, the scenarios in these studies are fairly removed from real-world applications. In the following sections, we discuss the implications of this model for adolescent social influence, with particular emphasis on adolescent health communication.

ADOLESCENT SOCIAL INFLUENCE

Consider the myriad of strategies that one might pursue to motivate healthier behaviors in teens. With smoking interventions, for instance, one strategy would be to emphasize the negative aspects of smoking. One could try to motivate teens not to smoke by showing them pictures of people with cancerous tumors in the mouth, tracheotomies in their necks to open airways, or have them listen to the stories of people who have been unable to overcome the physical addiction of smoking. These messages, if they are effective, would work by undermining the glamour associated with smoking. There may be concerns, however, that a strategy such as this would be off-putting to adolescents or that messages of this sort might be ignored because they are too emotionally distressing. Another strategy, then, would be to emphasize the positive aspects of not smoking. Such a campaign might feature star athletes who discuss their athletic accomplishments and how they were able to achieve them, only because they chose a healthy lifestyle. Or, one might expose high school students to information about college-student attitudes, showing that most college students live healthy lifestyles and prefer those who share these same tendencies. These messages, if they are effective, would work by improving the image of people who choose not to smoke.

These different campaigns reveal two distinct strategies for promoting health, the use of positively versus negatively framed health messages. A positively framed message emphasizes the positive consequences of engaging in a health behavior; whereas a negatively framed message emphasizes the negative consequences of engaging in unhealthy or health-risk behaviors. The dominant communication models that have led to predictions regarding framing effects have focused on the processing of emotionally valenced stimuli and the psychological factors that cause people to frame their health behaviors in terms of potential gains versus potential losses (for review, see Rothman & Salovey, 1997). DRT can also provide perspectives on message framing. However, it does so by focusing attention on the social norms surrounding behaviors and asks whether teens are living in an environment where they would stand out from the crowd for acting in a healthy manner or an unhealthy manner.

Framing Away from Norms

Consistent with the prior discussion, DRT argues that when the behavioral norm is to be unhealthy, one should emphasize the social benefits of healthy behaviors (i.e., use positive frames). Alternatively, when the behavioral norm is to be healthy, one should emphasize the social costs of unhealthy behaviors (i.e., use negative frames). In an initial test of this prediction, Blanton, Stuart, and VandenEijnden (2001) had college students read a bogus article stating that a flu epidemic was expected on campus. Half of the students read that the vast majority of students at the university were expected to get flu shots. With this manipulation, these researchers communicated that it was normative to get immunized and counternormative not to get immunized (behavioral norm is healthy). The other half were told a minority of students would get the shot. With this manipulation, these researchers communicated that it was normative not to get immunized and counternormative to get immunized (behavioral norm is unhealthy). Participants were then presented with a positively or negatively framed message encouraging immunization. The positively framed message emphasized the desirable attributes of someone who gets a flu shot (e.g., such people are being "responsible," and "considerate of others"); whereas the negatively framed message emphasized the undesirable attributes of someone who does not get a flu shot (e.g., such people are being "irresponsible," and "inconsiderate of others"). After reading the message, participants rated their intention to get a flu shot in the future.

The results of this study are displayed in Figure 5.1. Consistent with DRT, behavioral intentions were highest in the conditions that targeted deviant actions. When getting a flu shot was normative, intentions were higher following the negatively framed message (i.e., emphasizing the undesirable qualities of the deviant behavior). When not getting a flu shot was normative, intentions were higher following the positively framed message (i.e., emphasizing the desirable qualities of the deviant

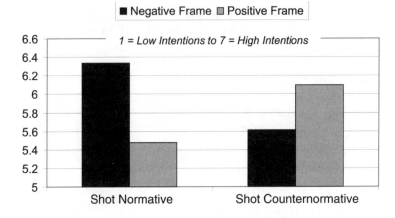

FIGURE 5.1. Predicting intention to get flu shot.

behavior). This pattern indicates that the health-related messages were more effective when they were associated with traits regarding the counter-normative behavior.

In a second study, the researchers examined intentions to use condoms. Rather than manipulating normative beliefs, however, this study examined natural variation in normative beliefs regarding condom use on campus. The same behavioral pattern emerged: The effects of the message-framing manipulation on behavioral intentions were again moderated by normative beliefs regarding condom use. Negative frames were most effective at promoting condom intentions among those who assumed that it was normative to use condoms; whereas, positive frames were most effective at promoting condom intentions among those who assumed it was normative not to use condoms. These effects held, even after controlling for a wide range of other attitudes and cognitions.

The findings in Blanton and colleagues (2001) suggest several straightforward recommendations regarding message framing: (1) When targeting a group with unhealthy norms, associate a positive image with health behavior; and (2) When targeting a group with healthy norms, associate a negative image with unhealthy behaviors. If only life were that simple.

Intervening and Interfering Processes

We fully appreciate that a wide range of psychological processes might intervene to prevent the predictions in DRT from being realized when they are applied in specific communication contexts. Consider, for instance, the earlier discussion regarding internalization of reference group norms. Many times, health communicators might frame their messages appropriately, but their efforts will fail because they are not meaningful reference others in the populations they wish to influence. In fact, messages might "backfire" if the target audience views the communicator as a "negative referent" who defines what is desirable through criticism (Newcomb, 1950). For instance, many teens may associate "positive" images with behaviors that are prohibited by authorities and, in these cases, negative framing will have the unfortunate quality of making relatively rare and unhealthy behaviors appear more desirable.

Exactly this sort of effect was recently observed in our laboratory. Blanton and Burpo (2006) exposed college students to positively or negatively framed messages promoting healthier drinking intentions. Although the DRT predictions held for those who had little history of drinking in the past, there was strong resistance to social influence among those with extensive drinking histories. Exposure to negatively framed messages that had decreased drinking intentions in the low-risk population actually increased intentions in this high-risk population. It appears that, among individuals with a history of drinking, they responded to the criticisms inherent in negative frames by moving toward their past actions, in much the way that people justify past behaviors in the face of threats (e.g., Cooper & Fazio, 1984). Similar forms "backfire effects" have been seen in other applied health settings, where attempts to reduce adolescent drinking and smoking at times increase these very same tendencies (Leventhal, 1970; Witte & Allen, 2000; see also Wakefield et al., 2006).

Implicit Theories

The possibility that adolescents will actively resist attempts to influence or alter their behavior can present serious challenges to applied researchers (see Prentice, Chapter 8, this volume). Nevertheless, we believe that the results of the above studies reveal some of the ways that people construct an identity out of difference, and this can guide efforts to affect change in adolescent populations. When there is little reason for targeted populations to resist influence attempts and when communicators can gain some modest degree of referent status, the principles in DRT can be harnessed to promote healthy behaviors. Not only do we believe that communicators should follow the advice of our model in such contexts, we think that many communicators do follow the advice of our model in most contexts.

One of the fundamental assumptions in DRT is that people have an implicit understanding of the first principle of deviance regulation; they know that difference is information. As a result, communicators spontaneously frame their communications with a negative tone when they are trying to discourage uncommon actions, to enforce conformity, or to promote moral codes of conduct. In contrast, communicators spontaneously frame their communications with a positive tone when they are trying to encourage rare actions, promote differentiation from the norm, or reinforce ideal standards of excellence. The best evidence we have for this comes from research showing that observers draw normative inferences from a speaker's chosen message frame.

To begin, notice some of the hidden assumptions people reveal from how they frame their communications. Consider the husband who compliments his wife for "not looking fat" in her new outfit or the wife who praises her husband for "being tolerable" at a dinner party. In both instances, these comments were framed positively and so they technically qualify as compliments. But, because of their framing, they also revealed negative assumptions about what is typical for these individuals, assumptions that would cause these "compliments" to sting a bit. As another set of examples, consider the inferences one would draw about a town from reading the newspaper headline "No Gang Shootings Downtown Last Month" or "Mayor: Likelihood of Being Murdered Low." In each of these instances, the editorial decision to comment on something positive revealed an implicit assumption that these positive events are "comment worthy"—or rare.

According to DRT, speakers' comments are assumed to reflect what they view to be the exception to the norm, because the norm does not merit comment (and see Grice, 1975). This simple fact provides new insights into the reasons why conformity pressure is typically negative in tone. If "everyone is doing it," then there is no information to be found in praising those who go with this same norm. Because the group only has limited power to associate images with distinction, it will be ineffective at promoting conformity to an existing norm through praise. A better strategy is to reduce the likelihood of deviation through criticism and rejection. Interestingly, however, if a group or a speaker were to ignore this basic reality and try to promote the norm directly, they could inadvertently reduce the likelihood that members will see the necessity of conforming. Consider, as an example, the implicit message revealed by parents who praise their children for telling the truth or for not hitting their siblings. By praising prosocial behaviors, these parents imply that these actions are exceptional and worthy of their praise. These secondary statements, if they were attended to by their children, could in fact lower commitment to truth telling and to nonviolence.

We were reminded of the downsides of praise when we first observed a contemporary health campaign designed to increase sexual abstinence among teenagers. The campaign of interest is titled Not Me, Not Now, and it was designed to promote sexual abstinence in high schools. Although the campaign title suggests otherwise, this campaign tends to pursue positively framed messages. It praises teens who abstain from sex and promotes teenage role models who abstain, portraying them as people who have good judgment, bright futures, and high aspirations.[1]

Although well meaning, we wondered if the decision to praise abstaining teens was not inadvertently communicating an unintended message that could reduce the campaign's effectiveness. Specifically, we wondered if the experts in health community who praised abstaining teens were not, unintentionally, communicating their belief that it is rare to abstain from sex. This secondary communication might lower inhibitions to have sex, as it would appear to teens that this is something that is age appropriate for their group.[2] Stuart and Blanton (2004) tested this logic by exposing college students to health communication texts that were adapted from the Not Me, Not Now campaign. For half of the conditions, however, they rephrased the original positively framed communications so that they now were negatively framed. Thus, an original message that praised the responsibility of teens who abstained was altered so that it focused on the irresponsibility of teens who are sexually active. After reading this material, participants then estimated the number of teens who have sex in high school. As predicted, participants who had read the positively framed messages estimated that there were fewer high school virgins than did those who read the negatively framed messages. It seems that, by holding up abstaining peers as role models, the positively framed material suggested to participants that such role models were the exception to the rule, not the norm.

In subsequent studies, Blanton and Hall (2006) found that these shifts could alter the effectiveness of communications designed to change behavior. In one study, a communication that praised students for refusing sex without condoms exerted less influence on behavioral intentions than a communication that criticized students for not using condoms, and this difference was partially mediated by changes in normative assumptions. Thus, students who read the positively framed communication (1) thought that it was less common to refuse sex without a condom

---

[1] *www.notmenotnow.org.*

[2] This assumption would be consistent with group theories that assume a motive to conform to social norms. As a rule, DRT focuses attention on the ability of social norms to alter the contingencies surrounding actions. However, this is not to say that people will not at times be motivated to conform to norms (or to react against them).

and (2) showed lower intentions to engage in this behavior themselves, compared to students who read negatively framed communications. Blanton and Hall then replicated this effect in a behavioral intervention designed to increase hand washing in public restrooms.

Going Negative

At first glance, DRT appears not to give greater emphasis to positive or negative communications. Blanton and colleagues (2001) in fact demonstrated that positively and negatively framed messages can be effective, depending on the norms surrounding the targeted behaviors. However, closer inspection reveals at least two reasons why negatively framed messages should exert more powerful influences on behavior than positively framed messages.

The first reason has to do with the effects of communications over time. Consider as an example a hypothetical campaign designed to encourage regular use of sunscreen. DRT suggests that, if sunscreen use is a normative choice in the population of interest, one should adopt a negatively framed message. Such a communication would associate negative images with those in the minority who do not use sunscreen. If the communication is effective in promoting sunscreen use, the number of people who use sunscreen will increase even more, and this increase in the desired behavior will only reinforce the effectiveness of the norm that promotes the use of a negative frame. Now imagine that sunscreen use is rare in the population. According to DRT, one should adopt a positively framed message in this normative context. Such a communication would associate a positive image with those few people who do use sunscreen. If this message is effective, however, the number of people using sunscreen will increase. Over time, this increase will change the norms that promote the use of positive frames and, thereby, will undermine the effectiveness of the positively framed message.

In short, negatively framed messages are more stable over time than positively framed messages. When a positively framed message is used effectively, it should undermine the norm that promotes the use of a positive frame. In contrast, when a negatively framed message is used effectively, it should reinforce the norm that promotes the use of a negative frame. This would suggest that there will be more contexts in which a communicator will want to adhere to negative communications rather than positive communications.

This prediction may seem to contradict strong theory and common wisdom. Many would argue, for instance, that it typically is more effective to teach new behaviors through positive reinforcement than negative reinforcement (Kazdin, 1994), and that it is easier to promote a behavior than discourage its alternative (e.g., Newman, Wolff, & Hearst, 1980; Sainsbury, 1971). Some evidence also suggests that communicators should strive for positive communications with target audiences to avoid putting off those they would like to influence (e.g., Keller, Lipkus, & Rimer, 2003; Thorsteinson & Highhouse, 2003). There also are no shortages of parenting books that emphasize the value of praise over criticism in raising a well-adjusted child (e.g., Latham, 1994; Spock, 2004). However, consider the many stable and negative communication structures that exist in our society and that guide our actions quite reliably.

For example, the legal system reinforces a large number of civil behaviors by punishing their alternatives. Society does not praise people who refrain from murdering or offer financial awards to those who elect to drive the speed limit. Society punishes those who engage in the alternates to these actions. As enduring social structures, most religions and informal codes of conduct also tend to punish those who pursue immoral actions more than they reward those who pursue moral actions. As just one illustration, it is informative that 8 of the 10 commandments in the Old Testament were written to sanction behaviors to avoid (that one "shalt not") pursue. Each of these actions reflects moralistic standards that one ought to live up to, and DRT has a ready explanation for why the commandments' author(s) typically chose negatively framed communications. Once behaviors take hold in a group and once they are more or less accepted as correct and right, the only way to reinforce these norms of action is through negative communications.

But what are the consequences of not pursuing negative communications? Our work on normative assumptions suggests a second reason to stick with negative communications, even when most people fall short of these standards. Suppose that a society decided to reward people who choose to drive the speed limit. One could make a case from the first principle of DRT that this is a reasonable strategy to pursue. After all, most people do not drive the speed limit, and so it is socially more informative to learn that someone never speeds. However, if our criminal code were restructured to reward legal driving, it would imply to all citizens that this action is an option. This secondary message could then undermine the very code of that society is trying to promote. In this light, DRT offers a somewhat forgiving take on the hypocrisies in societies and families. If authorities at times preach standards that they and most others fail to attain, at least these authorities can be respected for their assumptions, if not their actions.

Despite the two reasons why negative communications might exert more pull on individuals than positive, we do appreciate the reasons why popular and psychological wisdom emphasize the value of positive communications as socializing and learning forces. We suspect, however, that this bias toward the positive exists because people rarely focus attention on the behaviors that most people take for granted. Researchers do not think to persuade people not to murder, because these norms are so well entrenched in our society. However, the act of getting a teenager to stop smoking is a bit tricky. The behavior of such individuals might be framed negatively by concerned parents, to suggest to their teens that they are breaking from social norms in ways that might contaminate their identities. But, as noted above, such actions might generate motivated resistance by the teens who are feeling coerced by authorities or criticized by them. Moreover, if smoking is pervasive in a teen's life, then negatively framed communications will look silly to the target audience. This is because negatively framed statements try to associate an identity with a normal activity, and so it is reasonable for the teen to infer from the parents' tone that they are "out of touch."

So, although DRT argues that negatively framed communications are most effective in many instances, we rush to point out that this is most true for behaviors that are so well socialized that one rarely needs to continue communicating about them directly. Health communicators and parents more typically are trying to influence behaviors that are still open to change, open to interpretation, and observable from multiple frames of reference. These facts offer many applied challenges to researchers who wish to apply DRT or any other theory to influence adolescent behaviors.

It is also worth pointing out, however, that the negativity promoted by this model is not simply prescriptive (i.e., advocating how communicators should try to influence adolescents) but also descriptive (i.e., describing how adolescents typically influence one another). Most older adults who remember what it was like to be the target of peer pressure during their teen years probably also remember that peer pressure was not a positive force. The pressure to experiment with new ideas or action is often framed by adolescents, not as some fun new "option" that can be tried, but, rather, as an expectation that will be met with punishments, if it is not met. DRT can explain why peer pressure tends to be negative. Moreover, it suggests that peer pressure will become more negative over time.

Recall that DRT predicts that negative communications become more influential over time, once initial influence attempts begin to shape norms. Recall also that adolescents appear to have some insights into deviance regulation principles. This suggests that peers, as they develop and experiment with more risky behaviors, will go from rewarding positive distinctions that define "mature" behavior to punishing negative distinctions that define "immature" behavior. Consider as an example Juovenen's work (Chapter 11, this volume) showing that the tendency to view risky children (in her research "bullies") as "cool" was a predictor of antisocial outcomes in adolescents. Her findings strongly suggest that an appetitive/approach desire to be cool is a risk factor. However, DRT would suggest that, if the individuals in her studies were tracked over time, antisocial outcomes would be predicted more strongly by the tendency to view nonrisky kids as "uncool"—rather than the tendency to see risky peers as "cool." This is because, as risky behaviors become more pervasive in a given age group, attention will focus more on those who fail to take risks than those who opt in. As norms shift in these ways, those adolescents who are at most risk should not be those who intend to stand out to be cool. Rather, those at greatest risk should be those who are unwilling to deviate from the unhealthy norms of the group (see Gibbons, Chapter 3, this volume). This prediction goes beyond the empirical base of DRT, but we think it illustrates the potential insights that can be gained by using DRT to investigate adolescent peer influence.

CONCLUSION

Deviance regulation theory is built upon just two basic mechanisms. The first is a cognitive-perceptual mechanism that causes people to give greater weight to the consequences of counternormative (or "deviant") actions than normative actions. The second is a socialization mechanism that causes people to be most concerned with the opinions of important reference groups. Although there are many complications to consider when applying this (or any) theory, we have argued here that DRT offers a comprehensive framework that can offer many new insights into the nature of adolescent social influence processes.

REFERENCES

Asch, S. E. (1956). Studies of independence and conformity: I. A minority of one against a unanimous majority. *Psychological Monographs, 70*(9, Whole No. 416).

Baer, J. S., Stacy, A., & Larimer, M. (1991). Biases in the perception of drinking norms among college students. *Journal of Studies on Alcohol, 52,* 580–586.

Becker, H. S. (1963). *Outsiders: Studies in the sociology of deviance.* New York: Free Press.

Blanton, H., & Burpo, J. (2006). *Motivated rejection of negative frames.* Unpublished manuscript.

Blanton, H. B., & Christie, C. (2003). Deviance regulation: A theory of action and identity. *Review of General Psychology, 7,* 115–149.

Blanton, H., & Hall, D. (2006). *Knowing when to assume: Communicator knowledge as moderator of normative influence.* Unpublished manuscript.

Blanton, H., Hall, D., & Prentice, D. (2006). *Regulatory focus and distinctiveness motives*. Unpublished manuscript.

Blanton, H., & Sanchez-Burks, J. (2001). *Effects of attitudes and social norms on behavioral intentions*. Unpublished raw data.

Blanton, H., Stuart, A. E., & VandenEijnden, R. J. (2001). An introduction to deviance regulation theory: The effect of behavioral norms on message framing. *Personality and Social Psychology Bulletin, 27,* 848–858.

Bown, N. J., & Abrams, D. (2003). Despicability in the workplace: Effects of behavioral deviance and unlikeability on the evaluation of in-group and out-group members. *Journal of Applied Social Psychology, 33,* 2413–2426.

Brewer, M. B. (1991). The social self: On being the same and different at the same time. *Personality and Social Psychology Bulletin, 17,* 475–482.

Brewer, M. B. (1993). The role of distinctiveness in social identity and group behaviour. In M. A. Hogg & D. Abrams (Eds.), *Group motivation: Social psychological perspectives* (pp. 1–16). New York: Harvester Wheatsheaf.

Brewer, M. B., & Pickett, C. (1998). Distinctiveness motives as a source of the social self. In T. R. Tyler, R. M. Kramer, & O. P. John (Eds.), *The psychology of the social self* (pp. 71–90). Mahwah, NJ: Erlbaum.

Cooper, J., & Fazio, R. H. (1984). A new look at dissonance theory. In L. Berkowitz (Ed.), *Advances in experimental social psychology* (Vol. 17, pp. 229–264). Orlando, FL: Academic Press.

Crandall, C. S. (1988). Social contagion of binge eating. *Journal of Personality and Social Psychology, 55,* 588–598.

Deutsch, M., & Gerard, H. B. (1955). A study of normative and informational social influences upon individual judgment. *Journal of Abnormal and Social Psychology, 51,* 629–636.

Ditto, P. H., & Griffin, J. (1993). The value of uniqueness: Self-evaluation and the perceived prevalence of valenced characteristics. *Journal of Social Behavior and Personality, 8,* 221–240.

Erikson, E. H. (1950). *Childhood and society.* New York: Norton.

Festinger, L. (1950). Informal social communication. *Psychological Review, 57,* 271–282.

Festinger, L. (1954). A theory of social comparison processes. *Human Relations, 7,* 117–140.

Festinger, L., Gerard, H. B., Hymovitch, B., Kelley, H. H., & Raven, B. H. (1952). The influence process in the presence of extreme deviates. *Human Relations, 5,* 327–340.

Festinger, L., & Thibaut, J. (1951). Interpersonal communication in small groups. *Journal of Abnormal and Social Psychology, 46,* 92–99.

Forsyth, D. R. (2000). Social comparison and influence in groups. In J. Suls & L. Wheeler (Eds.), *Handbook of social comparison: Theory and research* (pp. 81–103). New York: Kluwer Academic/Plenum Press.

Fromkin, H. L. (1970). Effects of experimentally aroused feelings of indistinctiveness upon valuation of scarce and novel experiences. *Journal of Personality and Social Psychology, 16,* 521–529.

Fromkin, H. L. (1972). Feelings of interpersonal undistinctiveness: An unpleasant affective state. *Journal of Experimental Research in Personality, 6,* 178–182.

Gerrard, M., Gibbons, F., & Reis-Bergan, M. (2000). Self-esteem, self-serving cognitions, and health risk behavior. *Journal of Personality, 68,* 1177–1201.

Grice, H. P. (1975). Logic and conversation. In P. Cole & J. L. Morgan (Eds.), *Syntax and semantics, 3: Speech acts* (pp. 41–58). New York: Academic Press.

Haines, M. (1996). *A social norms approach to preventing binge drinking at colleges and universities* (NO. ED/OPE/96-18). Washington, DC: U.S. Department of Education.

Hammersley, R., Lavelle, T. L., & Forsyth, A. J. M. (1992). Adolescent drug use, health & personality. *Drug and Alcohol Dependence, 31,* 91–99.

Higgins, E. T. (1987). Self-discrepancy: A theory relating self and affect. *Psychological Review, 94,* 319–340.

Higgins, E. T., Shah, J., & Friedman, R. (1997). Emotional responses to goal attainment: Strength of regulatory focus as moderator. *Journal of Personality and Social Psychology, 72,* 515–525.

Hughes, E. (1945). Dilemmas and contradictions of status. *American Journal of Sociology, 50,* 353–369.

Hyman, H. H. (1960). The psychology of status. *Archives of Psychology, 38*(Whole No. 269).

Hyman, H. H., & Singer, E. (1968). Introduction. In H. H. Hyman & E. Singer (Eds.), *Readings in reference group theory and research* (pp. 3–20). New York: Free Press.

James, W. (1890). *Principles of psychology* (Vol. 1). New York: Holt.

Jones, E. E., & Davis, K. E. (1965). From acts to dispositions: The attribution process in person perception. In L. Berkowitz (Ed.), *Advances in experimental social psychology* (Vol. 2, pp. 220–266). New York: Academic Press.

Kazdin A. (1994). *Behavior modification in applied settings.* Pacific Grove, CA: Brooks/Cole.

Keller, P. A., Lipkus, I. M., & Rimer, B. (2003). Affect, framing, and persuasion. *Journal of Marketing Research, 40*(1), 54–64.

Kelley, H. H. (1972). Attribution in social interaction. In E. E. Jones, D. E. Kanouse, H. H. Kelley, R. E. Nisbett, S. Valins, & B. W. Weiner (Eds.), *Attribution: Perceiving the causes of behavior* (pp. 1–26). Morristown, NJ: General Learning Press.

Kitsuse, J. (1962). Societal reaction to deviance: Problems of theory and method. *Social Problems, 9,* 247–256.

Latham, G. I. (1994). *The power of positive parenting: A wonderful way to raise children.* Logan: University of Utah Press.

Leary, M. R., & Downs, D. L. (1995). Interpersonal functions of the self-esteem motive: The self-esteem system as a sociometer. In M. H. Kernis (Ed.), *Efficacy, agency, and self-esteem* (pp. 123– 144). New York: Plenum Press.

Leventhal, H. (1970). Findings and theory in the study of fear communications. In L. Berkowitz (Ed.), *Advances in experimental social psychology* (Vol. 5, pp. 119–186). New York: Academic Press.

Little, M., & Steinberg, L. (2006). Psychosocial correlates of adolescent drug dealing in the inner city: Potential roles of opportunity, conventional commitments, and maturity. *Journal of Research in Crime and Delinquency, 43,* 357–386.

Lynn, M., & Snyder, C. R. (2002). Uniqueness theory. In C. R. Snyder & S. J. Lopez (Eds.), *Handbook of positive psychology* (pp. 395–410). New York: Oxford University Press.

Maslow, A. H. (1968). *Toward a psychology of being.* Princeton, NJ: Van Nostrand.

McGuire, W. J., & McGuire, C. V. (1980). Salience of handedness in the spontaneous self-concept. *Perceptual and Motor Skills, 50,* 3–7.

McGuire, W. J., McGuire, C. V., Child, P., & Fujioka, T. (1978). Salience of ethnicity in the spontaneous self-concept as a function of one's ethnic distinctiveness in the social environment. *Journal of Personality and Social Psychology, 36,* 511–520.

McGuire, W. J., & Padawer-Singer, A. (1976). Trait salience in the spontaneous self-concept. *Journal of Personality and Social Psychology, 33,* 743–754.

Merton, R. K., & Kitt, A. S. (1950). Contributions to the theory of reference group behavior. In R. Merton & P. F. Lazarsfeld (Eds.), *Continuities in social research: Studies in the scope and method of the "The American Soldier"* (pp. 40–105). Glencoe, IL: Free Press.

Mullen, B., & Goethals, G. R. (1990). Social projection, actual consensus and valence. *British Journal of Social Psychology, 29,* 279–282.

Newcomb, T. M. (1950). *Social psychology.* New York: Dryden.

Newman, J., Wolff, W. T., & Hearst, E. (1980). The feature-positive effect in adult human subjects. *Journal of Experimental Psychology: Human Learning and Memory, 6,* 630–650.

Perkins, H. W. (1995, Fall). Scope of the problem: Misperceptions of alcohol and drugs. *Catalyst, 1,* 1–2.

Perkins, H. W. (Ed.). (2003). *The social norms approach to preventing school and college age substance abuse: A handbook for educators, counselors, and clinicians.* San Francisco: Jossey-Bass.

Perkins, H. W., & Berkowitz, A. D. (1986). Perceiving the community norms of alcohol use among students: Some research implications for campus alcohol education programming. *International Journal of the Addictions, 21,* 961–976.

Perkins, H. W., & Wechsler, H. (1996). Variation in perceived college drinking norms and its impact on alcohol abuse: A nationwide study. *Journal of Drug Issues, 26,* 961–974.

Pickett, C. L., Silver, M. D., & Brewer, M. B. (2002). The impact of assimilation and differentiation needs on perceived group importance and judgments of ingroup size. *Personality and Social Psychology Bulletin, 28,* 546–558.

Prentice, D. A., & Miller, D. T. (1993). Pluralistic ignorance and alcohol use on campus: Some consequences of misperceiving the social norm. *Journal of Personality and Social Psychology, 64,* 243–256.

Rogers, C. R. (1961). *On becoming a person.* Boston: Houghton Mifflin.

Rothman, A. J., & Salovey, P. (1997). Shaping perceptions to motivate healthy behavior: The role of message framing. *Psychological Bulletin, 121,* 3–19.

Sainsbury, R. S. (1971). The "feature-positive effect" and simultaneous discrimination learning. *Journal of Experimental Child Psychology, 11,* 347–356.

Schachter, S. (1951). Deviation, rejection and communication. *Journal of Abnormal and Social Psychology, 46,* 190–207.

Schroeder, C. M., & Prentice, D. A. (1998). Exposing pluralistic ignorance to reduce alcohol use among college students. *Journal of Applied Social Psychology, 28,* 2150–2180.

Shah, J., Higgins, E. T., & Friedman, R. S. (1998). Performance incentives and means: How regulatory focus influences goal attainment. *Journal of Personality and Social Psychology, 74,* 285–293.

Shedler J., & Block, J. (1990). Adolescent drug use and psychological health: A longitudinal inquiry. *American Psychologist, 45,* 612–630.

Sherif, M., & Sherif, C. W. (1964). La methode des categories personnelles et les recherches sur les attitudes [The own categories technique and research on attitudes]. *Bulletin d'Etudes et Recherches Psychologiques, 13,* 185–197.

Singer, E. (1981). Reference groups and social evaluations. In M. Rosenberg & R. Turner (Eds.), *Social psychology: Sociological perspectives* (pp. 66–93). New York: Basic Books.

Skowronski, J. J., & Carlston, D. E. (1987). Social judgment and social memory: The role of cue diagnosticity in negativity, positivity, and extremity biases. *Journal of Personality and Social Psychology, 52,* 689–699.

Skowronski, J. J., & Carlston, D. E. (1989). Negativity and extremity biases in impression formation: A review of explanations. *Psychological Bulletin, 105,* 131–142.

Snyder, C. R., & Endelman, J. R. (1980). Effects of degree of interpersonal similarity on physical distance and self-reported attraction: A comparison of uniqueness and reinforcement theory predictions. *Journal of Personality, 47,* 492–505.

Snyder, C. R., & Fromkin, H. L. (1977). Abnormality as a positive characteristic: The development and validation of a scale measuring need for uniqueness. *Journal of Abnormal Psychology, 86,* 518–527.

Snyder, C. R., & Fromkin, H. L. (1980). *Uniqueness: The human pursuit of difference.* New York: Plenum Press.

Spock, B. (2004). *Dr. Spock's baby and child care book: The one essential parenting book* (8th ed.). New York: Pocket Books.

Stuart, A. E., & Blanton, H. (2003). A conversational norms analysis of the effects of message framing on perceived behavioral prevalence. *European Journal of Social Psychology, 33,* 93–102.

Tafarodi, R. W., & Swann, W. B. (1996). Individualism-collectivism and global self-esteem: Evidence for a cultural trade-off. *Journal of Cross-Cultural Psychology, 27,* 651–672.

Thorsteinson, T. J., & Highhous, S. (2003). Effects of goal framing in job advertisements on organizational attractiveness. *Journal of Applied Social Psychology, 33*(11), 2392–2412.

Wakefield, M., Terry-McElrath, Y., Emery, S., Saffer, H., Chaloupka, F. J., Szczypka, G., et al. (2006). Effect of televised, tobacco company–funded smoking prevention advertising on youth smoking-related beliefs, intentions, and behavior. *American Journal of Public Health, 96,* 2154–2160.

Weinstein, N. D. (1980). Unrealistic optimism about future life events. *Journal of Personality and Social Psychology, 39,* 806–820.

Weinstein, N. D., & Klein, W. M. (2002). Resistance of personal risk perceptions to debiasing interventions. In T. Gilovich, D. Griffin, & D. Kahneman (Eds.), *Heuristics and biases: The psychology of intuitive judgment* (pp. 313–323). New York: Cambridge University Press.

Wellen, J. M., & Neale, M. S. (2006). Deviance, self-typicality, and group cohesion: The corrosive effects of the bad apples on the barrel. *Small Group Research, 37,* 165–186.

Witte, K., & Allen, M. (2000). A meta-analysis of fear appeals: Implications for effective public health campaigns. *Health Education and Behavior, 27*(5), 591–615.

PART III

ALTERING PEER INFLUENCE EFFECTS

Moderators and Interventions

CHAPTER 6

Variation in Patterns of Peer Influence

Considerations of Self and Other

William M. Bukowski, Ana Maria Velasquez,
and Mara Brendgen

The concept of peer influence refers to the processes by which children affect their agemates (Dishion & Dodge, 2005). According to this concept, children "acquire" the characteristics of the peers with whom they associate. Already there is a reasonably substantial database showing that over time children can acquire the characteristics of their peers (Bukowski, Brendgen, & Vitaro, 2007; Dodge, Dishion, & Lansford, 2006; Parker, Rubin, Erath, Wojslawowicz, & Buskirk, 2006; Rubin, Bukowski, & Parker, 2006). Insofar as there is evidence already that peers can influence each other's levels of aggression and of depression, these behaviors/characteristics have been conceived of as "contagious" behaviors in the sense that they can be passed to a child from her or his peers (Dishion & Dodge, 2005; Stevens & Prinstein, 2005).

In spite of the well-developed literature showing that peers can have an effect on each other, several fundamental questions about the breadth and the specificity of the processes underlying peer influence have been either unasked or unanswered. In this chapter we attempt to deal with some of these issues. Our overall concern has to do with identifying the factors or processes that account for variation in the effects of experiences with peers. In this way, the point of departure for our thinking is the premise that the effects of peer experiences are not fixed but instead vary as a function of person-related and peer-related characteristics. From our perspective, our most important concern is with theory. Although the broad literature on peer relations has often emphasized theory as well as established findings, the literature on peer influence sometimes appears to emphasize findings more so than theory. Having many exciting findings is, of course, a good thing as the current literature shows that peer influence is a real and powerful process. It is our view, however, that having a better understanding of what might explain why these effects happen and when they are most likely to occur would be a useful and important next step in this literature. The theory we develop represents a *rapprochement* between traditional theories about development and current thinking from social and developmental psychology about the self. Specifically we use the concept of discrepancy to organize a set of ideas drawn from different domains and to explain the processes of change underlying influence effects.

A second issue we raise has to do with recognizing that the effects of peer influence, and the variations in these effects, may occur at different levels of social complexity in the peer system. Peer experiences exist at multiple levels, most notably the dyad and the group. It is likely that peer influence may result from multiple phenomena taken from different levels. Our analysis is intended to show that peer influence is the result of several factors rather than just one. Finally, we point to some "cultural" processes that may affect the extent to which peers are likely to affect each other.

USING THE CONCEPT OF DISCREPANCY TO EXPLAIN PEER INFLUENCE EFFECTS

Discrepancy and Motivation for Change

The concept of peer influence is essentially an idea about change. Its central claim is that a child's behavior will change as a function of the child's experiences with peers. Accordingly, explanations of peer influence need to account for why this form of change occurs. Theoretical accounts of change are neither new nor unfamiliar to developmental psychologists. Theories of development are, to a great extent, theories of change. Beyond describing change, they explain why change occurs and when it is most likely to happen. Traditionally, theories of development have identified several processes and phenomena that are either internal or external to the person. An important distinction has been drawn between mechanistic theories, which claim that change is motivated or controlled by conditions that are external to the person, and organismic theories, which claim that the motivation for change derives from conditions within the person that reflect the interface between the person and a set of external conditions.

In spite of the central place of change in theories of development, developmental psychologists have done a better job of describing change than of showing when it is most likely to happen. Twenty-five years ago, it was noted that although developmental psychologists had become adept at demonstrating that change has occurred, they had done a poor job of identifying the antecedent conditions that lead to it (Ruble, Higgins, & Hartup, 1983). This observation is probably truer now than it was when it was made. This inattention to the conditions that make change likely is regrettable because there are multiple theories that explicitly describe the conditions that lead to change. Aside from mechanistic theories that simply emphasize external forces, organismic models typically argue that change occurs to repair discrepancies between a current state and a desired one. This concept is inherent in the Piagetian concept of disequilibrium. Disequilibrium occurs when one's functioning is discrepant from one's experience. According to a central premise of the Piagetian model, disequilibrium, as a form of discrepancy, motivates change.

A challenge to examining the role of disequilibrium as an antecedent condition to change has been our capacity to measure it. Insofar as disequilibrium is an internal state, it difficult to observe it directly. In infant research, disequilibrium has been simulated in babies when investigators have created conditions that are likely to lead to disequilibrium (e.g., by moving as hidden object). Nevertheless, even in these cases one has to assume that a discrepancy has occurred. In the study of peer relations with school-age children and early adolescents our measurement opportunities may be a bit richer because we can get access to children's internal states and because we can make reasoned assumptions about the states that children would desire. In these ways, measuring disequilibrium, or at least discrepancy, is a possibility in research on peer relations. As a result, assessing whether discrepancy, as a motivator of change, is an antecedent to a phenomenon such as peer influence is possible for persons who do peer research.

Friendlessness as Disequilibrium

But which disequilibria or discrepancies would we want to study as a source of motivation for peer influence? We propose that two interrelated kinds of discrepancy are likely motivators for a child to try to become like his or her peers. One is friendlessness, and the other is low self-esteem. The claim that friendlessness is a form of disequilibrium that will motivate a child to take on the characteristics of his or her peers is based on two premises. The first is that the disequilibrium associated with friendlessness derives from a nearly universal desire to have a friend. There is reason for us think that the desire for friendship is a basic feature of human nature. For example, Baumeister and Leary (1995) presented several forms of evidence that would support the view that friendedness is a basic human desire. Accordingly children who are without a friend will presumably recognize the discrepancy between their friendless condition and their desired state of having a friend.

A second premise of our idea is that the disequilibrium that results from friendlessness will be relieved by taking on the characteristics of one's desired peers. In other words, this idea presupposes that becoming like a desired peer will facilitate the process of becoming a friend of the peer. In this way, the process of acquiring the characteristics of the peer that a friendless child wants to have a friend is a form of accommodation. These ideas were recently tested using a longitudinal study of a group of early adolescent boys and girls (Adams, Bukowski, & Bagwell, 2005). Changes in levels of aggression across a 6-month period during the first year of secondary school were examined according to two aspects of the children's friendship experiences. The participants in the study were assessed twice, once 6 weeks after the school year stared and then again 6 months later. The two features of friendship that were tested were the level of aggression of the peer that the child chose as his or her best friend and whether or not the child's friendship choice was reciprocated. Adams and colleagues (2005) reported that changes in a child's level of aggression were strongest when the peer who was regarded as a best friend was aggressive and when this relationship was nonreciprocated. That is, greater effects were seen when the relationship was nonreciprocated than reciprocated. These findings are illustrated in Figure 6.1.

Two important conclusions can be drawn from the variations in the slopes shown in this figure. First the steepest slopes are for the children who chose an aggressive peer as a friend. This pattern is consistent with the basic concept of peer influence. The second critical finding is the larger divergence between the two slopes for the children without a reciprocated friend than between the slopes for the children with a reciprocated friend. The effect of choosing or not choosing an aggressive peer as one's friend was much stronger for the children without a reciprocated friend than for the children who had one. Among the possible interpretations is that when children were lacking the presence of a desired peer they were essentially in a state of disequilibrium and that they tried to repair this disequilibrium by acquiring the characteristics of the desired friend.

The proposal that peer influence effects will be seen most strongly for friendless children contradicts the usual practice of looking for the

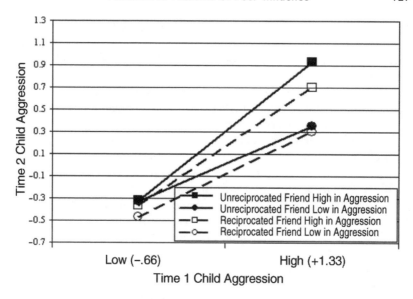

FIGURE 6.1. Association between time 1 and time 2 aggression as a function of friendship reciprocity and friend aggression.

effects of friendship in intact friendship pairs. Typically investigators have looked for the effect of peer relations by examining processes within friendship dyads that already exist. Our claim that the effects that a desired peer can have on a child will be stronger when the child is friendless does not mean that children who are not friends will not influence each other. Even in ongoing friendships there may be discrepancies and disequilibria, as well as other dynamics, that can lead to peer influence. Nevertheless, friendless children may be more motivated than friended children to take on the characteristics of a peer with whom they would like to be a friend.

The "Self" as Disequilibrium

One of these other kinds of discrepancy may derive from the self per se. The self-concept is one of psychology's oldest ideas. Typically it has been conceived as having two fundamental components. One concerns the characteristics that a person ascribes to the self, such as whether one sees oneself as smart, good looking, or athletic, while the other broad component refers to how one evaluates oneself. The evaluative component of the self refers to the extent to which someone is proud or satisfied with the way she or he is. Inherent in this idea is the notion that a person with low esteem for the self sees a difference between who he or she is and who he or she wants to be. Measures of self-esteem often refer directly to this discrepancy between what one is like and what one would like to be. For example in Harter's (1982) well-known Perceived Competence Scale for Children the items in the self-esteem subscale (i.e., the measure of general self-worth) refer to whether one would change things about oneself if these changes were possible.

This idea that self-esteem is essentially a measure of difference can be seen in Leary's conceptualization of self-esteem as a "sociometer" (Leary, 1999; Leary & Baumeister, 2000; Leary & Downs, 1995; Leary, Tambor, Terdal, & Downs, 1995). In his social psychological approach to the self, Leary saw the "self" as a descriptive construct and as a motivational construct. He argued that self-esteem functions as a monitor of the degree to which one is being included or excluded by other people and that will motivate a person to change so as to behave in ways that minimize exclusion. In this way, low self-esteem will motivate a person to change in ways that will increase his or her connections to others whereas persons who have high self-esteem will see no discrepancy between their social involvement and their desire to be included, and they will see no need for change.

An additional model from a social-psychological perspective reaches similar conclusion about self-esteem and patterns of influence. Like Leary, Rhodes and Wood (1992) saw motivational features in the concept of self-esteem. They argued that self-esteem affects the extent to which someone can be influenced by others. A feature of their analysis of the association between self-esteem and influence is that persons with low self-esteem are more likely to yield to the expectations of others. When applied to the concept of peer influence this view implies that children who are low in self-esteem may be more vulnerable to the influence or peers than are children with high self-esteem.

We tested the hypothesis that self-esteem would moderate the effects of peer influence in a longitudinal study of 225 10- to 13-year-old boys and girls (Bukowski & Hoza, 2007). At the first assessment, conducted during the first half of the school year, we had information about each child's disruptiveness and self-esteem and the disruptiveness of the peer the child chose as a best friend. We also knew whether the child's friendship choice was reciprocated. At the second assessment, held 6 months later, we knew how aggressive each child was. Controlling for the child's disruptiveness at time 1 (T1), we used the measures of the child's T1 self-esteem, the chosen peer's disruptiveness at T1, the measure of friendship reciprocity at T1 and the interaction between these variables as predictors of the child's aggressiveness at T2. Our analysis confirmed our expectation that friendship effects were stronger among children with low self-esteem than for those with high self-esteem. The most striking findings are shown in Figure 6.2. This figure shows that after controlling for disruptiveness at T1, aggression at T2 varied as a function of friendship status, self-esteem, and friend disruptiveness at T1. The highest level of aggression seen at T2 was for children who at T1 were unfriended, had low self-esteem, and chose a disruptive peer as their best friend. The findings also showed that the effects of friendship and friend aggression for children with high self-esteem were weaker than for children with low self-esteem.

Summary

At the outset of this section we noted that at the center of the concept of peer influence is the idea that peer experiences can lead to change. So far, the research on peer influence has been very successful at demonstrating that experiences with peers can lead to change. Nevertheless, efforts to specify what motivates these changes have been sparse. The organismic concept of discrepancy or disequilibrium is used as a general guide to identify how two constructs related to peer relations may explain the processes underlying peer influence. Specifically, friendlessness and low self-esteem were treated as forms of discrepancy that would motivate children to take on the characteristics of their peers. Accordingly, one

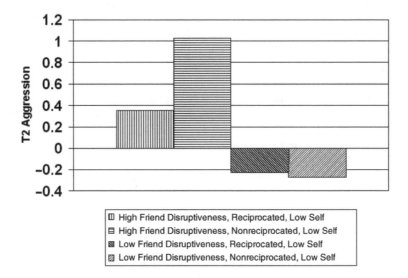

FIGURE 6.2. Levels of aggression at time 2 aggression as a function of friendship reciprocity and friend disruptiveness.

can hypothesize that the processes of peer influence are more likely to be evident among friendless children than friended children, and among children with low self-esteem than those high self-esteem.

In addition to their relevance to our understanding of what motivates children to take on the characteristics of their peers, these ideas are also relevant to our understanding of the processes of risk and protection. It is well known that friendedness and high self-esteem are likely to have immediate and positive effects on development. Aside from these effects, they may have indirect effects by either protecting children from influence by peers or by placing them at risk. If it is the case that children who are friended and children who have high self-esteem are less susceptible to the effects of peer influence, then these children may be spared from the negative effects that can result for peer interaction. On the other hand, if children who are friendless and children who have low self-esteem are more susceptible to the effects of peer influence, then they are at risk for negative influence. It is possible also that the likely combination of friendlessness and low self-esteem may be a particularly powerful form of risk.

VARIATIONS IN PEER INFLUENCE AS A FUNCTION OF THE "OTHER"

In the previous section we argued that some children are more likely to be influenced by their peers than are others. In this section we propose that some children have more influence on their peers than other children do. Our discussion here of the influence of the "other" covers two main points. First, insofar as peer experiences take many forms and occur at different levels of social complexity, any account of peer influence needs to recognize many different types of peer relations whose significance may vary from one child to another. In other words, there are multiple "others" who could influence any particular child. Second, that regardless of their other features some "others" have characteristics that give them a more prominent status among their peers. We start this discussion with a brief review of the multiple levels of the peer group.

Peer Relations as a Multilevel System

The term *peer relations* does not refer to one type of experience, but instead refers to a collection of experiences that occur at different levels of social complexity (Rubin, Bukowski, & Parker, 1998; Rubin et al., 2006). Specifically, the peer system consists of a set of interrelated experiences that take place in either dyadic or group contexts and that are a consequent and an antecedent of characteristics of the individual. According to this model, the level of the individual refers to the characteristics that children bring with them to their experiences with peers. These characteristics include more-or-less stable characteristics of the person such as social orientations, behavioral patterns, temperaments, social skills, forms of social perception, cognition, and social problem solving. Whereas *dyadic experiences* refer to the properties and characteristics of the relationships that a child has with a specific peer, most frequently a friend, *group context* refers to the structure and features of the set of peers in which the child and the child's relationships are embedded.

Phenomena from one level of experience are conceptually and experientially interdependent on phenomena at other levels such that individual, dyadic, and group variables influence and constrain each other. For example, when individuals enter into a relationship (i.e., a dyadic experience), they bring with them particular behavioral tendencies as well as a range of expectations and needs derived from their own relationship history. These factors, in turn, combine and interact with those of their friendship partner to determine the characteristics, continuity, and effects of the friendship. Moreover, the broader group provides a particular climate that may either favor or disfavor particular characteristics of individuals, thus making a particular child more or less popular (see, e.g., Boivin, Dodge, & Coie, 1995; Chang, 2004), and therefore affecting opportunities for friendship (Bukowski, Pizzamiglio, Newcomb, & Hoza, 1996).

An important repercussion of the interdependency of the phenomena that make up the peer system is that individual, dyadic, and group factors are confounded with each other. As a result they need to be studied together so that one can assess how these components fit and function together and to examine their combined and unique effects. That is, researchers need to account for the multiple pathways by which measures of peer relations may have an impact on development not only to be comprehensive, but also to account for the lack of independence among them. For the most part, researchers have been slow to achieve this objective in two ways. First, attention to the group has been rare (see Espelage, Holt, & Henkel, 2003, for an exception) and, second, efforts to combine an assessment of group and dyadic effects in the same study have been rarer. This overattention to the dyad may be lamentable, but it is understandable considering that most of the theory regarding the effect of peer relations has been dyad focused (Bukowski, Adams, & Santo, 2006). The particular challenge for studying peer relations has been to study the effects of the group and the dyad as distinct but intersecting phenomena.

Group and Dyadic Processes: Direct Effects and Moderators

Either explicitly or implicitly, most research on the effects of peer influence is predicated on the notion that this influence derives from direct experience with peers. Research on the effects of peer experience on outcomes has typically examined either the effects of the particular characteristics of the peers that a child associates with at either the group or dyadic level, or has attributed these effects to the support or reinforcement that peers give each other when they say or do things (see Bukowski et al., 2006, for a discussion). For example, in a study of preadolescents, Espelage and colleagues (2003) examined the effects of the level of aggression of one's peer group. They showed that the level of aggression in the members of the group that a child belonged to predicted changes in the child's level of aggression over time. In a study of particular processes of the interactions between boys, Dishion and colleagues (2006) reported that the rate of positive affect, such as laughing, between friends following comments that included aggressive content also predicted changes in a child's aggression over time. Another study focused on the effects of specific experience, specifically a process known as co-rumination in which friends provide opportunities and even positive regard for each other's expression of negative thoughts and depressed affect. Co-rumination has been shown to account for individual differences in levels of depressed affect (Rose, 2002). Together these studies appear to show that particular experiences at the level of the group or the dyad leads to changes in a child's behaviors or emotions.

Nevertheless, there is reason to think that these direct experiences do not account for all of the influence of peers, and it does not explain why peer influence may be stronger in some cases than in others. As other chapters in this volume show, studies by social psychologists have shown that individuals are concerned with social norms and that they will use norms to guide their own behavior (Miller & Prentice, 1994). For example, the prototypical study from this literature shows that college students adjust their consumption of alcohol so as to approximate what they believed to be the social norms of their campus even when the perceived norm differed from the actual norm. This concept of norm sensitivity and responsiveness to norms can be applied to the peer group. Specifically, the mechanism that underlies peer influence may derive from the desire of boys and girls to act in accordance with what they perceive to be the norm rather than the norm itself.

Consistent with the view of the peer system as having multiple levels of social complexity, any particular child could perceive multiple norms, including one for his or her friends, another for his or her group, and another for the entire school class. The norms that a child maintains could be calculated based on the actual ratings that a child makes of peers or they could exist more impressionistically that would need to be assessed as a general view rather than as an average of views of specific peers. A basic question for peer research is whether changes attributed to peer influence derive from responsiveness to perceived norms beyond the effects that can be traced to the actual characteristics of a child's peers at the group or dyadic level.

In a current study, we are trying to distinguish between dyadic and group effects. One part of our project consists of an assessment of children's perceptions of how much they and their peers tolerate aggression and how much they and their peers value academic success. Each of 415 11- to 13-year-old boys and girls evaluated two sets of items. One set of items referred to tolerance of aggression and the other referred to the amount of importance ascribed to doing well in school. Within each set, one item referred to the child ("I think it is ok to cause trouble or be aggressive"), one to the child's friends ("Most of my friends think it is ok to cause trouble or be aggressive"), and one to the peer group in general ("Doing well in school is important for most of the students in my grade"). The participants in the study rated each item on a 5-point scale according to how much they agreed with it.

Our preliminary analyses of these ratings have examined two questions. One analysis concerned the similarity between the children's views of aggression and school performance and their views of how their friends and other peers see aggression and school success. We also wanted to assess how much of a difference there was between ratings regarding the self and ratings of the friend and the broader peer group. In each case we assessed whether the patterns of our findings was the same for friended and friendless children. In regard to the first question, an initial set of correlational analyses showed that children's perceptions of their views of aggression were more strongly associated with their perceptions of how their friends viewed aggression ($r = .55$) than with their perceptions of how other peers viewed aggression ($r = .35$). (The difference between these correlations was significant.) When these analyses were repeated using the measures of school performance, similar but less powerful findings were observed. Children's perceptions of their views of the importance of doing well in school were more strongly associated with their perceptions of how their friends viewed school success ($r = .37$) than with their perceptions of how other peers viewed school success ($r = .26$). (Again, the difference between these correlations was significant.)

These findings indicate that children see themselves as being more similar to their friends than to peers in general in how they view two important domains of functioning. Children who saw themselves as being tolerant of aggression also saw their friends and, to a smaller extent, other peers as being tolerant. Similarly, children who ascribed importance to academic performance believed that their friends and other peers did so also. Again however, children see themselves as being more similar to their friends than to other children.

When we considered whether these patterns of findings were the same for friended and friendless children, we found different results for the aggression and the school success items. With the school success items the differences in the correlations were the same for friended and friendless children. With the aggression items, however, the correlation between the "child" score and the friend score was stronger for friended children ($r = .62$) than for friendless children ($r = .48$). No differences as a function of friendship status were seen in the correlations between the measure of how the children saw themselves and the measure of their perception of the group views. This difference suggests that children who are friended are more likely than friendless children to have a stronger identification with the peers they regard as their friends and, as a result, may be more likely to use them as a guide for what is normative.

A second set of analyses looked at differences between the mean values of these measures. Again a different pattern of results was observed with the aggression and the school success items. Children saw themselves as being lower in tolerance of aggression ($M = 1.66$, $SD = .86$) than their friends ($M = 2.02$, $SD = 1.06$) or the other children in their grade ($M = 2.50$, $SD = 1.08$). The difference between the child score and the friend score was significantly smaller than the difference between the child score and the peer score. This pattern of findings was more pronounced for the friended children than the friendless children. Specifically the difference between the child score and the friend score was smaller for friended children than friendless children. This pattern of findings is important as it suggests that friended and friendless children may have different referent points for the normativeness of aggression. Compared with friended children, friendless children claim that the peers whom they see as their friends have a higher tolerance of aggression. This perception among friendless children that their peers have a higher tolerance of aggression may put friendless children at risk for being more aggressive themselves.

With the school achievement items, the children's ratings indicated that they saw themselves as more concerned with school achievement ($M = 4.47$, $SD = .72$) than either their friends or the group in general ($M = 3.79$, $SD = .98$ for friends and $M = 3.79$, $SD = 1.00$ for the group).

In these ratings, friended and friendless children did not differ from each other.

In summary, it is likely that the effects of peer influence can be traced to associations with particular types of peers at either the dyadic or group level, or to specific aspects of interactions between peers. Insofar as the peer system consists of a set of interrelated experiences, efforts to account for the effects at one level need to account for effects at other levels as well. Different theories or ideas about the effects of peers have differentially emphasized either the dyad or the group. It may be that children themselves may differ from each other in their orientation toward either particular peers or to the group in general. Data from a recent study in our lab shows that children maintain different beliefs about friends and peers in general and that these differences are not the same for friended and friendless children. These differences may put friendless children at greater risk for some forms of peer influence.

CULTURE AND PEERS: REASONS TO EXPECT VARIATIONS BETWEEN CONTEXTS

In this final brief section we address the concept of culture. Many of the constructs that we have discussed in the previous sections are likely to vary across cultures and within cultures as a function of socioeconomic status (SES). As a function of culture descriptive constructs such as collectivism and individualism, children are likely to feel different pressures to conform or to be part of the social group. Central to the concept of collectivism is the idea that the group matters. It is possible that the effects of peer influence would be stronger for persons who are sensitive to the collectivistic orientation that may exist in their society. Persons who believe that their culture is characterized by individualism may be more likely to be immune to the effects of their peers.

Societies and cultures differ also in their norms. There are, for example, variations across groups and classrooms in levels of aggression, withdrawal, and helpfulness (see Rubin et al., 2006). Insofar as (1) children may be sensitive to and responsive to norms, and (2) that these norms may vary across contexts, then one would expect variations in peer influence across contexts as children comply with the norms or perceived norms of these contexts. Contexts may differ also in the self-esteem of the children in the context. It is known in particular that on average low SES children tend to have lower self-esteem that is seen among children from wealthier families (Harter, 1998). In this way, peer effects might be expected to be stronger for low SES children because they tend to have lower self-esteem.

Summary

Peer influence is likely to derive from processes and effects from different levels of social complexity. Although it has been studied primarily with aggression and, to a smaller extent, with depression, it is likely to affect several forms of outcomes. There is reason to expect that the effects of peer influence will be moderated by some personal characteristics, including a sense of disequilibrium between one's actual and desired peer experiences, one's perception of the norms of one's peers, and self-esteem. Cultural effects can be expected also. So far the literature on peer influence has shown the power of peer influence. Perhaps it is time for us to assess when and why peer influence is most likely to happen.

ACKNOWLEDGMENTS

Work on this chapter was supported by a grant from the Social Sciences and Humanities Research Council of Canada. We are grateful to Lina Maria Lopez for her assistance.

REFERENCES

Adams, R. E., Bukowski, W. M., & Bagwell, C. (2005). Stability of aggression during early adolescence as moderated by reciprocated friendship status and friend's aggression. *International Journal of Behavioral Development, 29*(2), 139–145.

Baumeister, R., & Leary, M. (1995). The need to belong: The desire for interpersonal attachments as a fundamental human motivation. *Psychological Bulletin, 117,* 497–529.

Boivin, M., Dodge, K. A., & Coie, J. D. (1995). Individual/group behavioral similarity and peer status in experimental play groups of boys: The social misfit revisited. *Journal of Personality and Social Psychology, 69*(2), 269–279.

Bukowski, W. M., Adams, R. E., & Santo, J. B. (2006). Recent advances for developmental psychopathology in the study of social and personal experiences. *International Journal of Behavioral Development, 30,* 26–30.

Bukowski, W. M., Brendgen, M., & Vitaro, F. (2007). Peers and socialization: Effects on externalizing and internalizing problems. In J. Grusec & P. D. Hastings (Eds.), *Handbook of socialization: Theory and research* (pp. 355–381). New York: Guilford Press.

Bukowski, W. M., & Hoza, B. (2007). *Self esteem moderates the effects of peer contagion in early adolescence.* Unpublished manuscript, Concordia University, Montreal.

Bukowski, W. M., Pizzamiglio, M. T., Newcomb, A. F., & Hoza, B. (1996). Popularity as an affordance for friendship: The link between group and dyadic experience. *Social Development, 5*(2), 189–202.

Chang, L. (2004). The role of classroom norms in contextualizing the relations of children's social behaviors to peer acceptance. *Developmental Psychology, 40*(5), 691–702.

Dishion, T. J., & Dodge, K. (2005). Peer contagion in interventions for children and adolescents: Moving towards an understanding of the ecology and dynamics of change. *Journal of Abnormal Child Psychology, 33*(3), 395–400.

Dishion, T. J., Dodge, K. A., & Lansford, J. E. (2006). Findings and recommendations: A blueprint to minimize deviant peer influence in youth interventions and programs. In T. J. Dishion, K. A. Dodge, & J. E. Lansford (Eds.), *Deviant peer influences in programs for youth: Problems and solutions* (pp. 366–394). New York: Guilford Press.

Espelage, D., Holt, M., & Henkel, R. (2003). Examination of peer-group contextual effects on aggression during early adolescence. *Child Development, 74,* 205–220.

Harter, S. (1982). The Perceived Competence Scale for Children. *Child Development, 53*(1), 87–97.

Harter, S. (1998). The effects of child abuse on the self-system. *Journal of Aggression, Maltreatment and Trauma, 2*(1), 147–169.

Leary, M. R. (1999). The social and psychological importance of self-esteem. In R. M. Kowalski & M. R. Leary (Eds.), *The social psychology of emotional and behavioral problems: Interfaces of social and clinical psychology* (pp. 197–221). Washington, DC: American Psychological Association.

Leary, M. R., & Baumeister, R. F. (2000). The nature and function of self-esteem: Sociometer theory. In M. P. Zanna (Ed.), *Advances in experimental social psychology* (Vol. 32, pp. 1–62). New York: Academic Press.

Leary, M. R., & Downs, D. L. (1995). Interpersonal functions of the self-esteem motive: The self-esteem system as a sociometer. In M. H. Kernis (Ed.), *Efficacy, agency, and self-esteem: Plenum Series in Social/Clinical Psychology* (pp. 123–144). New York: Plenum Press.

Leary, M. R., Tambor, E. S., Terdal, S. K., & Downs, D. L. (1995). Self-esteem as an interpersonal monitor: The sociometer hypothesis. *Journal of Personality and Social Psychology, 68,* 518–530.

Miller, D. T., & Prentice, D. A. (1994). Collective errors and errors about the collective. *Personality and Social Psychology Bulletin, 20*(5), 541–550.

Parker, J. G., Rubin, K. H., Erath, S. A., Wojslawowicz, J., & Buskirk, A. A. (2006). Peer relationships, child development, and adjustment: A developmental psychopathology perspective. In D. Cicchetti & D. Cohen (Eds.), *Developmental psychopathology, Vol 1: Theory and method* (2nd ed., pp. 419–493). Hoboken, NJ: Wiley.

Rhodes , N., & Woods, W. (1992). Self esteem and intelligence affect influenceability: The mediating role of message reception. *Psychological Bulletin, 111,* 156–171.

Rose, A. J. (2002). Co-rumination in the friendships of girls and boys. *Child Development, 73*(6), 1830–1843.

Rubin, K. H., Bukowski, W., & Parker, J. G. (1998). Peer interactions, relationships and groups. In W. Damon & N. Eisenberg (Eds.), *Handbook of child psychology* (5th ed., Vol. 3, pp. 619–700). New York: Wiley.

Rubin, K. H., Bukowski, W., & Parker, J. G. (2006). Peer interactions, relationships, and groups. In W. Damon, R. M. Lerner, & N. Eisenberg (Eds.), *Handbook of child psychology.* (6th ed., Vol. 3, pp. 571–645). New York: Wiley.

Ruble, D., Higgins, E. T., & Hartup, W. W. (1983). What's social about social cognitive development? In E. Higgins, D. Ruble, & W. W. Hartup (Eds.), *Social cognition and social development* (pp. 3–12). New York: Cambridge University Press.

Stevens, E. A., & Prinstein, M. J. (2005). Peer contagion of depressogenic attributional styles among adolescents: A longitudinal study. *Journal of Abnormal Child Psychology, 33*(1), 25–37.

CHAPTER 7

Adolescent Peer Influences

Beyond the Dark Side

Joseph P. Allen *and* Jill Antonishak

Evidence of negative peer influence in adolescence abounds. Smoking and substance use begin primarily in peer contexts (Oxford, Harachi, Catalano, & Abbott, 2001; Simons-Morton, 2002). Teenage boys are observed to drive faster in the presence of other teenage boys (Simons-Morton, Lerner, & Singer, 2005). Delinquent youths tend to cluster together and then enhance one another's levels of delinquency (Patterson, DeBaryshe, & Ramsey, 1989; Poulin, Dishion, & Haas, 1999). Even well-intentioned efforts to intervene to prevent adolescent problem behaviors often founder in the backwash created by negative peer influences (Dishion, McCord, & Poulin, 1999; Dishion, Poulin, & Burraston, 2001).

Although some peer influence effects may be smaller than they at first appear (because some of the observed similarities among deviant teens actually reflect their selection of similar peers as friends) (Kandel, 1978), the evidence of sizeable negative real influences remains. Some have even gone so far as to suggest that peer influences supersede virtually all parental socializing efforts (Harris, 1998). Although this extreme conclusion has been rightly contested (Collins, Maccoby, Steinberg, Hetherington, & Bornstein, 2000), it serves as just one indication of the extent of our concern over negative peer influences in adolescence.

In adolescence, peer influence clearly has a bad name. In this chapter, we would like to propose an alternative perspective. Although peer influences can often be negative and the effects of peer pressure can range from disturbing to dangerous, peer influence processes also have a far more positive side that is often overlooked. Even though peers can strongly influence adolescents, these influences need not always be negative. Quite the contrary, being influenced to behave in a way that one's peers find most acceptable and attractive is actually very close to being precisely the definition of what it means to be a well-socialized individual. In adulthood, being strongly influenced by one's peers is virtually isomorphic with the concept of socialization. If millions of people learn from friends that they can use the Internet to shop for some consumer goods, that a safety recall has been issued on a certain product, or that a new movie is hilariously funny, peer influence processes appear likely to be at work.

Being influenced by others to behave in a manner that they find broadly acceptable is generally not a concern within our society. The problem in adolescence is not that these socializing influences exist, but that they are increasingly from adolescent peers whose values at times run counter to those of parents and other adults. Even within adolescence, however, peers clearly can have positive socializing influences—teaching one another about everything from handling the give and take of group discussions to providing information about positive after school activities. And even regarding deviant behaviors, there is no logically a priori reason why influences should be negative. The existence of strong peer influence processes should make it as likely that a deviant youth would be influenced by a less deviant peer to reduce their deviance as that they would influence the less deviant peer to increase their deviant behavior. By adulthood, we expect and want individuals to be influenced by their peers so as to learn everything from workplace norms to appropriate social behavior in relationships. Thus, as we worry about peer influence, we need to recognize the extent to which it is not only inevitable, but also the extent to which it is closely tied to something much more positive, which is peer socialization.

We thus see it as relatively easy to make a theoretical case that adolescent peer influences are normal, inevitable, and at times even positive aspects of adolescent socialization. But to what extent does this view mesh with what we actually observe about adolescent behavior? Our goal in this chapter is to use data from several of our recent studies to weave together a story that illustrates the ways in which a more positive view of adolescent peer influences can help us understand a range of adolescents' behaviors with their peers. We seek to use these data to illustrate three overarching points: First, peer influence processes are not always pathological but rather may be either adaptive or maladaptive in nature. Second, peer influence processes are continuously reinforced via normal adolescent social interaction processes in a way that ingrains them into the very fiber of adolescent peer relationships. And third, though it may be virtually impossible and probably undesirable to stop peer influence processes in adolescence, strengthening adolescents' positive connections to peers and adults may help us steer these influences in more positive directions.

WHO GETS SOCIALIZED BY PEERS?

If the line between being influenced by one's peers and being well socialized by them is as evanescent as we are suggesting, then perhaps teens who are highly influenced by their peers won't necessarily always be the marginal, insecure adolescents depicted in popular media. On the contrary, we might expect that popular, well-socialized teens would be among the most likely to be influenced by their peers precisely because they are well socialized. To be popular, for example, typically means being well adapted to the norms of one's peer group. From this vantage point, popular adolescents should be open to socializing influences of peers—regardless of whether these socializing influences are in positive or in negative directions as viewed from the perspective of adult values. Popular adolescents thus pose an important test of our perspective suggesting that influence processes are closely associated with normal and frequently healthy socialization processes.

We have examined this perspective with a longitudinal data set that was specifically designed to assess peer functioning and peer influence over the course of adolescence. The Virginia Study of Adolescent Development began in 1998 by assessing a group of 184 male and female seventh and eighth graders in a public middle school in the urban ring of a small city in the eastern United States. The sample was demographically diverse and consisted of 69% European American adolescents and 31% African American adolescents. The sample was also diverse in terms of socioeconomic status, with a median family income of $38,000/year and a significant range around this median. This sample was drawn from a somewhat unique school system in which seventh- and eighth-grade students had been intact within their grade level since the fifth grade and would remain intact through the end of high school. Although physical transitions (i.e., to new buildings) occurred at the start of seventh and ninth grades, the peers within a given grade remained highly stable. In short, young people knew each other relatively well and peer dynamics had had time to unfold and become established well prior to our first assessment.

Our approach recognized that in assessing emotion-charged topics with high social-desirability quotients—such as peer interactions—it is quite difficult to get unbiased data solely via self-reports (Nisbett & Wilson, 1977). Thus, we also obtain data from adolescents' parents, their best friends, and others in their peer group, and we obtain these data repeatedly, with data collection occurring on an annual basis for most types of data.

For the present question, we wanted to identify a subsample of adolescents who would readily be recognized as well adapted and well socialized. For this purpose, popular adolescents appeared as an ideal subgroup. The term *popular* can actually refer to either of two slightly different constructs. Adolescents can be labeled as "perceived popular" if their peers judge them to have high status within the peer group, or they can be labeled "popular" simply because many other teens enjoy spending time with them (LaFontana & Cillessen, 2002). Although the former group of high-status adolescents has many positive traits and is respected within the peer group, these status adolescents are also often more dominant and antisocial in their behavior, and ironically, they are also often not particularly well liked on an individual basis (Gest, Graham-Bermann, & Hartup, 2001; LaFontana & Cillessen, 2002; Parkhurst & Hopmeyer, 1998; Prinstein, in press; Rodkin, Farmer, Pearl, & Van Acker, 2000). We chose to use the second definition of "popularity," which refers to young people who are named by others as being people with whom they would like to spend time. In childhood and adolescence, this approach to popularity appears to tap a quite well socialized group with characteristics ranging from greater social skills to lower levels of depression (Henrich, Blatt, Kuperminc, Zohar, & Leadbeater, 2001; Pakaslahti, Karjalainen, & Keltikangus-Jaervinen, 2002; Parkhurst & Hopmeyer, 1998).

Our own data confirmed that these popular, well-liked adolescents are indeed well adjusted by almost any standard (Allen, Porter, McFarland, Marsh, & McElhaney, 2005). Compared to their less popular peers for example, well-liked teens in our sample displayed higher levels of psychosocial maturity and attachment security. In comparison to less popular teens, our popular adolescents were also rated as more competent in close relationships by their best friends. And, lest we think that this success with peers reflected some type of precocious break from parents, we observed these teens interacting with their mothers and found that they displayed higher levels of warmth, engagement, and satisfaction in these interactions. In brief, when assessed in terms of concurrent functioning, popular adolescents look incredibly well socialized in terms of just about any measure we are able to examine.

The "catch" comes when we examine the behavior of popular teens as development unfolds. If we examine early use of alcohol and marijuana, for example, we find that if we stick with our concurrent assessments, we would see little to challenge our view of popular teens as faring well. Examining subsamples of adolescents who were above and below the mean in terms of popularity, the two groups differ little in levels of experimentation with alcohol and marijuana. Nine percent of popular adolescents report having used alcohol or marijuana in the prior 6 months, as compared to 7% of less popular teens—a statistically indistinguishable difference. Our initial analyses, however, suggested that a more disturbing pattern of differences begins to emerge in the following year (Allen et al., 2005) with popular adolescents increasing significantly in levels of alcohol and marijuana use. Our most recent subsequent analyses, presented in Figure 7.1, indicate that these differences remain quite substantial over time (Allen, 2006).

Figure 7.1 indicates that in the year following our assessment of adolescents' popularity, the percentage of popular teens that have used alcohol or marijuana in the prior 6 months has nearly tripled. Rather than being indistinguishable from the substance use rates of less popular teens, the popular teens' rates of substance use are now dramatically and significantly larger. Strikingly, this gap does not decline with age, and even though less popular teens also begin using alcohol and marijuana in significant numbers over time, the magnitude of the gap between these two groups continues to expand across adolescence. By age 18, the gap between the popular and less popular groups has reached more than 30 percentage points. Some research even suggests that if these teens are followed into adulthood, we may find that these differences persist well

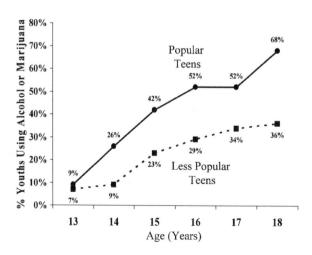

FIGURE 7.1. Percentage of youths who have recently used alcohol/marijuana.

into the early adult transition (Osgood, Ruth, Eccles, Jacobs, & Barber, 2005). Clearly something is going on.

By themselves, these differences are not necessarily evidence of peer influence processes. When we look more closely at just who popular teens have selected as friends, however, the evidence of influence processes appears more clearly. What we find, as depicted in Figure 7.2, is that popular teens are likely to increase most quickly in alcohol and marijuana use if at baseline they have selected friends who place more value upon engaging in such behaviors. The evidence thus suggests that these popular teens are closely attuned to and following the values of their peers. We have presented data regarding alcohol and marijuana use in detail here, though we find similar patterns of activity when we look at other forms of minor deviant behavior, including misdemeanor criminal acts such as vandalism and shoplifting (Allen et al., 2005).

These data thus support one facet of our proposed story: Peer influences do not appear to be reserved solely for disturbed or maladapted teens. Rather, in at least some cases they appear strongest among the teens who are best adjusted and most well socialized.

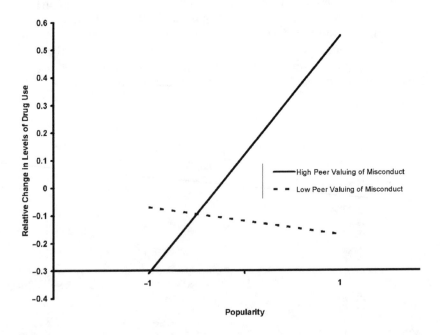

FIGURE 7.2. Interaction of popularity and peer valuing of misconduct in predicting relative changes in drug use from age 13 to age 14. From Allen, Porter, McFarland, Marsh, and McElhaney (2005). Copyright 2005 by Blackwell Publishing. Reprinted by permission.

WHEN PEER SOCIALIZATION IS A GOOD THING

If the other facets of our proposed story also hold—that socialization processes can be not just negative forces but also positive influences on development—we might expect to find evidence of this among our popular teens as well. And we do. What we see is that though popular teens are increasing in alcohol and marijuana use and minor levels of delinquency, they are not increasing in more serious forms of criminal behavior (e.g., felony offenses), which presumably are far less widely valued by peers. Even more important, popular peers are found to decrease over time in their levels of hostile behavior relative to their less popular counterparts (Allen et al., 2005). Notably, these hostile behaviors are clearly and widely devalued within the peer group. Hence, once again popular teens are increasingly behaving in ways consistent with the likely socializing influences of their peers.

So what's going on here? Popularity appears to be associated with increases in adaptive and maladaptive behaviors over time. From an adult-centered point of view, these findings seem puzzling. If we recognize, however, that well-socialized teens are in fact well socialized by their peers then these findings begin to fit nicely together. Popular teens' behavior appears to reflect that they are simply following the values of their peer group. For 13-year-olds, alcohol and marijuana use and even minor forms of delinquency are widely viewed as behaviors that "older" kids and adults pursue and are somewhat valued (Moffitt, 1993). Hostile behavior toward peers, in contrast, is not valued. Our popular teens are increasing in alcohol and marijuana use and decreasing in hostile behavior over time. In essence, they are behaving precisely like the well-socialized individuals that we thought them to be.

We see our popular teens as acting like minipoliticians. They are well regarded and may appear as leaders, but they are also carefully tracking the implicit "polls" of opinion among their peers and placing themselves out in front of the prevailing views. Popular teens need not be directly or even consciously pressured or influenced by their peers. Indeed, giving in to direct peer pressure is not valued by most adolescents (nor by most adult voters). Nevertheless, popular teens find themselves evolving in a way that keeps them in synch with the norms of their peers.

The problems with this socialization process are not that it occurs. Indeed, many positive traits, from turn-taking to improved hygiene are likely linked to peer socialization processes in adolescence. The problem is that the values toward which teens are being socialized are often less than ideal relative to the norms of adult society. To be well socialized is one thing; to be well socialized by a bunch of 13-year-olds is a less unambiguously positive experience, at least from an adult vantage point.

And though the troublesome behaviors described above, such as drinking and shoplifting, appear minor in some contexts, in many ways they are far from minor. Large numbers of teens as well as innocent bystanders are killed each year in alcohol-related accidents (Patel, Greydanus, & Rowlett, 2000). Recent evidence suggests that early use of alcohol may have long-term effects on brain development and may predispose at least some young brains toward a greater lifelong risk of substance abuse problems (American Medical Association, 2006). Homeowners, consumers, retail shopkeepers, and others bear tremendous costs from vandalism and shoplifting (Taylor & Mayhew, 2002). In short, so-called minor adolescent problem behaviors may reflect a passing stage in adolescent development for many, but they nonetheless create huge short- and long-term costs to society and to many of the adolescents involved.

But even if we wanted to stop the peer influence processes linked to these troubling behaviors, is that even possible? We take that up next.

THE HARDWIRING
OF THE PEER INFLUENCE PROCESS

In addition to perhaps subtle processes by which popular teens may absorb peers' values, there are also explicit dominance and submissiveness processes that often take a central role in interactions between adolescents and their peers. We believe that a close look at these processes suggests two conclusions: First, although being influenced by one's peers may be a net positive in some cases, being overtly submissive to peers probably is not. Second, and more important for our purposes, dominance processes may be rewarded in adolescent peer interactions in ways that increase the likelihood that peers will work hard to influence one another over time.

Researchers have been interested in dominant and submissive behaviors within adolescent peer interactions for at least the past several decades (Berndt, 1992; Costanzo & Shaw, 1966; Goethals & Darley, 1977; Steinberg & Silverberg, 1986). Understandably, most of this research has focused upon the myriad of problems created by adolescents' susceptibility to pressure to engage in deviant behaviors. This research has advanced the field significantly but also carries an important limitation. The measures used to assess peer pressure to engage in deviant behavior have typically confounded the assessment of susceptibility to peer influence with the assessment of a teen's willingness to engage in deviant acts (Berndt, 1992). The problem is that susceptibility and deviance proneness may have different correlates in development and may change in different ways over the course of adolescence. Combining the two into the same assessment makes it difficult to tease these effects apart.

Our approach to this problem has been to develop an experimental procedure for assessing susceptibility to being influenced by one's peers that focuses upon domains other than deviant behavior. For this procedure, we bring in a participant and his or her named closest friend. We then separate the two friends and have each teen individually complete a hypothetical decision-making task. For example, in one task, participants were told that surplus lottery money needed to be distributed among members of a group of hypothetical characters with various savory and unsavory characteristics. Participants and their friends initially made decisions regarding this task separately. They were then brought together, told of one another's decisions and given time to try to come to a set of consensus decisions. We began by simply tracking the extent to which our target participants rapidly changed their minds (i.e., with little time for persuasion) to give up their initial position. We labeled the resulting index—the percentage of decisions in which these rapid changes occurred—as "rapid susceptibility to peer influence."

Using the sample described above, what we found first of all were several links of our experimental measure of susceptibility to peer influence with evidence of problematic behavior and negative peer influence in actual peer interactions (Allen, Porter, & McFarland, 2006). Youths who were high in observed susceptibility were higher in levels of drug and alcohol use, were more likely to have engaged in precocious sexual experience, and were reported by their peers to be exposed to more negative peer pressure. Susceptibility also interacted with peer behavior, such that susceptible teens' alcohol and drug use was likely to be highest when the teens had peers who reported higher levels of substance use.

In addition, however, we found that susceptible youths were not doing well on other fronts. For example, they had lower levels of competence in close friendships, as reported by themselves and their closest friend. Furthermore, as we followed them, we found that they were more likely to experience increases in depressive symptoms over the following year. In short, though being socialized by one's peers and adapting to their values can be positive, doing so in the explicit, submissive manner that we observed in our experimental task had nothing but negative correlates.

Perhaps the most interesting aspect of this study, however, lies in the converse presentation of these findings. Our peer influence measure was symmetric, such that youths who were low on our susceptibility measure were those who rarely changed their positions, but rather whose friends' positions rapidly changed. Thus, our findings can all be read as applying in opposite directions to the more dominant youth in our observed interactions. These more dominant youths, who rarely changed their positions but persuaded their friends to do so instead, thus fared quite well—with lower levels of deviance, greater friendship competence, and relative decreases in levels of depressive symptoms over time.

These positive correlates of dominant behavior would at first seem to cast a more positive light on peer influence processes. In important ways, however, this perspective is at least as disturbing as the more negative perspective with which we began. For what this finding suggests is that the process of being dominant over one's peers—of leading a disagreement such that one's peer rapidly accepts one's point of view—actually appears adaptive in some respects in early adolescence (in their association with relative decreases in levels of depressive symptoms, for example). Said in a different way, this finding represents our first evidence that the contexts that may create peer pressure for some adolescents in adolescence are actually adaptive in some ways for other adolescents to promote.

Other evidence supports this view. For example, we have found that when we observe teens' actual behavior in interactions with their peers around disagreements, those who are most forceful in presenting their arguments also tend to be most highly regarded within their broader peer group (McFarland & Little, 2004). Similarly, we find that levels of successful dominance-seeking behavior that we directly observe and code from interactions are linked to an array of markers of adaptive functioning with peers and to higher self-esteem (Antonishak, Allen, & McElhaney, 2007). These findings are consistent with findings linking dominance to social status in other studies (Hawley, 1999; Hawley & Vaughn, 2003). Notably, even within other species of mammals, it is widely observed that successful dominance-seeking behaviors are almost universally rewarded (Hawley, 1999).

In addition to these dominance effects, we also find that those adolescents who simply talk most in discussions among peers are the adolescents who are most likely to behave deviantly themselves and thus hold deviant values (Allen, Porter, & Tencer, 2002). This means that what an adolescent hears when listening to a group of peers talk is not necessarily an unbiased representation of the values of that group. Rather, those within the group who have more deviant values may well talk more, and thus the overall group discussion is likely to have a more deviant slant to it than the views of the average member would support.

We thus have several converging lines of evidence not only that submitting to peer pressure is negative—as has long been believed—but also that creating peer pressure may be socially adaptive. To the extent such behavior is rewarded within the peer group, then efforts to counteract it may be swimming against a very powerful current of reinforcers. Clearly there are different types of peer influence processes—from the submissive behavior that predicts increasing depression over time to popular teens' absorption of peer values in ways that reflect their high degree of skill and sensitivity. Equally clearly, intervening to reduce the power of these processes is likely to be an exceedingly difficult task at best.

ORIGINS OF PEER VALUES

If preventing peer influences is often likely to be futile, then attention might more profitably shift to a focus upon the content of the values that is passed among peers. Once we make this shift, we must immediately confront the question: From where do negative peer influences arise? Any individual parent might point to other adolescents as a source of negative influence on their teen. When we view adolescents collectively, however, we recognize that pointing to peer influences as the source of negative adolescent behavior entails an inherent circularity: It is neither logically sufficient nor particularly useful to state that adolescents as a group sometimes behave badly because as a group they influence one another to do so. Blaming peer influences for negative adolescent values and behaviors may ultimately make about as much sense as blaming TV transmission towers for disturbing images that appear on TV. With regards to peer influence, Marshal McLuhan's dictum is emphatically not correct: The medium is not the message. Peer influences transmit values, they don't create them.

So, if "peer influences" is ultimately a circular answer to the question of where adolescents get their somewhat deviant values, what is a more appropriate answer? One way we have sought to examine this issue is by presenting our findings to focus groups of successful late adolescents. A clear message comes back in response: Adolescent peer culture places significant value upon teens acting in ways that demonstrate that they are becoming independent from their parents' control. The best-adjusted adolescents may find the least harmful ways of demonstrating such behaviors but demonstrate them they will. Knocking over mailboxes with a baseball bat while driving along a country road, drinking alcohol, and sneaking into movies without paying are all ways of demonstrating one's independence from parents' rules. In some ways these behaviors thus appear normative and some might say inevitable. Normative, however, does not mean healthy. The common cold is normative, as is greater susceptibility to broken bones in old age. Neither condition is healthy or desirable. More important, what is normative may nevertheless still be preventable. Deaths from simple infections were normative prior to the development of penicillin.

These focus group results are consistent with Terri Moffitt's theories regarding adolescence-limited delinquency (Moffitt, 1993). Moffitt (1993) noted the rapid rise in deviant behavior that occurs at the onset of adolescence. One explanation for this rise, she posited, is that adolescents' are seeking ways of appearing more mature. Ironically, alcohol and drug use and minor forms of criminal behavior all can serve this purpose for early adolescents. Even more ironic, these behaviors are often adopted by those who are arguably our best-adjusted adolescents. If the desire to appear more mature, even via pseudo-mature behaviors, drives part of early adolescents' valuing of deviant behavior, then the next question that arises is why adolescents' don't favor more adaptive means of appearing mature? Two factors seem highly relevant to consider: adolescents' lack of access to adult values and their lack of access to adult-like ways of engaging with the larger society.

It may be true that nothing grows in a vacuum, but observing the development of adolescents' social values in postmodern society certainly pushes this principle to its limits. To a remarkable extent, adolescents live in a vacuum vis-à-vis the norms of the larger adult world. Adults avoid adolescents, and adolescents in turn often reciprocate. We see adults crossing to the other side of shopping malls to avoid "gangs" of teens approaching. Teens are not generally welcome in serious adult workplaces. Save for major holidays, adults are more likely to plan parties with complete strangers than with their own teens. Most teens feel and act similarly in return. And teenagers have only limited contact with adults in school, and then primarily in ratios of many teenagers to few adults. The same is true of athletic teams after school. Teens do have more direct, one-on-one contact with their parents, but even this contact often is sharply limited in adolescence, and any communication regarding values must first cut through the static of the extended autonomy negotiations that characterize this period.

In all of this, what is clear is that there is very little direct, intensive, extrafamilial contact between teens and the adults of our society. Given this lack of contact, how precisely would we expect adolescents and their peers to be absorbing the values of the larger society? Magically through the air? In actuality, of course, much value transmission does occur through the air, not via magic or wishful thinking, but rather through the airwaves that transmit signals from TV, radio, cell phones, and wireless connections to the Internet. And the values that are transmitted via these airwaves are often a distorted caricature reflecting the worst of American culture—and certainly a far cry from the values most parents would seek to inculcate within their homes.

The social vacuum in which large groups of adolescents live and interact is not just one of values, but also of meaningful activity. Social psychologists have long recognized that our values are often as likely to follow from our actions as to precede them (Bem, 1972). What is striking about adolescence as it currently plays out in our society is the near total absence of opportunities to engage in actions that truly contribute to others in society or even to have an impact within it. From this perspective, large numbers of adolescents are placed together with their peers in a vacuum not only lacking contact with adult values but also lacking opportunities to meaningfully engage in the larger society.

One way to get a feel for the impact of this vacuum is to imagine as an adult engaging in one's current job but being told that everything about the job was hypothetical. A teacher would be teaching only to a video-camera that recorded the teacher's actions. Doctors would treat only actors with hypothetical illnesses. Mechanics would work only on mock-ups of real cars. Every 3 months or so, these workers would get feedback on their performance in the form of five letters printed on a piece of paper indicating how well they had done. And they would be told that this process would continue for 5 to 15 years, that they should learn as much as possible from it (though much would not be relevant to their ultimate work), and at the end of it the work they would then be allowed to do would be somewhat influenced by these letter grades. It is not difficult to speculate that under these conditions, many adults would be far less motivated and have far less positive values toward their work—or perhaps even toward the society which created this scenario for them. In some ways, the real situation that adolescents confront is even worse, as they must face a very similar enforced sequestration from meaningful work at the same time that they are reaching their absolute peak in terms of levels of physical energy and intellectual processing speed. It is not accidental that in other periods of history, 15- to 20-year-olds could take on tremendously central roles in society, often commanding large armies and running governments (Barzun, 2000). Today, the only armies teens can command are on the screens of their video games and the passion they bring to these games is in all likelihood just an echo of the passion once brought to truly meaningful activities.

Any organism, even well down the evolutionary chain, that is systematically deprived of the opportunity to use a large number of its capacities is likely to face significant motivational difficulties and increased likelihood of aimless and destructive behavior. It probably helps only minimally to tell adolescents that their boredom is a result of an extended preparation period necessary to master the increasingly complex and technological nature of work in our society. Even successful groups of 14-year-olds with high educational aspirations are likely facing a decade or more of extended preparation before being able to actually do something to have an impact in the larger world. Under these circumstances, the sense of having a direct and immediate impact that derives from knocking over someone's mailbox is at least a bit easier to comprehend. Discovering other peers who are experiencing the same inactivity and feeling the same sense of frustration and powerlessness may feel like a breath of fresh air to teens under these circumstances, however tired and stale the resulting behaviors are to adults.

Together, all of these factors create a powerful convergence of forces—a perfect storm that seems more than able to account for the rapid rise in problematic behavior seen in groups of early adolescents. Together, these factors also help explain why efforts to intervene to prevent or treat behavior problems in adolescence are so challenging. And these results are consistent with findings that programs that bring at-risk adolescents together often lead to iatrogenic effects as a result of negative peer influences (Dishion et al., 1999, 2001; Poulin et al., 1999). Within these programs, even adolescents who become more prosocially motivated may find themselves isolated and influenced by teens still experiencing a profound sense of alienation from societal institutions and norms.

IF WE CAN'T FIGHT IT . . .

If there is a way out of this process, it appears likely to occur not at the level of stopping the transmission of information and values among adolescents, but rather in changing the content of the values transmitted within adolescent peer groups. Some of the most promising work in this regard comes from efforts to engage adolescents in the actual tasks of the larger adult society. We have, of course, known for a long time that adolescents who were positively engaged within their families were at lower risk for deviant behaviors (Baumrind, 1988; Henggeler, 1991; Patterson et al., 1989; Steinberg, 1987). More recently, we have begun to examine promising extra-familial approaches to intervention that work along these lines.

One such program with which we have been involved—the Teen Outreach Program—engages young people in voluntary community service and links this service to intensive, small group discussions with an adult facilitator who helps ease the transition into adult-like roles and helps adolescents integrate what they learn in these roles (Allen, Kuperminc, Philliber, & Herre, 1994). This service learning approach has shown remarkable potential in evaluations to date. For example, interested youths who were randomly selected to participate in this program displayed 50% reductions in school failure, school suspensions, and teen pregnancy rates over the course of the following year relative to a no-treatment control group (Allen, Philliber, Herrling, & Kuperminc, 1997). Notably, pregnancy and school failure reductions took place even though there was extremely minimal focus within the program upon either sexual behavior or education.

Youths in the program reported that it gave them a strong positive feeling from being able to help others, as well as a sense of what life might be like beyond high school. The sense of being able to actively engage in help-giving tasks (known as the helper-therapy principle) (Riessman, 1965), and the vision of a potential future role in adult life appear in sharp contrast to the relative isolation from the world of meaningful adult activity in which most groups of adolescents live their daily lives. These results have been replicated with other similar programs and with this specific program under a variety of other conditions (Allen et al., 1994; Allen & Philliber, 2001; Moore & Allen, 1996) and thus form the beginnings of a way to address the problem of negative adolescent peer values that are broadly communicated in our society.

The Teen Outreach Program frequently brings together at-risk young people and thus faces the same potential iatrogenic effects from grouping adolescents as do other prevention programs (Dishion et al., 1999, 2001). Yet, when we examine how the program differs in effectiveness depending upon the degree of psychosocial risk experienced by those within it, we find it has its greatest impact (assessed in terms of pre- and postchange) when serving groups of youths who began the program at greatest demographic risk (Allen & Philliber, 2001). *Risk* in this case was defined in terms of prior histories of academic suspensions, prior pregnancies, and growing up in a family with low levels of parental education. These program data suggest that placing even at-risk youths together in a behavioral and social context in which they can productively engage with the adult world can supersede negative peer influences within adolescent culture and produce significant reductions in problematic behavior. For decades, parents have tried to find ways to occupy adolescents to reduce their opportunities to "get into trouble" outside of school. Although the research on the advantages of limiting adolescent free time is mixed (Steinberg, Fegley, & Dornbusch, 1993), the instinct to not simply occupy adolescents but engage them in the tasks of the larger society appears quite promising indeed.

Even enhancing adolescents' sense of engagement and connection within their own peer groups appears to potentially have positive value. In some of our most recent analyses, we have begun to examine the ways in which strong connections to peers might serve, not as a risk factor, but as a buffer against some forms of risky adolescent behavior. For example, we find that when tracked across a multiyear period, there is a consistent lagged prediction from close friendship quality to lower levels of aggressive behavior in interactions with peers (Antonishak, Allen, & McFarland, 2006). This lagged relationship exists in both directions. Teens who are connecting well with close friends become less aggressive over the following year. Teens who become less aggressive in turn connect more effectively with their close friends over the subsequent year and so on. We have observed this process consistently over a 5-year period thus far, suggesting the opportunity for a significant buildup of the effects of strong connections to close friends as a buffer against antisocial behavior. Conversely, of course, one can view these relationships from the opposite perspective. Youths who are alienated from close friends become more aggressive over time, which in turn predicts greater alienation and so on. The bottom line with this finding for our purposes is clear: Rather than seeing strong connections to peers as an out-of-control force to be feared and opposed, we perhaps should be thinking about ways to appropriately harness and direct this force in positive ways.

PEER INFLUENCES IN CONTEXT

These final two more positive examples highlight the need for a more contextualized view of peer influence processes. Specific peer influence processes (e.g., dominance and submissiveness within dyads and groups) are likely to interact with the broader context of social values within the peer group. Findings regarding the Teen Outreach Program and the positive effects of engagement with close peers are instances in which teens are likely to be exposed to peer values that are relatively prosocial in nature. It seems unquestionable, for example, that within the Teen Outreach Program, peers continue to influence one another via the dominance and modeling processes described above. Two factors potentially operate to moderate these influences, however, and increase their likelihood of playing out in adaptive fashion. First, the overall context of the program potentially alters the values existing within the peer group in a more prosocial direction. Peers may continue to strongly transmit values in these programs, but what's going out over the peer airwaves is now of a somewhat different quality.

Perhaps equally important, this program is exposing young people to meaningful roles in the adult world. The peer world may have its greatest power (indeed too much power) in contexts in which a teenager views it as his or her only meaningful social outlet. Programs that help teens escape from the hothouse of a social milieu comprising solely peer influences removed from meaningful adult contact may provide adolescents with opportunities and motivation to open themselves up to other, more adaptive, socializing influences. Conversely, in a more typical adolescent setting, in which direct adult contact and adult influences are distant or absent, we may find that the magnitude of adolescent peer influences will be at their zenith (where else can the teen turn for validation?) and that the valence of these influences is more likely to be deviant in relation to (relatively distant) adult norms. In these cases, the more frightening picture of the role of peers in adolescent development that we painted at the beginning of this chapter—with strong, multifaceted peer influences toward behaviors that are not in keeping with adult norms—may indeed be likely to emerge in dramatic and disturbing fashion.

CONCLUDING THOUGHTS

We have tried in this chapter to make an overarching case that we must move beyond a focus upon the existence of strong peer influences as a fundamental cause of adolescent problem behaviors. We began by suggesting that peer influences did not solely occur in groups of maladjusted, vulnerable adolescents and were not always negative in nature. Even highly popular youths were capable, and indeed likely, to absorb values from their peers—positive and negative. We have also sought to argue that these peer influences are, for all practical purposes, unstoppable. To be well influenced by one's peers is quite close to the definition of being well socialized. We presented evidence that the process of values transmission among peer groups was normative and reinforced within the peer group. We recognized that the values that were transmitted could be either adaptive or maladaptive from the perspective of the larger society. Finally, we offered some speculations about the reasons why groups of adolescents might develop values that diverge from those of adult society. We noted the isolation of adolescents in the postmodern era from the values and the actual work of the larger adult society. And we presented evidence to suggest that programs that seek to engage youths in this work have remarkable effects in reducing many seemingly unrelated problem behaviors at once.

As we see it, this evidence does not lead to the conclusion that the existence of strong peer influences is a fundamental problem in adolescence. If adolescents were primarily helping pass along positive adult values to other adolescents (much as they pass along a sense that hostile behavior is unacceptable), then we might even argue that peer influences were not strong enough. Conversely, if what adults have passed on to adolescents in terms of values consists more of static than actual signal, then disabling the adolescent messengers who retransmit these garbled messages is unlikely to have much benefit. Peer influences may be unstoppable in adolescence, and we may not even want to stop them. But we will want to pay great attention to ways of enhancing adult inputs into the values that circulate among adolescents and their peers.

ACKNOWEDGMENTS

This chapter was supported by grants from the National Institute of Mental Health (R01-MH44934, R01-MH58066, and F31-MH65711-01).

REFERENCES

Allen, J. P. (2006, May). *Teens, peers, and driving: The perfect storm?* Paper presented at the National Research Council of the National Academy of Science, Board on Children, Youth, and Families, Committee on the Contributions from the Behavioral Sciences in Reducing and Preventing Teen Motor Crashes, Washington, DC.

Allen, J. P., Kuperminc, G., Philliber, S., & Herre, K. (1994). Programmatic prevention of adolescent problem behaviors: The role of autonomy, relatedness, and volunteer service in the Teen Outreach Program. *American Journal of Community Psychology, 22,* 617–638.

Allen, J. P., & Philliber, S. P. (2001). Who benefits most from a broadly targeted prevention program? Differential efficacy across populations in the Teen Outreach Program. *Journal of Community Psychology, 29,* 637–655.

Allen, J. P., Philliber, S., Herrling, S., & Kuperminc, G. P. (1997). Preventing teen pregnancy and academic failure: Experimental evaluation of a developmentally based approach. *Child Development, 68,* 729–742.

Allen, J. P., Porter, M. R., & McFarland, C. F. (2006). Leaders and followers in adolescent close friendships: Susceptibility to peer influence as a predictor of peer pressure, risky behavior, and depression. *Development and Psychopathology, 18,* 155–172.

Allen, J. P., Porter, M. R., McFarland, C. F., Marsh, P. A., & McElhaney, K. B. (2005). The two faces of adolescents' success with peers: Adolescent popularity, social adaptation, and deviant behavior. *Child Development, 76,* 747–760.

Allen, J. P., Porter, M. R., & Tencer, H. (2002,). *New mechanisms of negative peer influence: The role of the dominant deviant.* Paper presented at the Biennial Meetings of the Society for Research on Adolescence, New Orleans, LA.

American Medical Association. (2006). *Harmful consequences of alcohol use on the brains of children, adolescents, and college students.* Washington, DC: Author.

Antonishak, J., Allen, J. P., & McElhaney, K. B. (2007, April). The role of social competencies in peer group selection and peer contagion. In W. J. Burk (Chair), *Under the influence?: Explaining behavioral homogeneity in adolescent peer groups.* Symposium presented at the Biennial Meetings of the Society for Research in Child Development, Boston.

Antonishak, J., Allen, J. P., & McFarland, F. C. (2006, March). *Social competencies and peer relationships: Longitudinal associations with peer group and adolescent aggression.* Paper presented at the Biennial Meetings of the Society for Research on Adolescence, San Francisco.

Barzun, J. (2000). *From dawn to decadence: 500 years of western cultural life 1500 to the present*. London: HarperCollins.

Baumrind, D. (1991). Effective parenting during the early adolescent transition. In P. A. Cowan & E. M. Hetherington (Eds.), *Family transitions* (pp. 111–164). Hillsdale, NJ: Erlbaum.

Bem, D. J. (1972). Self-perception theory. *Advances in Experimental Social Psychology, 6*, 1–62.

Berndt, T. J. (1992). Friendship and friends' influence in adolescence. *Current Directions in Psychological Science, 1*, 156–159.

Collins, W. A., Maccoby, E. E., Steinberg, L., Hetherington, E. M., & Bornstein, M. H. (2000). Contemporary research on parenting: The case for nature and nurture. *American Psychologist, 55*, 218–232.

Costanzo, P. R., & Shaw, M. E. (1966). Conformity as a function of age level. *Child Development, 37*, 967–975.

Dishion, T. J., McCord, J., & Poulin, F. (1999). When interventions harm: Peer groups and problem behavior. *American Psychologist, 54*, 755–764.

Dishion, T. J., Poulin, F., & Burraston, B. (2001). Peer group dynamics associated with iatrogenic effects in group interventions with high-risk young adolescents. In D. W. Nangle & C. A. Erdley (Eds.), *The role of friendship in psychological adjustment* (New Directions for Child and Adolescent Development, No. 91) (pp. 79–92). San Francisco: Jossey-Bass.

Gest, S. D., Graham-Bermann, S. A., & Hartup, W. W. (2001). Peer experience: Common and unique features of number of friendships, social network centrality, and sociometric status. *Social Development, 10*, 23–40.

Goethals, G. R., & Darley, J. M. (1977). Social comparison theory: An attributional approach. In J. M. Suls & R. L. Miller (Eds.), *Social comparison processes: Theoretical and empirical perspectives* (pp. 259–278). Washington, DC: Hemisphere/Halstead.

Harris, J. R. (1998). *The nurture assumption: Why children turn out the way they do*. New York: Free Press.

Hawley, P. H. (1999). The ontogenesis of social dominance: A strategy-based evolutionary perspective. *Developmental Review, 19*, 97–132.

Hawley, P. H., & Vaughn, B. E. (2003). Aggression and adaptive functioning: The bright side to bad behavior. *Merrill–Palmer Quarterly, 49*, 239–243.

Henggeler, S. W. (1991). *Multidimensional causal models of delinquent behavior and their implications for treatment*. Hillsdale, NJ: Erlbaum.

Henrich, C. C., Blatt, S. J., Kuperminc, G. P., Zohar, A., & Leadbeater, B. J. (2001). Levels of interpersonal concerns and social functioning in early adolescent boys and girls. *Journal of Personality Assessment, 76*, 48–67.

Kandel, D. B. (1978). Homophily, selection and socialization in adolescent friendships. *American Journal of Sociology, 84*, 427–436.

LaFontana, K. M., & Cillessen, A. H. (2002). Children's perceptions of popular and unpopular peers: A multimethod assessment. *Developmental Psychology, 38*, 635–647.

McFarland, F. C., & Little, K. C. (2004, March). *Links between adolescent popularity and promotion of autonomy and relatedness with parents and peers*. Paper presented at the Biennial Meetings of the Society for Research on Adolescence, Baltimore.

Moffitt, T. E. (1993). Adolescence-limited and life-course-persistent antisocial behavior: A developmental taxonomy. *Psychological Review, 100*, 674–701.

Moore, C. W., & Allen, J. P. (1996). The effects of volunteering on the young volunteer. *Journal of Primary Prevention, 17,* 231–258.

Nisbett, R. E., & Wilson, T. D. (1977). Telling more than we can know: Verbal reports of mental processes. *Psychological Review, 84,* 231–259.

Osgood, D. W., Ruth, G., Eccles, J. S., Jacobs, J. E., & Barber, B. L. (2005). Six paths to adulthood: Fast starters, parents without careers, educated partners, educated singles, working singles, and slow starters. In R. A. Settersten, Jr., F. F. Furstenberg, Jr., & R. G. Rumbaut (Eds.), *On the frontier of adulthood: Theory, research, and public policy* (pp. 320–355). Chicago: University of Chicago Press.

Oxford, M. L., Harachi, T. W., Catalano, R. F., & Abbott, R. D. (2001). Preadolescent predictors of substance initiation: A test of both the direct and mediated effect of family social control factors on deviant peer associations and substance initiation. *American Journal of Drug and Alcohol Abuse, 27,* 599–616.

Pakaslahti, L., Karjalainen, A., & Keltikangas-Jaervinen, L. (2002). Relationships between adolescent prosocial problem-solving strategies, prosocial behaviour, and social acceptance. *International Journal of Behavioral Development, 26,* 137–144.

Parkhurst, J. T., & Hopmeyer, A. (1998). Sociometric popularity and peer-perceived popularity: Two distinct dimensions of peer status. *Journal of Early Adolescence, 18,* 125–144.

Patel, D. R., Greydanus, D. E., & Rowlett, J. D. (2000). Romance with the automobile in the 20th century: Implications for adolescents in a new millennium. *Adolescent Medicine, 11,* 127–139.

Patterson, G. R., DeBaryshe, B. D., & Ramsey, E. (1989). A developmental perspective on antisocial behavior. *American Psychologist, 44,* 329–335.

Poulin, F., Dishion, T. J., & Haas, E. (1999). The peer influence paradox: Friendship quality and deviancy training within male adolescent friendships. *Merrill–Palmer Quarterly, 45,* 42–61.

Prinstein, M. J. (in press). Assessment of adolescents' preference- and reputation-based popularity using sociometric experts. *Social Development.*

Riessman, F. (1965). The helper-therapy principle. *Social Work, 10,* 27–32.

Rodkin, P. C., Farmer, T. W., Pearl, R., & Van Acker, R. (2000). Heterogeneity of popular boys: Antisocial and prosocial configurations. *Developmental Psychology, 36,* 14–24.

Simons-Morton, B. G. (2002). Prospective analysis of peer and parent influences on smoking initiation among early adolescents. *Prevention Science, 3,* 275–283.

Simons-Morton, B., Lerner, N., & Singer, J. (2005). The observed effects of teenage passengers on the risky driving behavior of teenage drivers. *Accident Analysis and Prevention, 37,* 973–982.

Steinberg, L. (1987). Familial factors in delinquency: A developmental perspective. *Journal of Adolescent Research, 2,* 255–226.

Steinberg, L., Fegley, S., & Dornbusch, S. M. (1993). Negative impact of part-time work on adolescent adjustment: Evidence from a longitudinal study. *Developmental Psychology, 29,* 171–180.

Steinberg, L., & Silverberg, S. B. (1986). The vicissitudes of autonomy in early adolescence. *Child Development, 57,* 841–851.

Taylor, N., & Mayhew, P. (2002). *Financial and psychological costs of crime for small retail businesses.* Griffith: Australian Institute of Criminology.

CHAPTER 8

Mobilizing and Weakening Peer Influence as Mechanisms for Changing Behavior

Implications for Alcohol Intervention Programs

Deborah A. Prentice

The dominant approach to reducing alcohol consumption on college campuses involves giving students accurate statistics on what their peers think, feel, and do in drinking situations. This so-called social norms approach to alcohol intervention grew out of two consistent empirical findings. First, perceptions of peers' alcohol use is strongly correlated with own alcohol use (Perkins, Haines, & Rice, 2005; Perkins & Wechsler, 1996). This finding has been taken as evidence that students are affected by what they think their peers are doing, even though very little of the evidence supports a causal inference. Second, students misperceive their peers, assuming more drinking, more heavy drinking, and more comfort with heavy drinking than is actually the case (Borsari & Carey, 2003; Perkins et al., 2005). This finding has been viewed as a golden opportunity: If, in fact, heavy drinking by college students is driven by an overestimation of this behavior among peers, then providing students with true, accurate information about their peers' behavior should reduce alcohol use.

Inspired by the promise and apparent simplicity of this approach, colleges and universities have adopted it with abandon. For example, in a survey of 118 four-year colleges and universities across the United

States, Wechsler and colleagues (2003) found that 57 of them (48%) had implemented a social norms campaign. However, as studies evaluating these campaigns accumulate, it is clear that their success in reducing drinking among college students is mixed at best (Lewis & Neighbors, 2006; Wechsler et al., 2003). One source of variability in the success of these campaigns is their uneven implementation, but another is an incomplete understanding of what social norms are and how they influence drinking behavior.

In this chapter, I examine how, when, and why social norms influence alcohol use among college students and consider the implications of this analysis for alcohol intervention programs. My argument, in a nutshell, is that social norms offer numerous routes to changing drinking behavior, routes that differ in whether they mobilize peer influence processes or weaken peer influence processes. Moreover, these two routes differ in the populations and contexts for which they are best suited, the details of their implementation, and the consequences, positive and negative, of their success. I begin by describing the properties of social norms that determine how and how much they influence behavior.

SOCIAL NORMS

Social norms are properties of groups; they characterize where a group is located along an attitudinal or behavioral dimension (Miller & Prentice, 1996). Researchers have found it useful to distinguish between two types of norms: descriptive norms, which characterize what group members are like, and injuctive norms, which characterize what group members are supposed to be like to fit in (Cialdini, Kallgren, & Reno, 1991). Descriptive norms for college students might include studying during the week, partying on the weekends, going to home football games, wearing jeans, participating in many extracurricular activities, and holding moderate political views. Some of these might also be injuctive norms (e.g., partying on the weekends, going to home football games), whereas others might not (e.g., studying during the week, wearing jeans). In addition, there might be injuctive norms that prescribe behaviors that the majority of students cannot quite attain (e.g., being highly socially skilled). Thus, descriptive and injuctive norms are typically overlapping, but not isomorphic.

Two properties of a social norm determine its influence on group members' behavior. One is its central tendency—that is, where, on the dimension in question, the group is located. For example, college students tend, in general, to dress casually, party often, and spend a lot of time on e-mail. Of course, not every college student manifests these qualities, but the average student, the typical student, and most students do. This property of the norm determines what attitudes and behaviors the group promotes in its members, the direction of its influence.

A second important property of the norm is its dispersal—that is, how uniform the group is on the dimension in question. For example, suppose on one campus, students average 20 hours of study time a week, with a range from 15 to 25 hours. On another campus, students also average 20 hours of study time a week, but here the range is 0–40 hours. The central tendency of the norm, and therefore the direction of its influence, is the same on these two campuses; however, the strength of that influence is likely to be very different. On the first campus, studying behavior is highly uniform; everybody does pretty much the same thing. On the second campus, the range is so great that almost anything goes. As a consequence, the studying norm is likely to have much stronger influence on the first campus than on the second.

PERCEPTION VERSUS REALITY

Thus far, I have considered norms as objective properties of groups that can be assessed through scientific measurement and calculation. However, people rarely measure and calculate the norms of their social groups. Instead, they construct these norms in their heads, as they perceive and communicate with their fellow group members. Elsewhere, I have considered this construction process in considerable detail (Miller & Prentice, 1996). Here, I simply note that the process can lead to systematic discrepancies between the actual norms of the group and the norms that group members perceive. These discrepancies are important, for it is the perceived norms, not the actual norms, that influence group members' behavior.

Consider, for example, the norms for alcohol use on college campuses. Researchers have documented several systematic discrepancies between the aggregate of how students represent themselves (the actual campus norms) and the representations they have of their campus as a whole (the perceived campus norms). These discrepancies take the following forms.

First, students overestimate how much their peers drink. For example, in a study of 76,000 students at 130 colleges and universities, Perkins and colleagues (2005) found that 71% of students overestimated the amount their peers drank, whereas just 15% of students underestimated the amount. Discrepancies of this magnitude have been obtained in countless other studies (e.g., Baer, Stacy, & Larimer, 1991; Haines &

Spear, 1996; Steffian, 1999). These findings reveal that students err systematically in where they locate the descriptive drinking norm. Interestingly, studies have revealed a similar overestimation for other kinds of drug use (Perkins, Meilman, Leichliter, Cashin, & Presley, 1999) and for other health-risk behaviors (Gibbons, Helweg-Larsen, & Gerrard, 1995). The majority of studies of norm misperception have focused on this error in locating the descriptive drinking norm.

Second, students overestimate how comfortable their peers feel with heavy drinking. For example, Prentice and Miller (1993) asked students to indicate their own comfort with alcohol use on campus and the comfort of the average student. Male and female students rated the average student as more comfortable than they were (see also Schroeder & Prentice, 1998). This discrepancy, too, has been replicated in numerous other studies (e.g., Bourgeois & Bowen, 2001; Perkins & Berkowitz, 1986; Suls & Green, 2003). Thus, students err not just in where they locate the descriptive drinking norm but also in where they locate the injunctive drinking norm. In fact, in a recent meta-analysis, Borsari and Carey (2003) found that the latter error was larger in magnitude than the former. This discrepancy, too, has been found for other health-risk behaviors, and also for comfort with media portrayals of health-risk behaviors (see Hines, Saris, & Throckmorton-Belzer, 2002; Lambert, Kahn, & Apple, 2003).

Finally, students underestimate the variability in how comfortable their peers feel with heavy drinking. That is, students range more widely in their attitudes toward alcohol use than they themselves recognize. An illustration of this error comes from Prentice and Miller (1993, Study 1). They asked students to estimate not just the comfort of the average student but also the range within which the comfort levels of 50% of students fall. Students' underestimated this range by a full point on the 11-point rating scale, indicating that they perceived more uniformity of student opinion than was actually the case. Note that the error students make in estimating the dispersion of the injunctive norm is independent of the error they make in estimating its location. Whether they make a similar error in estimating the dispersion of the descriptive norm has not, to my knowledge, been examined.

SOURCES OF NORM MISPERCEPTION

Faced with this catalogue of errors, one obvious question is how students could be so wrong. After all, people are usually quite good at estimating the attitudes and behaviors of their peers (Morrison & Miller, 2006; Nisbett & Kunda, 1985). The most common answer to this question traces misperception of the drinking norms to a psychological state known as "pluralistic ignorance."

Pluralistic ignorance is a psychological state characterized by the belief that one is feeling differently from others even though one is acting similarly (Miller & McFarland, 1991; Prentice & Miller, 1996). It typically arises in situations in which people act in ways that belie their private feelings, perhaps out of fear of embarrassment, fear of social censure, or just plain uncertainty (Miller & McFarland, 1991). Under these circumstances, a curious divergence between self- and other-perception emerges. People intepret their own behavior in terms of their internal states but take others' similar behavior at face value. That is, they assume that others are acting on their own private desires and convictions.

Numerous studies have documented pluralistic ignorance in the context of alcohol use on campus (Prentice & Miller, 1993; Schroeder & Prentice, 1998; Suls & Green, 2003). These studies have shown that students overestimate their peers' comfort, conform to those overestimates, and feel alienated when they perceive their alcohol-related attitudes to vary from those of their peers (Prentice & Miller, 1993). Male students, in particular, feel embarrassed by their concern about drinking and believe they would experience negative social consequences if they expressed it (Suls & Green, 2003). In addition, interventions that dispell pluralistic ignorance reduce drinking, particularly among students who are socially anxious (Schroeder & Prentice, 1998). All of these findings support the claim that students experience pluralistic ignorance in the context of alcohol use on campus and that this state has the effect of increasing their alcohol consumption.

At the same time, pluralistic ignorance can account for only some of the misperceptions students have of the drinking norms. The prototypical situation in which pluralistic ignorance arises is one in which everybody at a party is drinking and appears to be having a good time but is privately harboring misgivings. Here, uniformity of behavior across self and other yields to divergent interpretations of that behavior. This situation produces overestimations of peers' comfort and of the uniformity of that comfort, but it does not produce overestimations of peers' drinking. In fact, pluralistic ignorance only occurs in situations in which everybody was drinking and recognized that everybody was drinking. Thus, pluralistic ignorance can explain misperceptions of the location of and consensus around the injunctive norm. It cannot explain misperceptions of the descriptive norm.

What does explain misperceptions of the descriptive norm? Researchers have documented a number of psychological and social processes that lead certain behaviors to be overrepresented in the norm. For example, the presence of behaviors is more noticeable than their absence (e.g., drinking as compared with not drinking); some behaviors are more noticeable than others (e.g., heavy drinking as compared with light drinking); and some behaviors are more likely to be discussed than others (Miller & Prentice, 1996). Indeed, it is much easier to tell a good story about a night of heavy drinking than about a night of moderation (Berger & Heath, 2005). For all of these reasons, examples of excessive drinking are likely to be perceptually salient, memorable, and therefore prominent in students' thoughts about their peers' alcohol use. More generally, the important point here is that pluralistic ignorance is not the only process that produces misperceptions of drinking norms. These misperceptions are overdetermined phenomena, with multiple processes giving rise to them.

In summary, I have distinguished between different types of drinking norms (descriptive versus injunctive), different misperceptions of these norms (of their location versus dispersion), and different psychological and social processes that underlie these misperceptions. The view of alcohol use among college students that emerges from this analysis is complex, but necessarily so. The various norms, misperceptions, and processes I have documented are all relevant to an understanding of why students often drink to excess, as well as to the crafting of intervention strategies designed to change students' drinking behavior. I now turn attention to these intervention strategies.

STRATEGIES FOR CHANGING DRINKING BEHAVIOR

Alcohol intervention programs are nothing new on college campuses, and neither is the recognition of peer influences on drinking. Traditionally, most intervention programs dealt with peer influence by fortifying individuals to withstand it. Students were taught the deleterious consequences of excessive alcohol consumption, how to monitor their own alcohol intake, and how to say no. These programs foundered by failing to recognize that students typically do not want to resist peer pressure. They want to be accepted by their peers and to fit in with their peer group (Baumeister & Leary, 1995). Indeed, peer influence is best conceived not as a weakness to overcome, but instead as a basic feature of human psychology (Turner, 1991).

Now, with the discovery that students misperceive drinking norms, alcohol intervention programs have a new focus. Rather than fortifying individuals to withstand peer influence, recent programs have sought to alter the norms to which they conform. Peer influence processes can then proceed unfettered and result in a healthier level of alcohol consumption. There are two variants on this general strategy, which map onto the two types of errors students make in perceiving drinking norms.

Mobilizing Peer Influence

The first strategy is to mobilize peer influence by giving students information about what their peers actually think, feel, and do. This information has the potential to reduce alcohol use to the extent that students overestimate their peers' level of drinking and/or comfort with heavy drinking. By providing them with accurate information about their peers, this strategy alters the direction of peer influence toward a more moderate, less permissive norm. It thereby co-opts the peer influence process to promote healthier behavior.

One of the great advantages to this strategy is that it can be implemented, via media campaigns, at low cost and on a large scale. Thus, it is not surprising that dozens of campuses have experimented with this approach, producing posters, leaflets, table tents, greeting cards, and advertisements designed to convey accurate information about students' drinking. The vast majority of these so-called social norms marketing campaigns have focused on correcting misperceptions of the descriptive norm on campus—that is, communicating that most students drink in moderation. By publicizing, for example, that "64% of . . . students have 0–5 drinks at a time" (Granfield, 2002) or that "70% of . . . students have never let drinking get in the way of academics" (Mattern & Neighbors, 2004), these campaigns signal that moderation is the norm and excessive drinking is deviant. An excellent and very creative example of a poster from a social norms marketing campaign is shown in Figure 8.1.

This approach to alcohol intervention has had some notable successes at reducing excessive drinking behavior (see, e.g., Glider, Midyett, Mills-Novoa, Johannessen, & Collins, 2001; Haines & Spear, 1996; Mattern & Neighbors, 2004). However, it has also had at least as many outright failures. In some cases, norms campaigns have yielded reductions in drinking for certain groups of students (e.g., women, novices; see Granfield, 2002; Werch et al., 2000). However, more typically, these campaigns have changed students' perceptions of the amount their peers drink without changing their own drinking behavior (e.g., Clapp, Lange, Russell, Shillington, & Voas, 2003; Gomberg, Schneider, & DeJong, 2001; Granfield, 2005; Thombs & Hamilton, 2002). This latter result has also emerged in studies in which norm-correcting information was administered in a group setting (e.g., Peeler, Far, Miller, & Brigham, 2000; B. H. Smith, 2004; Stamper, Smith, Gant, & Bogle, 2004; Steffian, 1999).

Why have so many of these social norms marketing campaigns failed to reduce drinking? One culprit is their message. Social norms campaigns

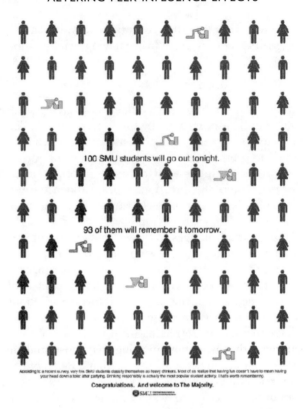

FIGURE 8.1. Poster from a social norms marketing campaign designed to correct misperceptions of the location of the descriptive drinking norm. Reprinted with permission of Southern Methodist University.

rely on statistical information to convince students' that their perceptions of alcohol use on campus are erroneous. Those statistics may be true, according a campus survey, but usually they are not true to students' experiences. Faced with a discrepancy between their own experiences and a message on a poster, which do students believe? Evidence suggests that their experiences often dominate the message (Polonec, Major, & Atwood, 2006; Russell, Clapp, & DeJong, 2005; S. W. Smith, Atkin, Martell, Allen, & Hembroff, 2006; Thombs, Dotterer, Olds, Sharp, & Raub, 2004).

A second weakness of social norms campaigns is their broad-based, scattershot approach. Imagine a college health administrator, concerned about alcohol use on her campus and eager to implement a social norms intervention. She makes up table tents, such as that in Figure 8.1, that give accurate statistical information, distributes them in dining halls across campus, and waits. What is she hoping will happen? She is hoping that heavy drinking students will see the table tent. She is hoping that they will take in its message. She is hoping that they will think about its relevance to their own behavior ("I guess I was in the 10% of students who consumed more than five drinks last Saturday night"). The problem is there is no guarantee that any of these things will happen. Heavy drinking students may not see the table tent, may not read it, and may not compare their own behavior to the campus standards it invokes. As easy as social norms marketing campaigns are to implement, they are also easy for students to ignore.

An alternative approach that deals with this set of issues is the personalized normative feedback (PNF) intervention. The theory behind this approach is identical to that of the social norms marketing campaigns: Give students accurate information about the prevalence of heavy drinking on campus so that they will bring their behavior into line with more moderate campus norms. However, it recognizes, in addition, that normative information must be connected to the self if it is to lead to changes in personal standards and behaviors (Agostinelli & Grube, 2005). Thus, unlike norms marketing campaigns, PNF interventions provide students with personalized information on their own levels of alcohol consumption and where they stand relative to the norm. In addition, these interventions typically target heavy drinkers—the population of most concern and the one most likely to be affected by accurate information about drinking norms. This approach is still in its early days, but the initial evaluations of it are quite promising (Neighbors, Larimer, & Lewis, 2004; Neighbors, Lewis, Bergstrom, & Larimer, 2006; although see Collins, Carey, & Sliwinski, 2002, and Neal & Carey, 2004, for more qualified results).

Thus far, I have attributed the mixed success of social norms marketing campaigns to their implementation; now, let me turn to the limitations inherent in the approach. I describe three such limitations.

First, social norms marketing campaigns are least effective where they are most common (and perhaps most needed). Wechsler and colleagues (2003), in their nationwide survey of norms marketing campaigns, found that these campaigns were most likely to be implemented at large, heterogeneous, public universities with sizable commuter populations. This finding is not surprising, in that these are the schools with high levels of alcohol consumption and, often, serious budget constraints. However, by design, norms marketing campaigns are, in fact, best suited to reduce alcohol use on small, homogeneous, and residential campuses, campuses that function as a single community. These are the campuses on which the "typical student" is a meaningful entity, and pressures to conform to the typical student are strongest.

Second, students' tendency to misperceive drinking norms is inversely related to the power of those norms to influence their behavior.

As I have documented, misperceptions of the drinking of the "typical student" are widespread and robust; however, misperceptions of "one's friends" are usually much closer to self-ratings (see Borsari & Carey, 2003, for a review). This finding, too, is not surprising, in that students are likely to have a great deal of firsthand information about their friends' drinking and are also likely to assume that their friends drink more or less as they do. However, given that students are much more likely to be influenced by perceptions of their friends than by perceptions of the typical student (Campo et al., 2003), the fact that people do not misperceive their friends calls into question the effectiveness of a norm-correcting approach. In other words, the norms students misperceive are not the ones that influence their behavior, and the norms that influence their behavior are not the ones they misperceive. This disjunction between misperception and influence may help to explain why norms campaigns so often influence perceptions but not behavior. It may also help to explain why these campaigns prove to be ineffective for athletes (Thombs & Hamilton, 2002), fraternity members (Carter & Kahnweiler, 2000), and other groups whose local norms promote heavy drinking.

Finally, there is a paradox embedded in the logic of these programs. The main message they seek to communicate to students is that most of their peers drink in moderation, that the norms for alcohol use on campus are healthy. One obvious implication of this message is that widespread problem drinking is illusory, and thus there no need for concern. However, the very existence of the message signals concern. Moreover, we know from other data that students themselves feel concern. Information about the moderate drinking habits of the typical student is unlikely to address this perfectly legitimate feeling. And, to the extent that is does address their feelings, it may leave them unconcerned about the risks of heavy drinking rather than committed to a course of moderation (see Buunk, van den Eijnden, & Siero, 2002, for a discussion of a similar dynamic regarding condom use). In short, the messages conveyed by norms marketing campaigns may not be as simple and straightforward as their architects intend.

One way to deal with this problem is to shift the focus of norm correction from the descriptive norm to the injunctive norm, from "most students don't drink heavily" to "most students don't approve of heavy drinking." This focus creates a much more coherent message, and one that is less vulnerable to disconfirmation from simple behavioral observation. Indeed, because they target private thoughts and feelings, injunctive norms campaigns are likely to be more believable than descriptive norms campaigns. Moreover, to the extent that students themselves harbor disapproval, they may resonate to the idea that others do too. The potential downside of this approach is its judgmental tone, which runs contrary to campus norms of tolerance and freedom from restraint. However, on campuses that have experienced a lot of negative events tied to excessive drinking, this judgmental tone may capture well the community's sentiment and thus may be quite effective. Unfortunately, this is all speculation, as injunctive norms campaigns have not yet come under systematic investigation. However, a number of campuses have implemented such campaigns; a clever poster from one of these is shown in Figure 8.2.

In summary, mobilizing peer influence around a more moderate, and accurate, drinking norm can be an effective intervention strategy. It works best for heavy drinkers (Borsari & Carey, 2000), on small, residential campuses (Wechsler et al., 2003), and when accompanied by personalized feedback (Lewis & Neighbors, 2006). It also works best when the message about the true norms falls within students' latitude of accep-

FIGURE 8.2. Poster from a social norms marketing campaign designed to correct misperceptions of the location of the injunctive drinking norm. Reprinted with permission of Southern Methodist University.

tance (S. W. Smith et al., 2006), and when it encompasses a group with which students identify (e.g., fraternity members, teammates, friends). Obviously, these are mighty qualifiers that seriously restrict the viability of this approach, but it is important to remember that all approaches are limited. Correcting the location of the drinking norm is a useful tool, in combination with others and under the right circumstances (DeJong, 2002). Let me consider now a second strategy for intervening in the peer influence process.

Weakening Peer Influence

As I noted earlier, social norms have two important properties: their location and their dispersion. Location determines the direction of peer influence, and dispersion determines its strength. Both of these properties of drinking norms are misperceived and thus offer possibilities for intervention. Having explored the former, I now turn to the latter.

Correcting misperceptions of the dispersion of the norm involves drawing people's attention to the variability in their peers' thoughts, feelings, and behaviors. This serves to weaken the influence of the norm by dispelling the perception that there is a right way to think, feel, or behave. In the case of alcohol use on campus, heightening students' awareness of the variability of their peers' attitudes and behaviors should dispel the perception that everybody is drinking to excess. It should free students up to act on their own attitudes and dispositions, which, given what we know about those attitudes and dispositions, should promote a more moderate level of alcohol consumption. This effect should be most apparent for students who are most influenced by their peers, in particular, social drinkers and students high in social anxiety.

The effectiveness of this intervention strategy is difficult to evaluate, as few programs have explicitly sought to change students' perceptions of the dispersion of the norm. Nonetheless, it is quite likely that many norms marketing campaigns have influenced perceptions of the norm's dispersion, as well as its location. Consider, for example, the message that "64% of . . . students have 0–5 drinks at a time" (Granfield, 2002). Is this a message about the location of the norm or the dispersion of the norm? In fact, it contains information about both. Interventions involving small-group discussion may also have produced effects on the perceived variability of student opinion and behavior, although without appropriate measures, one cannot know for sure.

The most direct evidence for the effectiveness of weakening peer influence as an intervention strategy comes from Schroeder and Prentice (1998). Their intervention focused on dispelling pluralistic ignorance in a small-group setting. Students were presented with evidence that they themselves overestimated their peers' comfort with heavy drinking and then discussed, as a group, the phenomenon of pluralistic ignorance and what might give rise to it in drinking situations. The message of the intervention was just because everybody is doing it does not mean they all feel good about it. The result was a 40% drop in drinking behavior, relative to a control intervention, at a follow-up assessment 4 to 6 months after the discussions.

Additional findings suggested that this reduction in drinking was a result of a weakening of peer influence, not a relocation of the norm. First, there was no evidence for a change in perceptions of the average student's comfort with drinking as a consequence of the pluralistic ignorance intervention (in fact, perceptions of average-student comfort dropped in all conditions), nor any evidence that a change in the perceived location of the norm-mediated drinking behavior. Second, the intervention was most effective at reducing heavy drinking among students high in social anxiety, suggesting a reduction in perceived peer pressure. Third, the intervention left nondrinking students feeling more comfortable on campus, again suggesting a reduction in perceived peer pressure (see Prentice & Miller, 1996). All of these finding point to a weakening of peer influence as a consequence of the pluralistic ignorance discussions.

With so few studies available that explore the utility of weakening peer influence as an intervention strategy, it may be premature to speak of its prospects and limitations. Nevertheless, let me make three observations about the potential limitations of this approach. First, like all norms-based approaches, its effectiveness for reducing alcohol consumption depends on the extent to which it targets the norms that are driving drinking behavior. Thus, interventions that target the typical student or the average student will only work on campuses where this entity has some meaning and importance for students—that is, small, homogeneous, residential campuses. Interventions that target more proximal groups are likely to have more impact, but fewer misperceptions available to dispell. An exception to this generalization is the misperceptions associated with pluralistic ignorance, which occurs in groups of all sizes. Indeed, pluralistic ignorance regarding alcohol use is likely to be strongest in face-to-face groups that engage in heavy drinking. This suggests that dispelling pluralistic ignorance may be an effective intervention strategy for sports teams, fraternities, and other traditionally challenging populations.

Second, as liberating as it might be, the strategy of weakening peer influence deprives students of something they very much want and need: a way to fit in with their peer group. Group norms are double-edged swords: They thwart individuality but at the same time provide identity and belongingness (Prentice, 2006). If students cannot connect themselves to the group and establish themselves as good group members by drinking alcohol, they may very well find another way to do it. Or, they may seek out like-minded peers, who share their perceptions and habits, with whom they can establish more well-grounded norms. The point is that intervention efforts may be able to weaken peer influence in a particular domain, but they will not be able to eliminate it across domains. Nor should they try. Instead, they should include activities that provide students with alternative (healthier) ways of establishing their connection with the group. This inclusion is likely to be especially important in interventions with pre-college-age populations, whose sense of self is less well developed and whose need for peer approval is especially strong.

Third, the success of a norm-weakening approach to alcohol intervention rests entirely on the question of what will guide students' behavior once peer pressure is reduced. The assumption we have made is that students will fall back on thoughts and feelings that encourage moderation. This assumption may be more valid for some populations and on some campuses than others. At highly selective, private universities, where a night of heavy drinking is merely a temporary respite from the relentless drive to achieve and succeed, it may be a perfectly reasonable assumption. In other contexts and with other populations, it may not. However, even if weakening the norm is not sufficient to produce desirable behavior, it may be a necessary component of an effective intervention. Combined with strategies that teach students how to drink responsibly, it may be effective for a wide range of populations.

Summary

In summary, I have outlined four broad types of norms-based alcohol interventions that vary in whether they target the descriptive or the injunctive norm and whether they seek to correct misperceptions about the norm's location or its dispersion. The vast majority of intervention programs have taken just one of these four forms: They have sought to correct misperceptions of the location of the descriptive norm and thereby to mobilize peer influence around a more moderate norm. At the same time, many of these programs have implicitly or explicitly included information in their messages about the dispersion of the norm. The results have been mixed, with some successes, but many failures (Wechsler et al., 2003). The foregoing analysis suggests the following three conclusions about the design of norms-based interventions going forward.

First, correcting the location of the norm and the dispersion of the norm are viable intervention strategies, though they operate through very different psychological mechanisms. In fact, it may be ill advised to combine these two strategies, for the mechanisms by which they change behavior may interfere with each other. As an illustration of this point, consider once again the message, "64% of . . . students have 0 to 5 drinks at a time." This message includes information about the location of the norm (the average level of alcohol consumption on any drinking occasion is somewhere between zero and five), and also its dispersion (64% of students have fewer than five drinks and 36% have more than five drinks at a sitting). The first piece of information seeks to set a moderate norm, and the second undermines it by highlighting the variability in students' behavior. Campaigns that use messages like this often show effects on perceptions but not behavior, and it is easy to see why. Students can remember the percentage of students who drink zero to five drinks at a time without perceiving any clear implications of this information for their own drinking behavior.

Second, injunctive norms may offer better alcohol intervention possibilities than do descriptive norms. In fact, one of the biggest problems with interventions that target descriptive norms is that students do not believe their message about the level and prevalence of alcohol consumption. Their own observations and experiences belie claims of widespread moderation. Interventions that target injunctive norms are much less likely to run into this problem, in that students' attitudes—their approval of and comfort with heavy drinking—are much less easy to observe. Students cannot know for sure how their peers feel, and their own discomfort lends credence to claims about widespread misgivings. Moreover, norm misperception is considerably greater for injunctive than for descriptive norms (Borsari & Carey, 2003). For all of these reasons, injunctive norms present a very attractive intervention target.

Third, weakening peer influence may be a more reliable intervention strategy than redirecting it (though it may have unintended consequences). Students often misperceive the location of the drinking norm, but they almost always misperceive its uniformity. And even when behavior is uniform (e.g., in heavy-drinking subpopulations), attitudes almost never are. Thus, the most consistently vulnerable flank of a drinking norm is the perception that everybody privately supports it. That vulnerability can easily be exploited in intervention programs that reveal the variability in students' private views. Of course, as I have noted, the ultimate effects of such programs depend on what guides behavior once peer influence is weakened.

As for remaining questions, the most important and pressing one, in my view, is how norms-based interventions influence behavior in real time. That is, what do students do differently by virtue of having participated in one of these interventions? Do they drink a little less at every party? Attend fewer parties? Choose their activities differently? Choose their friends differently? Broadly speaking, do these interventions lead students to see situations differently and therefore respond to them differently (what I will call the perceptual view)? Or do the interventions lead students to choose different types of situations (the behavioral view)? One of the most striking findings of the Schroeder and Prentice (1998) intervention study was that most of the students did not remember participating in the alcohol discussion groups by the time of the follow-up assessment. This finding seems to argue against the perceptual view, for if students were perceiving situations differently by virtue of the intervention, one would expect them to remember why. More likely, the alcohol discussions, which occurred during students' first week on campus, initiated a pattern of behavior that became self-sustaining, even after its source was forgotten. Empirical research on this point is sorely needed.

CONCLUDING REMARKS

Despite the uneven success of norms-based alcohol intervention programs to date, the foregoing analysis provides ample reason for optimism. In particular, it suggests that there are many different ways to intervene in the peer influence processes that drive so much excessive drinking behavior, and that these interventions can have strong and lasting effects. However, it also highlights the importance of attention to details, including many details that have been overlooked in previous intervention efforts. Decisions about who participates, which norms and misperceptions are targeted, how messages are constructed, what medium is used, and what additional features are included in the intervention all must be tailored to the particulars of the campus and its drinking situation. Peer influence may be a ubiquitous feature of drinking among college students, but each case of peer influence is different. The first step in any successful intervention is to identify whether and how peer influence processes are operating to produce excessive drinking and what opportunities exist to redirect or weaken them. In this chapter, I have suggested a set of distinctions and considerations that are important to this task.

The relevance of this analysis extends well beyond the domain of alcohol use by college students. In fact, norm misperception and peer influence characterize alcohol and drug use by preadolescents and high school students as well (e.g., Hansen & Graham, 1991; Martino-McAllister & Wessel, 2005; Ott & Doyle, 2005), though how these processes operate in younger populations is not well understood. Younger cohorts differ systematically from college students in their life circumstances and developmental stages. Peer relations have different dynamics and alcohol use a different social meaning in these cohorts. Thus, the peer influence processes that facilitate drinking among adolescents and younger children are likely to be importantly different from those that facilitate drinking among college students. An understanding of exactly how these processes work will be critical for the development of successful intervention strategies to curb drinking in these younger age groups.

REFERENCES

Agostinelli, G., & Grube, J. (2005). Effects of presenting heavy drinking norms on adolescents' prevalence estimates, evaluative judgments, and perceived standards. *Prevention Science, 6*(2), 89–99.

Baer, J. S., Stacy, A., & Larimer, M. (1991). Biases in the perceptions of the consequences of alcohol use among college students. *Journal of Studies on Alcohol, 52,* 580–586.

Baumeister, R. F., & Leary, M. R. (1995). The need to belong: Desire for interpersonal attachments as a fundamental human motivation. *Psychological Bulletin, 117*(3), 497–529.

Berger, J. A., & Heath, C. (2005). Idea habitats: How the prevalence of environmental cues influences the success of ideas. *Cognitive Science, 29*(2), 195–221.

Borsari, B., & Carey, K. B. (2000). Effects of a brief motivational intervention with college student drinkers. *Journal of Consulting and Clinical Psychology, 68*(4), 728–733.

Borsari, B., & Carey, K. B. (2003). Descriptive and injunctive norms in college drinking: A meta-analytic integration. *Journal of Studies on Alcohol, 64*(3), 331–341.

Bourgeois, M. J., & Bowen, A. (2001). Self-organization of alcohol-related attitudes and beliefs in a campus housing complex: An initial investigation. *Health Psychology, 20*(6), 434–437.

Buunk, B. P., van den Eijnden, R. J., & Siero, F. W. (2002). The double-edged sword of providing information about the prevalence of safer sex. *Journal of Applied Social Psychology, 32*(4), 684–699.

Campo, S., Brossard, D., Frazer, M. S., Marchell, T., Lewis, D., & Talbot, J. (2003). Are social norms campaigns really magic bullets? Assessing the effects of students' misperceptions on drinking behavior. *Health Communication, 15*(4), 481–497.

Carter, C. A., & Kahnweiler, W. M. (2000). The efficacy of the social norms approach to substance abuse prevention applied to fraternity men. *Journal of American College Health, 49*(2), 66–71.

Cialdini, R. B., Kallgren, C. A., & Reno, R. R. (1991). A focus theory of normative conduct: A theoretical refinement and reevaluation of the role of norms in human behavior. In M. P. Zanna (Ed.), *Advances in experimental social psychology* (Vol. 24, pp. 201–234). Orlando, FL: Academic Press.

Clapp, J. D., Lange, J. E., Russell, C., Shillington, A., & Voas, R. B. (2003). A failed norms social marketing campaign. *Journal of Studies on Alcohol, 64*(3), 409–414.

Collins, S. E., Carey, K. B., & Sliwinski, M. J. (2002). Mailed personalized normative feedback as a brief intervention for at-risk college drinkers. *Journal of Studies on Alcohol, 63*(5), 559–567.

DeJong, W. (2002). The role of mass media campaigns in reducing high-risk drinking among college students. *Journal of Studies on Alcohol, 14*(Suppl.), 182–192.

Gibbons, F. X., Helweg-Larsen, M., & Gerrard, M. (1995). Prevalence estimates and adolescent risk behavior: Cross-cultural differences in social influence. *Journal of Applied Psychology, 80*(1), 107–121.

Glider, P., Midyett, S. J., Mills-Novoa, B., Johannessen, K., & Collins, C. (2001). Challenging the collegiate rite of passage: A campus-wide social marketing media campaign to reduce binge drinking. *Journal of Drug Education, 31,* 207–220.

Gomberg, L., Schneider, S. K., & DeJong, W. (2001). Evaluation of a social norms marketing campaign to reduce high-risk drinking at the University of Mississippi. *American Journal of Drug and Alcohol Abuse, 27*(2), 375–389.

Granfield, R. (2002). Believe it or not: Examining to the emergence of new drinking norms in college. *Journal of Alcohol and Drug Education, 47*(2), 18–31.

Granfield, R. (2005). Alcohol use in college: Limitations on the transformation of social norms. *Addiction Research and Theory, 13*(3), 281–292.

Haines, M., & Spear, S. F. (1996). Changing the perception of the norm: A strategy to decrease binge drinking among college students. *Journal of American College Health, 45*(3), 134–140.

Hansen, W. B., & Graham, J. W. (1991). Preventing alcohol, marijuana, and cigarette use among adolescents: Peer pressure resistance training vs. establishing conservative norms. *Preventive Medicine, 20,* 414–430.

Hines, D., Saris, R. N., & Throckmorton-Belzer, L. (2002). Pluralistic ignorance and health risk behaviors: Do college students misperceive social approval for risky behaviors on campus and in media? *Journal of Applied Social Psychology, 32,* 2621–2640.

Lambert, T. A., Kahn, A. S., & Apple, K. J. (2003). Pluralistic ignorance and hooking up. *Journal of Sex Research, 40*(2), 129–133.

Lewis, M. A., & Neighbors, C. (2006). Social norms approaches using descriptive drinking norms education: A review of the research on personalized normative feedback. *Journal of American College Health, 54*(4), 213–218.

Martino-McAllister, J., & Wessel, M. T. (2005). An evaluation of a social norms marketing project for tobacco prevention with middle, high, and college students: Use of funds from the Tobacco Master Settlement (Virginia). *Journal of Drug Education, 35*(3), 185–200.

Mattern, J. L., & Neighbors, C. (2004). Social norms campaigns: Examining the relationship between changes in perceived norms and changes in drinking levels. *Journal of Studies on Alcohol, 65*(4), 489–493.

Miller, D. T., & McFarland, C. (1991). When social comparison goes awry: The case of pluralistic ignorance. In J. M. Suls & T. A. Wills (Eds.), *Social comparison: Contemporary theory and research* (pp. 287–316). Hillsdale, NJ: Erlbaum.

Miller, D. T., & Prentice, D. A. (1996). The construction of social norms and standards. In E. T. Higgins & A. W. Kruglanski (Eds.), *Social psychology: Handbook of basic principles* (pp. 799–829). New York: Guilford Press.

Morrison, K. R., & Miller, D. T. (2006). *Distinguishing between silent and vocal minorities: Not all deviants feel marginal.* Unpublished manuscript, Stanford University.

Neal, D. J., & Carey, K. B. (2004). Developing discrepancy within self-regulation theory: Use of personalized normative feedback and personal strivings with heavy-drinking college students. *Addictive Behaviors, 29*(2), 281–297.

Neighbors, C., Larimer, M. E., & Lewis, M. A. (2004). Targeting misperceptions of descriptive drinking norms: Efficacy of a computer-delivered personalized normative feedback intervention. *Journal of Consulting and Clinical Psychology, 72*(3), 434–447.

Neighbors, C., Lewis, M. A., Bergstrom, R. L., & Larimer, M. E. (2006). Being controlled by normative influences: Self-determination as a moderator of a normative feedback alcohol intervention. *Health Psychology, 25*(5), 571–579.

Nisbett, R. E., & Kunda, Z. (1985). Perception of social distributions. *Journal of Personality and Social Psychology, 48*(2), 297–311.

Ott, C. H., & Doyle, L. H. (2005). An evaluation of the small group norms challenging model: Changing substance use misperceptions in five urban high schools. *High School Journal, 88*(3), 45–55.

Peeler, C. M., Far, J., Miller, J., & Brigham, T. A. (2000). An analysis of the effects of a program to reduce heavy drinking among college students. *Journal of Alcohol and Drug Education, 45*(2), 39–54.

Perkins, H. W., & Berkowitz, A. D. (1986). Perceiving the community norms of alcohol use among students: Some research implications for campus alcohol education programming. *International Journal of the Additions, 21*, 961–976.

Perkins, H. W., Haines, M. P., & Rice, R. (2005). Misperceiving the college drinking norm and related problems: A nationwide study of exposure to prevention information, perceived norms and student alcohol misuse. *Journal of Studies on Alcohol, 66*(4), 470–478.

Perkins, H. W., Meilman, P. W., Leichliter, J. S., Cashin, J. R., & Presley, C. A. (1999). Misperceptions of the norms for the frequency of alcohol and other drug use on college campuses. *Journal of American College Health, 47*(6), 253–258.

Perkins, H. W., & Wechsler, H. (1996). Variation in perceived college drinking norms and its impact on alcohol abuse: A nationwide study. *Journal of Drug Issues, 26*(4), 961–974.

Polonec, L. D., Major, A. M., & Atwood, L. E. (2006). Evaluating the believability and effectiveness of the social norms message "Most students drink 0 to 4 drinks when they party." *Health Communication, 20*(1), 23–34.

Prentice, D. A. (2006). On the distinction between acting like an individual and feeling like an individual. In T. Postmes & J. Jetten (Eds.), *Individuality and the group: Advances in social identity* (pp. 37–55). London: Sage.

Prentice, D. A., & Miller, D. T. (1993). Pluralistic ignorance and alcohol use on campus: Some consequences of misperceiving the social norm. *Journal of Personality and Social Psychology, 64*(2), 243–256.

Prentice, D. A., & Miller, D. T. (1996). Pluralistic ignorance and the perpetuation of social norms by unwitting actors. In M. Zanna (Ed.), *Advances in experimental social psychology* (Vol. 28, pp. 161–209). San Diego, CA: Academic Press.

Russell, C. A., Clapp, J. D., & DeJong, W. (2005). Done 4: Analysis of a failed social norms marketing campaign. *Health Communication, 17*(1), 57–65.

Schroeder, C. M., & Prentice, D. A. (1998). Exposing pluralistic ignorance to reduce alcohol use among college students. *Journal of Applied Social Psychology, 28*(23), 2150–2180.

Smith, B. H. (2004). A randomized study of a peer-led, small group social norming intervention designed to reduce drinking among college students. *Journal of Alcohol and Drug Education, 47*(3), 67–75.

Smith, S. W., Atkin, C. K., Martell, D., Allen, R., & Hembroff, L. (2006). A social judgment theory approach to conducting formative research in a social norms campaign. *Communication Theory, 16*(1), 141–152.

Stamper, G. A., Smith, B. H., Gant, R., & Bogle, K. E. (2004). Replicated findings of an evaluation of a brief intervention designed to prevent high-risk drinking among first-year college students: Implications for social norming theory. *Journal of Alcohol and Drug Education, 48*(2), 53–72.

Steffian, G. (1999). Correction of normative misperceptions: An alcohol abuse prevention program. *Journal of Drug Education, 29*(2), 115–138.

Suls, J., & Green, P. (2003). Pluralistic ignorance and college student perceptions of gender-specific alcohol norms. *Health Psychology, 22*(5), 479–486.

Thombs, D. L., Dotterer, S., Olds, R. S., Sharp, K. E., & Raub, C. G. (2004). A close look at why one social norms campaign did not reduce student drinking. *Journal of American College Health, 53*(2), 61–68.

Thombs, D. L., & Hamilton, M. J. (2002). Effects of a social norm feedback campaign on the drinking norms and behavior of division I student-athletes. *Journal of Drug Education, 32*(3), 227–244.

Turner, J. C. (1991). *Social influence*. Pacific Grove, CA: Brooks/Cole.

Wechsler, H., Nelson, T. F., Lee, J. E., Seibring, M., Lewis, C., & Keeling, R. P. (2003). Perception and reality: A national evaluation of social norms marketing interventions to reduce college students' heavy alcohol use. *Journal of Studies on Alcohol, 64*(4), 484–494.

Werch, C. E., Pappas, D. M., Carlson, J. M., DiClemente, C. C., Chally, P. S., & Sinder, J. A. (2000). Results of a social norm intervention to prevent binge drinking among first-year residential college students. *Journal of American College Health, 49*(2), 85–92.

CHAPTER 9

Identity Signaling, Social Influence, and Social Contagion

Jonah Berger

Certain products catch on and spread like wildfire. Consider Livestrong wristbands. These yellow bands were produced in the summer of 2004 to support cyclist Lance Armstrong and his nonprofit cancer foundation. At first they were worn by mostly celebrities and athletes but soon spread and achieved broad popularity in the general population. The wristbands first sold for a dollar, but stores quickly burned through their original allotments, and the bands soon appeared on eBay for upwards of $10. Similar levels of widespread success have been achieved by catchphrases like "sweet," hairstyles like the "fauxhawk" (a short mohawk first worn by soccer superstar David Beckham), and management practices like Six Sigma quality management.

   Although some cultural products see widespread popularity, sharp declines in interest often soon follow. Livestrong wristbands were hugely popular for a few years but disappeared soon after. Teens have stopped saying "sweet," interest in the fauxhawk has declined, and the number of companies practicing Six Sigma has greatly decreased (London, 2003). Although some theories of fads and fashions would suggest cultural products are abandoned because people continually want something novel (Sproles, 1981), such boredom-based explanations have trouble explaining why certain cultural products persist longer than others, or why some cultural practices (e.g., Mohawks) never see a decline. So what drives fluctuations in the popularity and spread of culture?

Before introducing the perspective of this chapter, it is worth first defining what is being studied. Cultural scholars define *culture* as a set of "meanings and practices" (Markus & Kitayama, 2003) or "beliefs, customs, symbols, or characteristics that is shared by one population of people, and which is different from the set of beliefs, customs, symbols, or characteristic shared by other distinct populations" (Conway & Schaller, in press; see also Schaller & Crandall, 2004). Culture can include the products people buy, the attitudes they hold, and the behaviors they engage in. Culture encompasses the style of shoes people wear, their decision to smoke cigarettes, and the catchphrases they say. To refer to such meanings and practices, this chapter will use the terms *cultural practices*, *products*, or *tastes*. Although different cultural products may each have specific nuances that help their success (and influence their failure), a closer look suggests a similar underlying social process that drives many of the observed fluctuations. Researchers have examined the diffusion of innovations (Rogers, 1995), fluctuation in children's names (Lieberson, 2000), adoption of consumer products (Bass, 1969), and variation in linguistic patterns (Eckert, 1989, 2000). Though each area has particular characteristics, many of the social dynamics are the same. By looking at culture more broadly, we can gain insight into factors that lead many products, ideas, and behaviors, to catch on and become popular, as well as die out, and become abandoned.

This chapter examines the role of the communication of identity in social influence and social contagion. The first portion of the chapter introduces an identity-signaling perspective, or how cultural tastes can act as symbols of identity. This perspective will then be used to help explain why people abandon cultural tastes, as well as why they adopt them in the first place. Special care will also be given to how such principles can be used in interventions to improve adolescent health. Building on these findings, the second portion of the chapter examines how such dynamics can lead to fluctuations in the popularity of cultural tastes. It investigates how identity-signaling concerns lead culture to spread, but also how the same dynamics that drive increases in popularity can also drive people to abandon the taste. Finally, the third portion of the chapter discusses how these ideas help shed light on where culture that eventually becomes popular might originate.

AN IDENTITY-SIGNALING APPROACH TO THE ADOPTION AND ABANDONMENT OF CULTURE

Some insight into why people adopt cultural tastes can be gained from focusing on the other end of the process, or why people abandon culture. One important factor that influences taste abandonment is divergence from other social groups: People often abandon tastes when members of other social groups adopt them. Kids abandon slang their parents start using, and traditional champagne buyers were turned off once the "chavs," a subculture of brash, materialistic young adults with a penchant for soccer hooliganism made the beverage a staple of their lifestyle (Clevstrom & Passariello, 2006). Similarly, the Toyota Scion was targeted at young adults, but once it became popular with senior citizens (they enjoyed its low ride and ample headroom), adoption among the target market was stymied.

An identity-signaling approach (e.g., Berger, 2008; Berger & Heath, 2007, 2008) helps explain why social groups diverge from one another. People buy products, hold attitudes, and engage in behaviors not only for their functional value but also for what they symbolize (Levy, 1959). Cultural tastes can act as signals of identity, communicating aspects of individuals (e.g., group memberships or other preferences) to others in the social world (Douglas & Isherwood, 1978; Solomon, 1983; Wernerfelt, 1990). If we see someone driving a hybrid car, we're likely to think they are a liberal tree-hugger, if someone loves opera we're likely to assume they prefer wine over beer, and if someone says "radical" and "sweet" we assume they prefer skateboarding to golf.

Importantly, cultural tastes gain meaning, or signal value, through their association with groups, or similar types of individuals. Tastes are not inherently associated with one meaning or another, rather, they gain meaning based on the set of people that hold them (Douglas & Isherwood, 1978; McCracken, 1988). If extreme sports fanatics start saying "radical," then the phrase will get associated with that type of people. In contrast, if golfers and opera lovers were the first people to start saying "radical," the phrase would signal a different identity entirely.

Consequently, though a taste may signal a certain identity at one point in time, if outsiders adopt the taste, the signal may change. If lots of people who love the outdoors start driving SUVs, then SUVs may come to signal a rugged identity. But once soccer moms or weekend warriors start driving SUVs, the meaning of driving one starts to shift. Regardless of whether these outsiders adopt SUVs because they like the functionality (e.g., they have lots of kids) or because they want to seem outdoorsy, driving an SUV may now come to communicate an entirely different meaning (i.e., soccer mom).

Original taste holders may then diverge, or abandon the taste, to avoid signaling undesired identities. By converging with similar others, people can imbue tastes with meaning and ensure they signal desired characteristics. But when outsiders start using the same product or saying the same phrase, its meaning can change, and it can lose its ability to signal desired identities effectively. As a result, people may diverge, abandoning a taste to avoid being thought of as a member of another social group (Berger & Heath, 2007, 2008; Bourdieu, 1979/1984; Hebdige, 1987; Simmel, 1904/1957).

Demonstrations of Divergence

Consider the following experiment which examined whether college undergraduates would abandon a cultural product once "geeks" adopted it (Berger & Heath, 2008). Before Livestrong wristbands became popular, research assistants (RAs) went door-to-door in college dorms, handing out yellow flyers with information about cancer, and selling the yellow wristbands to raise cancer awareness. The RAs sold wristbands to one campus dorm (target dorm), and then later, sold the same wristbands to the academic theme dorm, or "geeks," next door. Different experimenters used an ostensibly unrelated survey to measure how many target dorm members were wearing the wristband before, and after, the geeks adopted it.

Consistent with an identity-signaling perspective, students abandoned the wristband once it was adopted by the geeks. Almost one-third of dorm members who had worn the wristband previously stopped wearing it once the geeks adopted. Furthermore, an additional control condition cast doubt on the possibility that the results were driven by boredom over time. Instead, the study suggested that concerns of sending undesired identity signals, in this case, looking like a geek, led people to abandon the cultural taste.

Similar divergence dynamics extend to a broad range of social groups. White-collar professionals were the first group to give their children suffixes like Jr. but abandoned this practice once the working class began to imitate it (Taylor, 1974); undergraduates reported that they would abandon a catchphrase if other social groups (e.g., business executives, high school students, or students from a local university) adopted it (Berger & Heath, 2008); and African Americans who live in predominantly black communities tend to avoid giving their children first names that are popular among whites (Fryer & Levitt, 2004). Thus people may avoid, or abandon, cultural tastes to avoid signaling undesired social identities (also see Cooper & Jones, 1969).

Relation of Divergence to Conformity

These findings illustrate that people often diverge from the behavior of others, but other work also suggests that people converge, or do the

same thing as others. Decades of work in psychology suggest that people imitate the behaviors of those around them (e.g., Asch, 1956; Deutsch & Gerard, 1955; Sherif, 1936). Participants judging the length of lines, for example, tended to select answers that other participants had chosen, even though they were wrong (Asch, 1956). Similar dynamics are discussed in economics (bandwagon effects—Liebenstein, 1950; herding behavior and information cascades—Banerjee, 1992; Bikhchandani, Hirshleifer, & Welch, 1992) and sociology (e.g., mimetic isomorphism—DiMaggio & Powell, 1983). These theories all suggest that people imitate others, and thus people's behavior should converge, so what determines when people conform versus diverge?

An identity-signaling perspective predicts that the identity of the other taste holders and how much people use the taste domain to infer others' identity will determine whether social influence leads people to conform or diverge (Table 9.1). Certain domains of social life tend be seen as more symbolic of identity than others (e.g., cars and clothes as opposed to pens and dish soap—Belk, 1981; Shavitt, 1990). When people were asked to select cues that would aid in inference making about others, for example, most people selected clothing (Burroughs, Drews, & Hallman, 1991). Similarly, when people rated different taste domains (e.g., cars, clothes, dish soap, toothpaste, and music) based on how much they use them to infer others' identity there was high consensus across participants. People reported using things like cars, clothes, and music to infer others' identity, rather than dish soap, toothpaste, on pen color (Berger & Heath, 2007).

Identity-signaling predicts that the identity of the other taste holders should have a greater effect on behavior in these symbolic or identity-relevant domains (Berger, 2008). In domains where choice is less identity rele-

TABLE 9.1. Whether People Conform to, or Diverge from, Others Depends on Their Identity and Whether People Use the Choice Domain to Infer Identity

	Group people want to signal membership in (e.g., in-group or aspiration group)	Group people want to avoid signaling membership in (e.g., out-group or avoidance group)
Less identity-relevant domains	Convergence	Convergence
More identity-relevant domains	Convergence	Divergence

Note. Convergence means that people deciding which behavior to adopt will conform to the behavior of others, and if they already hold a behavior, they will continue to do so even after others adopt it. Divergence means that people will avoid behaviors associated with that particular group, and will abandon a behavior if members of that group adopt it.

vant, consistent with research that has found conformity, people should converge with others regardless of their identity. In these domains, the fact that someone else is doing something suggests that this thing is good, and others will be more likely to do it. Experts should have more influence than others (Kaplan & Martin, 1999), but in general, people will conform. In identity-relevant domains (e.g., cars and clothes), however, whether social influence will lead to conformity or divergence should depend on the identity of the taste adopters. If members of a group people want to signal membership in (e.g., in-group members or aspiration groups—e.g., Englis & Solomon, 1995) adopt their tastes, people will continue using the taste because it signals a desired identity. However, if members of a group people do not want to signal membership in (e.g., out-group members or avoidance groups—Englis & Solomon, 1995; White & Dahl, 2006) start adopting their tastes, people will abandon the taste to avoid sending undesired identity signals.

Support for these predictions was found using a broad sample of varying ages (Berger, 2008). Participants listed either an in-group or an out-group and then rated how they would react if that group started adopting their preference in each of a variety of taste domains (e.g., favorite music artist, clothing, and dish soap). They also rated how much they would or would not like other people to think they were a member of the group they listed. As predicted, in less identity-relevant choice domains (e.g., dish soap or toothpaste), people conformed to others' behavior (e.g., reported greater likelihood of using that toothpaste brand), regardless of whether they were in-group or out-group members. In more identity-relevant domains, however, whether people conformed to or diverged from others' behavior depended on the others' group membership. People reported they would converge with in-group members and continue using identity-relevant tastes that were adopted by in-groups. But social influence had the opposite effect when the adopters were out-group members; people reported they would diverge from out-groups and abandon identity-relevant tastes that were adopted by out-group members. Furthermore, consistent with an identity signaling perspective, a mediational analysis indicated that whether people conformed or diverged from others in identity-relevant domains was driven by whether they did, or did not, want other people to treat them as a member of that group.

Using Identity Signaling to Improve Adolescent Health

These findings suggest the utility of identity-based interventions to improve adolescent health. The prototype model of risk behavior (Gibbons

& Gerrard, 1995, 1997) suggests that the decision to engage in health behaviors is driven, in part, by people's desire to acquire positive (or avoid negative) characteristics associated with that behavior. People have a prototype, or social image, they associate with health behaviors, and the favorability of this image helps determine whether they will engage in that behavior. Young people who had more favorable perceptions of the type of people who smoke cigarettes or engage in unprotected sex, for example, reported higher willingness to smoke cigarettes or engage in unprotected sex (Gerrard, Gibbons, Stack, Vande Lune, & Cleveland, 2005; Gibbons, Gerrard, Blanton, & Russell, 1998).

Consequently, it may be possible to help adolescents avoid risky health behaviors by associating those behaviors with social identities they do not want to signal. Gerrard and colleagues (2006), for example, found that an intervention that associated negative characteristics with early alcohol consumption was able to alter the positivity of adolescents' risk prototypes, as well as their actual alcohol consumption. Other research provides further evidence that social concerns of communicating identity are at least partially responsible for such effects. Linking junk food consumption to a social group undergraduates did not want to signal membership in led them to choose less junk food, particularly when their choices were publicly visible to others (Berger & Heath, 2008). These effects are also stronger for people who want to avoid signaling membership in the social group linked to the behavior. One study placed posters in a college dorm suggesting that a particular campus group was known to binge drink (Berger & Rand, in press). Two weeks later, the dorm members reported their recent alcohol consumption and their desire to avoid others thinking they were akin to different social groups. As predicted, undergraduates who did not want others to think they were akin to the social group linked to binge drinking reported consuming less alcohol. These findings suggest that shifting the identity associated with risky health behaviors to one which adolescents do not want to signal can be a useful intervention to improve adolescent health.

IDENTITY-SIGNALING DYNAMICS AND THE SPREAD OF CULTURE

More broadly, an identity-signaling perspective also provides insight into social contagion and the lifecycle of culture. Most existing research has examined individuals abandoning tastes at one time or another based on adoption by, or association with, avoidance group members. But these individual decisions are part of a dynamic system, and aggregated over time, they lead to fluctuations in the popularity of culture.

Music artists, clothing styles, slang, and other cultural tastes often start out by being associated with members of a certain subculture. Punks wear mohawks and tattoos and listen to punk, ska, or other types of hardcore music. Inner-city teens wear baggy pants and sideways hats, listen to hip-hop and rap music, and use phrases like "tight" and "phat." Similarly, hardcore business people may drive BMWs, use Blackberries, and talk about the "800-pound gorilla" and the "low hanging fruit."

Once cultural tastes gain value as signals however, out-group members may start poaching them as a way of trying to signal desired meaning. In some cases, these poseurs may poach tastes so that other people will treat them like members of a desired social group. Recent MBA graduates may copy the lingo of business execs, or buy the "right" Personal Digital Assistant (PDA) in an attempt to "pass" or be treated as business executives. In other cases, poaching is not due so much to a desire to be thought of as an out-group member, but rather to be thought of as having some of the characteristics associated with that group. Suburban teens poach the lingo or styles of inner-city teens in an attempt to seem tough or cool.

This poaching then starts a cycle of meaning change. Imagine social groups as layers of an onion, or concentric circles, with the original taste holders as the core (see Figure 9.1). Each layer is another social group or type, with groups that have a greater interest in looking like members of the subculture as more central layers, and groups that are less interested in, or want to avoid signaling subcultural identity as more distal layers. If enough outsiders, or poseurs, start adopting a subculture's taste, its meaning may shift, and original taste holders may abandon the taste to avoid signaling undesired identities. While listening to a certain music artist, saying a certain slang phrase, or wearing a certain style of clothing may once have signaled subculture membership, adoption by outsiders dilutes or confuses the meaning of the signal. The subculture will then abandon the taste to avoid signaling undesired identities, and a new signal of group identity will emerge (see Heath, Ho, & Berger, 2008, for a broader discussion).

But the cycle doesn't stop there; original taste holders may be long gone, but as the taste starts getting sucked outward, other social types who actually like the new diluted signal may start to adopt. Once the subculture abandons the taste, it may become even more associated with the second group that adopted it, and this may be appealing to more mainstream social groups. Through the diffusion process, a catchphrase that started with inner-city teens may move to suburban teens who want to look cool. But consequently, it loses some of its value as a signal of toughness as it becomes associated with suburban teens. This causes the

Original group   Poseurs poach the   Original group
adopts taste   taste, signal shifts   abandons taste

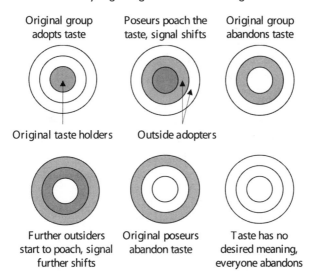

Original taste holders   Outside adopters

Further outsiders   Original poseurs   Taste has no
start to poach, signal   abandon taste   desired meaning,
further shifts   everyone abandons

FIGURE 9.1. Movement of cultural tastes and shifts in signal meaning. A group adopts a cultural taste (indicated in gray). Outsiders (i.e., poseurs) adopt the taste in an attempt to signal membership in that group, but by doing so, they begin to change the signal associated with the taste. Original taste holders then abandon to avoid signaling an undesired identity. But because the signal has shifted, the taste becomes appealing to further outsiders, and they adopt, further shifting the meaning. The original poseurs then abandon to avoid communicating the new, undesired, signal. Eventually the taste has no desired meaning to anyone, and is abandoned by all.

original subculture to abandon it but may interest suburban parents who want to show they are hip to pop culture. Their adoption further changes the signal value of the taste and may lead suburban teens to abandon it. Consequently, a taste that started with one group moves further afield, and the cycle continues until the taste no longer has a desirable meaning to anyone and is abandoned by all. Importantly, though individual cultural units themselves may "die," or become abandoned, group members just shift and adopt or feature other units of culture to maintain distinction, and the cycle starts anew (Mason & Berger, 2008).

This process suggests that all identity-relevant cultural tastes may be in danger of eventually perishing, but certain factors should moderate the speed of diffusion, and consequently, the longevity of the taste (Berger, Heath, & Ho, 2008). Public visibility is one such factor. Tastes that are publicly visible (e.g., the clothes people wear or the car they drive) are easy for others to see and, consequently, easy for poseurs to poach. Public visibility makes it easier for people to identify insiders as a member of a certain social group, but it also makes it easier for outsiders who want to signal certain identities to steal signals and adopt them as their own. Thus more visible tastes should have a shorter lifecycle.

Cost is another factor that should moderate diffusion speed and taste longevity. Tastes can be costly in a monetary sense (i.e., a car brand that is expensive to buy), but they can also vary in terms of opportunity costs. Having a mohawk or cornrows may make it hard to get a job in certain corporate settings, and this cost impedes weekend warriors from poaching the taste. Tastes can also be costly in terms of time or knowledge; though people can hear a catchphrase in passing and then try to use it themselves, unless they frequently interact with others who actually use the phrase, it will be hard for them to actually say it the right way. Similarly, to find out about the next hot independent rock band, a person has to spend time in the right places talking to the right people (though easy access to information over the Internet has greatly reduced what once was a high cost). Tastes that are more costly, in any sense, should be harder for outsiders to poach and thus have a longer lifecycle.

WHERE TASTES THAT BECOME POPULAR ORIGINATE

Today's margin becomes tomorrow's mainstream.
—BEALE (2005)

An identity-signaling perspective also provides insight into a seemingly perplexing question: Why does what eventually becomes cool sometimes originate with outsiders or traditionally marginalized social group? Academics and cultural observers alike have noted that what eventually becomes popular often starts with outsiders (Blumberg, 1974; Field, 1970; Meyersohn & Katz, 1957; Peterson & Anand, 2004; Pountain & Robins, 2000). The *New York Times* noted "the subtle power of lesbian style" in fashion (Trebay, 2004) and that everyone from celebrities to music stars seemed to be imitating the clothing and hairstyles of homosexual men (Coleman, 2005). Much of the slang and styles of the late 1990s (e.g., baggy pants and fitted hats) originated with inner-city teens. Similarly, observers of culture have noted that "the originators of cool have always been outsiders" (Belk, Tian, & Paavlova, 2006, p. 10) and that "the groups responsible for the radical reform of cultural meaning are those existing at the margins of society, e.g., hippies, punks, or gays," (McCracken, 1986, p. 76).

Such suggestions are intriguing because they contradict the traditional perspective on the way culture spreads. The trickle-down theory of fashion (Robinson, 1961; Simmel, 1904/1957; Veblen, 1899/1912) suggests that people adopt from those above them in the status food chain. Fashions are initiated by the higher class and imitated by the lower classes. These theories suggest that everyone wants to look wealthy and they well explain why the middle-class poaches the status symbols of the rich. But such trickle-down dynamics are less useful in explaining why people would ever poach the styles of inner-city teens, gays and lesbians, trailer-park inhabitants, or other traditionally marginalized minority groups. Most members of the mainstream would shun association with any of these groups, yet there are many examples of the mainstream eventually adopting things that were once associated with marginalized groups. Why?

An identity-signaling perspective helps shed light on this question; tastes that originate among traditionally marginalized groups often become popular because people poach them as away to distinguish themselves from the mainstream. To illustrate this notion, we can focus on three types of social groups: the mainstream, marginalized or oppositional groups, and hipsters. Briefly, the mainstream is the majority culture, marginalized groups are groups that are discriminated against by the mainstream, and hipsters are usually connected with the mainstream but want to distinguish themselves from it. There are obviously multiple groups at each of these levels and even groups in between, but focusing on these three groups simplifies the perspective.

Minority culture often differs from mainstream culture. Some cultural differences may just result from different backgrounds of the two groups; immigrants, for instance, bring with them different cultural traditions from their homeland. In other cases, minorities may actively create culture that distances themselves from the mainstream (see Ogbu, 1992, for the distinction between primary and secondary cultural differences). Whether due to their race, sexual preference, or some other factors, outsiders are often discriminated against by the mainstream and thus often can't gain status within mainstream society. Discrimination often leads to an oppositional identity (Solomon, 1992), and psychological threat may lead oppositional groups to "disidentify" (Major, Spencer, Schmader, Wolfe, & Crocker, 1998; Steele, 1997) with mainstream culture. Rather than embrace the mainstream culture that spurns them, these groups may instead create a status hierarchy and cultural system of their own.

Originally, mainstream people will avoid signals associated with marginalized groups to avoid signaling a marginalized identity. Social identities are often defined and maintained in opposition to other groups and just as marginalized groups may define their identity in relation to the mainstream, the mainstream may define their identity as separate from marginalized groups. In addition, some mainstream individuals may already have a lot in common with members of marginalized groups and thus are particularly wary of having overlapping tastes. People who once lived in a trailer park, for instance, may move to the city and renounce the culture of their old life because they see doing so as "moving up" in the world. Thus members of the mainstream attempt to stay far way from anything that would signal they are a member of a marginalized group.

There are also segments of society who exist within the mainstream, or just outside it, who prefer a social identity that is distinct from the mainstream (in this model, hipsters). Tastes are less useful in distinguishing between different types when too many people hold them, and consequently, groups form smaller units as a way of coordinating more effectively. By sharing culture with a cohesive set of others, these individuals can more easily recognize people who share similar interests (e.g., track bicycles), or know who to talk to when looking for information about the next hot band. Such individuals may have high needs for uniqueness (Snyder & Fromkin, 1977; Tian, Bearden, & Hunter, 2001) or desires to be early adopters (e.g., the first to wear a new style or listen to new music, Rogers, 1995; also see Moore, 1991), but more generally, they are united by their desire for identities that separate them from the mainstream. Consequently, members of such groups want to hold cultural tastes that provide them with the desired distinction.

Unfortunately for hipsters, their sources of distinction are never safe; mainstreamers who want to seem hip or cool may poach hipster tastes to try and signal that identity. Although mainstreamers do not want to be the first to pilot new cultural tastes, some of them are fast followers, and by poaching the tastes of another group, these poseurs create the signal dilution or confusion outlined earlier. By poaching hip tastes, they destroy the previous mark of distinction, and now hipsters must adopt a new taste to avoid signaling undesired identities.

One powerful way hipsters can try to reinstate their distinction is by poaching the cultural tastes of traditionally marginalized groups. The tastes of marginalized groups should be appealing for two reasons. First, though hipster-types could (and sometimes do) create new culture, it is often easier and more efficient to poach existing symbols of differentiation. As groups get larger, their coherence, or the percentage of characteristics they have in common often decreases, and thus it should be easier for cultural tastes to gain meaning when they are associated with social groups that are not overly large. Furthermore, because the meaning of signals is socially constructed, adopting a new cultural taste, and attempting to imbue it with meaning, takes time. Mountaineers can get together and decide that wearing a red-striped hat will be their group identifier, but it will take nonmountaineers a number of times of inter-acting with a striped-hatted person, and learning they are a mountaineer, to realize that this is how they should interpret the signal. Those receiv-ing the signal determine how to treat the signaler, and thus a more effi-cient way for people to ensure they are treated as different from the mainstream is to adopt existing tastes that already communicate the de-sired differentiation.

Second, hipsters should find the tastes of marginalized groups par-ticularly appealing because mainstreamers want to avoid them. The hip-sters are engaged in a repeated chase with mainstreamers. Every time the hip adopt a new taste, the mainstream soon follows, and so hipsters are constantly looking for something new. But because the mainstream wants to avoid the signals of the marginalized, those tastes may be a par-ticularly good place for hipsters to poach. By adopting tastes that the group they are trying to get away from wants to avoid, hipsters can de-crease the likelihood that the mainstream will immediately poach their new tastes.

But when hipsters adopt the cultural taste of a marginalized group, it often ensures the taste's death. Although tastes associated with marginalized groups might originally have been appealing due to their distinction from the mainstream, by adopting the taste, hipsters change its meaning. What was once a signal of a marginalized identity shifts to-ward becoming a signal of being hip. This ultimately leads the tastes to look more appealing to the mainstream. Although mainstreamers want to avoid looking like the outsiders, some of them also have at least some desire to look cool or hip. Consequently, once the hipsters adopt, some mainstreamers, and soon the broader masses, will flock in, and the taste slowly gets sucked into the mainstream. Thus a taste that started out as a signal of marginalized status, can, by nature of its value as a signal of distinction, gain broader appeal, which will then lead to its eventual abandonment.

Outsider Innovation

Marginalized tastes should also be appealing to those looking for dis-tinction from the mainstream because they are innovative relative to the current standard. Most of the discussion so far has treated signals like they are sent and received with full fidelity, but the process is often noisy. The meaning of a taste is shared socially, but individuals may vary slightly in their exact conception of what signals a certain group identity. Furthermore, tastes are often continuous rather than discrete; a shaved head is different from a crew cut, but it is hard to distinguish between someone who has forgotten to shave their head for a week and someone who received a crew cut that was too short. Consequently, signals are more likely to be received correctly the more they differ from one another. If most people are letting their hair grow long, getting a midlength cut doesn't provide much differentiation. Shaving one's head is a better signal of distinction. Thus, doing the opposite is a good way of avoiding undesired signals (Heath et al., 2006; also see the ratchet effect, Lieberson, 2000).

Such separation should increase the appeal of tastes associated with any group that is relatively distant from mainstream culture. The prior discussion focused mainly on the tastes of marginalized groups, but similar dynamics should apply to any group whose tastes differ from what is popular at the time. Before they became popular in the late 1990s, Hush Puppies were work mainly by senior citizens and were obviously not in fashion. Hipsters started wearing them, however, "precisely because no one else would wear them" (Gladwell, 2000, p. 5). Similarly, some of the hottest cars for young people today are models usually identified with seniors, for example, old Buicks and Chevrolets; they have the cool factor of being so "out" they are "in" (Saranow, 2006). Because what is popular with seniors is so distant from most of what is popular currently, adopting tastes associated with this group provide a good way of distinguishing oneself from the rest of the mainstream.

Change in Culture Itself Due to the Onset of Popularity

Tastes originally linked with marginalized groups may eventually become popular, but at least some change to the taste itself often occurs along the way. People often suggest culture is watered down for mainstream consumption, and marginalized tastes likely undergo shifts to make them more palatable. Unless mainstream taste has radically changed, the marginalized taste's edginess that once opposed the mainstream must now be rounded and brought into the fold. People who listened to bands before they became popular, for instance, often remark that they much preferred the band's original albums to their newer work.

In some cases though, the perception that the cultural unit has changed may result more from the new taste holders, rather than the actual culture itself. Once an independent music artist becomes popular, listening to that artist is no longer a sign that one is "indie" and instead becomes a signal of being mainstream. Thus even if the music itself doesn't change much over the progression of albums, people may perceive it as having changed based on the identity of the new adopters.

CONCLUSION

This chapter has focused on the role of identity signaling in social influence, social contagion, and fluctuations in the popularity of cultural tastes. What we buy or how we behave can act as signals of social identity, but when outsiders adopt these tastes, what it means to buy that product or engage in that behavior can change. Consequently, original taste holders may diverge to avoid signaling undesired identities. This process has a number of implications for understanding the spread of culture. Tastes may gain popularity if they signal a desired identity, but once outsiders adopt, they will lose that desired signal and may eventually be abandoned they no longer communicate desired meaning for anyone. Furthermore, because traditionally marginalized groups are often seen as outsiders in society, cultural tastes that these groups pioneer may eventually become popular because they provide a way for hipsters, or other social groups, to differentiate themselves from the mainstream. By focusing on how cultural tastes can act as signals of identity, we gain greater insight into why products, ideas, and behaviors catch on as well as why they die out.

This identity-signaling perspective is particularly useful for understanding the behavior of adolescents because they are at a time in their life where identity concerns have great importance. Teens care a lot about fitting in, finding friends, and meeting romantic partners, and consequently, they care a great deal about what their behavior communicates about their place in the social hierarchy. One of the main reasons adolescents smoke cigarettes, for example, is to "look cool" or appear rebellious (Delorme, Kreshel, & Reid, 2003). Although this increased emphasis on identity means that adolescents may be more tempted to engage in counternormative behaviors for signaling purposes, it also suggests that identity-shifting interventions may be particularly effective among this population. By shifting the identity associated with a risky behavior to one which adolescents do not want to communicate, we may be able to reduce their likelihood of engaging in risky behaviors (see Berger & Rand, in press).

This perspective also speaks to the growing body of work seeking to understand the propagation of culture. Recent work on cultural psychology has examined how the meanings and practices inherent in a culture influence human psychology, but much less research has examined the reciprocal process, or how human psychology influences the meanings and practices that persist in a culture (Schaller & Crandall, 2004). Researchers have just begun to examine how aspects of human psychology, such as emotion (e.g., Heath, Bell, & Sternberg, 2001) or memory (e.g., Norenzayan & Atran, 2004; Rubin, 1995), properties of culture itself, such as its communicability (e.g., Schaller, Conway, & Tanchuk, 2002) or fit with the surrounding environment (e.g., Berger & Heath, 2005), and social network structure (e.g., Mason, Jones, & Goldstone, 2008) influence the spread and persistence of culture. By understanding the communication of identity, hopefully we can gain greater insight into culture more broadly.

ACKNOWLEDGMENTS

Ben Ho and Winter Mason provided helpful comments on the chapter, and I am greatly indebted to Chip Heath for the numerous discussions that helped develop many of the ideas mentioned here.

REFERENCES

Asch, S. E. (1956). Studies of independence and conformity: A minority of one against a unanimous majority. *Psychological Monographs, 70*(Whole no. 416).

Banerjee, A. V. (1992). A simple model of herd behavior. *Quarterly Journal of Economics, 107*, 797–817.

Bass, F. M. (1969). A new product growth model for consumer durables. *Management Science, 13*, 215–227.

Beale, L. (2005, June 19). John Hughes versus the vampires: The dilemma of the midnight movie. *New York Times*, p. 22.

Belk, R. W. (1981). Determinants of consumption cue utilization in impression formation: An associational deviation and experimental verification. *Advances in Consumer Research, 8*, 170–175.

Belk, R. W., Tian, K. T., & Paavola, H. (2006). *The meanings of cool: Transformations and continuities within global consumer culture* (Working paper).

Berger, J. (2008). *Conformity versus divergence: The role of identity-signaling in responses to social influence*. Manuscript submitted for publication.

Berger, J., & Heath, C. (2005). Idea habitats: How the prevalence of environmental cues influences the success of ideas. *Cognitive Science, 29*(2), 195–221.

Berger, J., & Heath, C. (2007). Where consumers diverge: Identity-signaling and product domains, *Journal of Consumer Research, 34*(2), 121–134.

Berger, J., & Heath, C. (2008). *Who drives divergence?: Identity-signaling, outgroup dissimilarity, and the abandonment of cultural tastes*. Manuscript submitted for publication.

Berger, J., Heath, C., & Ho, B. (2008). *Divergence in cultural practices: Tastes as signals of identity* (Working paper).

Berger, J., & Rand, L. (in press). Shifting signals to help health: Using identity-signaling to reduce risky health behaviors. *Journal of Consumer Research, 35*(3).

Bikhchandani, W., Hirshleifer, D., & Welch, I. (1992). A theory of fads, fashion, custom, and cultural change as informational cascades. *Journal of Political Economy, 100*, 992–1026.

Blumberg, P. (1974). The decline and fall of the status symbol: Some thoughts on status in post-industrial society. *Social Problems, 21,* 480–498.

Bourdieu, P. (1984). *Distinction: A social critique of the judgment of taste* (R. Nice, Trans.). Cambridge, MA: Harvard University Press. (Original work published 1979)

Burroughs, W. J., Drews, D. R., & Hallman, W. K. (1991). Predicting personality from personal possessions: A self-presentational analysis. *Journal of Social Behavior and Personality, 6*(6), 147–163.

Coleman, D. (2005, June 19). Gay or straight? Hard to tell. *New York Times,* Sunday Styles, p. 1.

Conway, L. G., III, & Schaller, M. (in press). How communication shapes culture. In K. Fiedler (Ed.), *Frontiers of social psychology: Social communication.* New York: Psychology Press.

Cooper, J., & Jones, E. E. (1969). Opinion divergence as a strategy to avoid being miscast. *Journal of Personality and Social Psychology, 13,* 23–30.

Clevstrom, J., & Passariello, C. (2006, August 18). No kicks from "Chavpagne." *Wall Street Journal,* p. A11.

Delorme, D., Kreshel, P. J., & Reid, L. N. (2003). Lighting up: Young adults' autobiographical accounts of their first smoking experiences. *Youth and Society, 34*(4), 468–496.

Deutsch, M., & Gerard, H. B. (1955). A study of normative and informational social influences upon individual judgment. *Journal of Abnormal and Social Psychology, 51,* 629–636.

DiMaggio, P., & Powell, W. (1983). The iron cage revised: Institutional isomorphism and collective rationality in organizational fields. *American Sociological Review, 48,* 147–160.

Douglas, M., & Isherwood, B. (1978). *The world of goods: Towards an anthropology of consumption.* New York: Norton.

Eckert, P. (1989). *Jocks and burnouts: Social identity in the high school.* New York: Teachers College Press.

Eckert, P. (2000). *Linguistic variation as social practice.* Oxford, UK: Blackwell.

Englis, B. G., & Solomon, M. R. (1995). To be and not to be? Lifestyle imagery, reference groups, and the clustering of America. *Journal of Advertising, 24,* 13–28.

Field, G. A. (1970). The status float phenomenon—The upward diffusion of innovation. *Business Horizons, 8,* 45–52.

Fryer, R. G., Jr., & Levitt, S. D. (2004). The causes and consequences of distinctively black names. *Quarterly Journal of Economics, 119,* 767–805.

Gerrard, M., Gibbons, F. X., Brody, G. H., Murry, V. M., Cleveland, M. J., & Wills, T. A. (2006). A theory-based dual focus alcohol intervention for pre-adolescents: Social cognitions in the Strong African American Families Program. *Psychology of Addictive Behaviors, 20,* 185–195.

Gerrard, M., Gibbons, F. X., Stock, M. L., Vande Lune, L. S., & Cleveland, M. J. (2005). Images of smokers and willingness to smoke among African American pre-adolescents: An application of the prototype/willingness model of adolescent health risk behavior to smoking initiation. *Journal of Pediatric Psychology, 30,* 305–318.

Gibbons, F. X., & Gerrard, M. (1995). Predicting young adults' health risk behavior. *Journal of Personality and Social Psychology, 69,* 505–517.

Gibbons, F. X., & Gerrard, M. (1997). Health images and their effects on health behavior. In B. P. Buunk & F. X. Gibbons (Eds.), *Health, coping and well-being: Perspectives from social comparison theory* (pp. 63–94). Mahwah, NJ: Erlbaum.

Gibbons, F. X., Gerrard, M., Blanton, H., & Russell, D. W. (1998). Reasoned action and social reaction: Willingness and intention as independent predictors of health risk. *Journal of Personality and Social Psychology, 74,* 1164–1181.

Gladwell, M. (2000). *The tipping point: How little things can make a big difference.* New York: Little, Brown.

Heath, C., Bell, C., & Sternberg, E. (2001). Emotional selection in memes: The case of urban legends. *Journal of Personality and Social Psychology, 81,* 1028–1041.

Heath, C., Ho, B., & Berger, J. (2006). Focal points in coordinated divergence. *Journal of Economic Psychology, 27*(5), 635–647.

Hebdige, D. (1987). *Subculture: The meaning of style.* London: Routledge.

Kaplan, M. F., & Martin, A. M. (1999). Effects of differential status of group members on process and outcome of deliberation. *Group Processes and Intergroup Relations, 2,* 347–364.

Leibenstein, H. (1950). Bandwagon, snob, and Veblen effects in the theory of consumers demand. *Quarterly Journal of Economics, 65,* 183–207.

Levy, S. J. (1959). Symbols for sale. *Harvard Business Review, 33,* 117–124.

Lieberson, S. (2000). *A matter of taste: How names, fashions, and culture change.* New Haven, CT: Yale University Press.

London, S. (2003, June 12). Why are the fads fading away? *Financial Times,* p. 14.

Major, B., Spencer, S., Schmader, T., Wolfe, C., & Crocker, J. (1998). Coping with negative stereotypes about intellectual performance: The role of psychological disengagement. *Personality and Social Psychology Bulletin, 24*(1), 34–50.

Markus, H. R., & Kitayama, S. (2003). Culture, self, and the reality of the social. *Psychological Inquiry, 14,* 277–283.

Mason, W., & Berger, J. (2008). *How culture spreads: Social networks, identity-signaling, and the diffusion of culture* (Working paper).

Mason, W., Jones, A., & Goldstone, R. L. (2008). *Propagation of innovations in networked groups.* Manuscript under review.

McCracken, G. (1986, June). Culture and consumption: A theoretical account of the structure and movement of the cultural meaning of consumer goods. *Journal of Consumer Research, 13,* 71–84.

McCracken, G. (1988). *Culture and consumption: New approaches to the symbolic character of consumer goods and activities.* Bloomington: Indiana University Press.

Meyersohn, R., & Katz, E. (1957, May). Notes on the natural history of fads. *American Journal of Sociology, 62,* 594–601.

Moore, G. (1991). *Crossing the chasm: Marketing and selling technology products to mainstream customers.* New York: HarperBusiness.

Norenzayan, A., & Atran, S. (2004). Cognitive and emotional processes in the cultural transmission of natural and nonnatural beliefs. In M. Schaller & C. Crandall (Eds.), *The psychological foundations of culture* (pp. 149–169). Hillsdale, NJ: Erlbaum.

Ogbu, J. U. (1992). Understanding cultural diversity and learning. *Educational Researcher, 21*(8), 5–14.

Peterson, R. A., & Anand, N. (2004). The production of culture perspective. *Annual Review of Sociology, 30,* 311–334.

Pountain, D., & Robins, D. (2000). *Cool rules: Anatomy of an attitude*. London: Reaktion.

Robinson, D. E. (1961). The economics of fashion demand. *Quarterly Journal of Economics, 75,* 376–398.

Rogers, E. M. (1995). *Diffusion of innovations*. New York: Free Press.

Rubin, D. C. (1995). *Memory in oral traditions: The cognitive psychology of epic, ballads, and counting-out rhymes*. New York: Oxford University Press.

Saranow, J. (2006, May 9). Hip to be square: Why young buyers covet "Grandpa" cars. *Wall Street Journal,* p. A1.

Schaller, M., Conway, L. G., III, & Tanchuk, T. L. (2002). Selective pressures on the once and future contents of ethnic stereotypes: Effects of the communicability of traits. *Journal of Personality and Social Psychology, 82,* 861–877.

Schaller, M., & Crandall, C. S. (2004). *The psychological foundations of culture*. Mahwah, NJ: Erlbaum.

Shavitt, S. (1990). The role of attitude objects in attitude functions. *Journal of Experimental Social Psychology, 26,* 124–148.

Sherif, M. (1936). *The psychology of social norms*. New York: Harper.

Simmell, G. (1957). Fashion. *American Journal of Sociology, 62,* 541–548. (Original work published 1904)

Snyder, C. R., & Fromkin, H. L. (1977). Abnormality as a positive characteristic: The development and validation of a scale measuring need for uniqueness. *Journal of Abnormal Psychology, 86,* 518–527.

Solomon, M. R. (1983). The role of products as social stimuli: A symbolic interactionism perspective. *Journal of Consumer Research, 10,* 319–329.

Solomon, P. R. (1992). *Black resistance in high school*. Albany: State University of New York Press.

Sproles, G. B. (1981). Analyzing fashion life cycles: Principles and perspectives. *Journal of Marketing, 45,* 116–124.

Steele, C. (1997). A threat in the air: How stereotypes shape intellectual identity and performance. *American Psychologist, 52,* 613–629.

Taylor, R. (1974). John Doe, Jr: A study of his distribution in space, time, and the social structure. *Social Forces, 53,* 11–21.

Tian, K. T., Bearden, W. O., & Hunter, G. L. (2001). Consumers' need for uniqueness: Scale development and validation. *Journal of Consumer Research, 28,* 50–66.

Trebay, G. (2004, June 27). The subtle power of lesbian style. *New York Times,* Sunday Styles, p. 1.

Veblen, T. (1912). *The theory of the leisure class*. New York: Viking Press. (Original work published 1899)

White, K., & Dahl, D. (2006). To be or not be?: The influence of dissociative reference groups on consumer preferences. *Journal of Consumer Psychology, 16*(4), 404–414

Wernerfelt, B. (1990). Advertising content when brand choice is a signal. *Journal of Business, 63,* 91–98.

PART IV

UNDEREXPLORED CONTEXTS FOR POTENTIAL PEER INFLUENCE EFFECTS

CHAPTER 10

Homophily in Adolescent Romantic Relationships

Wyndol Furman *and* Valerie A. Simon

It's actually, it's really gotten me out of this big hole I used to be in. I used to go off and I smoked weed a lot, drank a whole [obscenity], a lot, I mean I used to love to party 24-7 and all that, and during this time, my grades just went down to like crap. And she's helped me a lot and all that, and I mean, she's helped me actually get interested in school again, and be able to go off and just be actually be, I mean, she got me out of the rut. I mean I hardly drink. I don't smoke no more. I mean things like that.
—A 12TH-GRADE BOY

The chapters in this volume examine adolescent peer influence processes. Most of the chapters, however, focus on the influence of adolescent friends and peer groups, and the mechanisms underlying such influences. Relatively little is said (or known) about the influence of romantic partners on adolescents.

Yet the preceding quote suggests that romantic partners may play an important role as well. Certainly, romantic relationships are a central part of most adolescents' social worlds. In a survey of adolescents in a Midwestern city in the United States (Giordano, Manning, & Longmore, 2006), 32% of seventh graders, 41% of ninth graders, and 59% of eleventh graders report having a romantic relationship in the last year. Many early adolescent girls expect to be in love all the time (R. W. Simon, Eder, & Evans, 1992). By the tenth grade, adolescents interact more frequently with romantic partners than they do with parents, siblings, or friends (Laursen & Williams, 1997). Moreover, other-gender peers occupy much of heterosexual adolescents' attention even when they are not interacting with them. Romantic relationships are a frequent topic of conversation among most adolescents (Eder, 1985). Even when they are not with the other gender, high school students also spend much of their time thinking about actual or potential romantic partners (Richards, Crowe, Larson, & Swarr, 1998). Most report thinking about sex "often" or "very often" as well (Juhasz, Kaufman, & Meyer, 1986).

Romantic partners are also a major source of support for many adolescents. By the tenth grade, they are tied for second with mothers in the hierarchy of support figures (Furman & Buhrmester, 1992). In college (19 years of age), romantic relationships are the most supportive relationship for males and are among the most supportive relationships for females. For heterosexual youth, the other gender is also a frequent source of strong emotions as well—in fact, a more frequent source of emotions than same-gender peers, parents, or school issues (Wilson-Shockley, 1995, as cited Larson, Clore, & Wood, 1999). It seems very likely that romantic partners are also frequent sources of emotion for sexual minorities.

Romantic experiences not only are central in the daily lives of adolescents, but also they are thought to shape intimacy and identity development (Erikson, 1968; Furman & Shaffer, 2003). They may also help adolescents successfully establish autonomy as they explore extra-familial relationships and come to rely less on parents (Dowdy & Kliewer, 1998; Furman & Shaffer, 2003). Adolescent romantic experiences may even influence the nature of subsequent close relationships, including marriages (Erikson, 1968; Furman & Flanagan, 1997; Sullivan, 1953). These ideas about the long-term influence of romantic experiences, however, are simply speculations, as little work has examined such questions. In fact, we know relatively little about the short-term or immediate impact of romantic experiences on adolescents. Particularly absent is work on the selection of romantic partners and the effect the characteristics of the partner may have on psychosocial development and adjustment.

In this chapter, we examine the issue of *homophily* in adolescent romantic relationships—that is, the degree of similarity between adolescents and their partners. Such homophily can occur by selection or assortative pairing; that is, individuals have long been hypothesized to be attracted to those who are similar to each other (Byrne, 1971; Newcomb, 1961). Additionally, the socialization influences of partners may lead adolescents to become more similar to them. Finally, relationships with dissimilar partners may end more quickly than those with similar ones (i.e., deselection).

The issue of homophily in adolescent romantic relationship has received virtually no attention. Accordingly, we begin by briefly summarizing the literature on homophily in marriages and adult romantic relationships. We then discuss how homophily may or may not be different in adolescent romantic relationships. Next we describe the results of two empirical studies examining homophily. Finally, we delineate a series of issues that warrant attention in subsequent work. Our comments refer to heterosexual relationships, because unfortunately research has not examined this issue in gay or lesbian relationships.

HOMOPHILY IN ADULT COUPLES

Numerous studies have assessed the degree of homophily in adult romantic couples, especially marriages. Although it is beyond the scope of this chapter to review this literature (see Buss, 1985; Epstein & Guttman, 1984; Kalmijn, 1998; McPherson, Smith-Lovin, & Cook, 2001), several key conclusions warrant mentioning. First, people tend to partner within their social group (endogamy) and to people close in status (homogamy). Married couples are much more likely to be similar to each other than complement each other. The degree of homophily in cohabiting and dating couples is almost as great as in married couples (Blackwell & Lichter, 2004). In fact, virtually no evidence exists that opposites attract. Instead, homophily occurs on status and value dimensions (Lazerfeld & Merton, 1954). That is, homophily occurs on features associated with formal, informal, or ascribed status, such as age, ethnicity, education, intelligence, religion, and physical attractiveness. Additionally, homophily occurs in values, attitudes, and beliefs. The degree of homophily in personality characteristics, however, is modest (see Buss, 1985; Klohnen & Mendelsohn, 1988).

Theoretical explanations for these findings suggest that we tend to select similar partners because of the genetic and social advantages it confers to individuals and groups (Kalmijn, 1998; Thiessen & Gregg, 1980). However, methodological limitations of most homophily studies make it difficult to determine the degree to which observed similarities reflect selection or other processes that would lead to similarity, such as socialization or deselection. For example, most homophily studies are cross-sectional and examine couples in longstanding marriages. Accordingly, observed partner similarity could reflect either the initial selection of partners, the influence of partners during the time of courtship or early years of marriage, or the deselection of partners through divorce. Moreover, even longitudinal studies that begin substantially after couples have met (let alone marry) may underestimate the influence of socialization effects as such effects may have already occurred prior to the onset of the study.

A few studies have examined whether similarity is greater in longer lasting relationships as deselection or socialization accounts would expect. These investigations have yielded mixed results (Anderson, Keltner, & John, 2003; Butterworth & Rodgers, 2006; Caspi & Herbener, 1990; Epstein & Guttman, 1984; Gruber-Baldini, Schaie, & Willis, 1995; Huston & Levinger, 1978). Other research has shown that married partners who are more similar are more compatible and less likely to divorce, which suggests deselection may be one significant factor (Acitelli, Kenny, & Weiner, 2001; Levinger, 1976). Likewise, similarity is associated with satisfaction among premarital couples (Houts, Robins, & Huston, 1996) and dissimilarity seems predictive of break-ups (Hill, Rubin, & Peplau, 1976).

Evidence of romantic partner socialization can be found in longitudinal research examining continuity in behavior. A supportive, nondeviant adult partner can disrupt patterns of childhood conduct disorder, whereas a deviant one promotes its continuity (Laub, Nagin, & Sampson, 1998; Quinton, Pickles, Maughan, & Rutter, 1993; Werner & Smith, 2001).

HOMOPHILY IN ADOLESCENT ROMANTIC RELATIONSHIPS

Surprisingly, virtually no work has examined homophily in adolescent romantic relationships. For example, in Feingold's (1988) review of similarity in physical attractiveness of romantic couples, only 1 of the 34 studies used an adolescent population, and it was an unpublished conference presentation (Price, Dabbs, Clower, & Resin, 1974, as cited in Feingold, 1988). In fact, aside from this presentation, we have been unable to locate studies that examined homophily in adolescent romantic relationships.

Moreover, the literature on interpersonal attraction in adolescence is also quite limited and dated. Most of it comprises studies of characteristics perceived to be desirable in romantic partners. The factors listed as important for adolescent romantic relationships are intelligence and interpersonal skills, such as being friendly, relaxed, pleasant, considerate, dependable, and funny (Hansen, 1977; Regan & Joshi, 2003; Roscoe, Diana, & Brooks, 1987). Physical appeal, such as being sexually responsive or passionate or being well dressed, are also mentioned, especially for casual sexual partners (Regan & Joshi, 2003). Similarity to self and prestige factors, such as material wealth or social status receive lower ratings (Hansen, 1977; Regan & Joshi, 2003). Finally, adolescent females and males prefer a partner a little older than themselves, although males have a wide range of acceptability, being willing to go out with someone younger than themselves (Kenrick, Gabrielidis, Keefe, & Cornelius, 1996).

Such self-reports of preferences, however, have significant limitations. As one may discern from the preceding descriptions, they seem to be markedly influenced by social desirability; for example, adolescents list features such as being popular, having a car, and knowing how to dance as important for their peers' preferences, but not their own (Hansen, 1977). The typical questionnaire assessment of preferences also makes all characteristics artificially equally accessible and does not take into account the indirect influence of these characteristics on judgments of the likelihood of other less accessible characteristics (Feingold, 1992). Hence, self-reports are not necessarily accurate reflections of one's actual preferences. For example, women say that physical attractiveness is less important than men do, but this gender difference is much smaller in actual behavioral choices (Feingold, 1990). Additionally, behavior is determined by more than one's own choice. Most individuals may be attracted to particularly attractive, intelligent, wealthy, socially skilled individuals, but the limited number of such individuals may make one choose alternatives. One's own characteristics, social stratification, courtship roles, cultural constraints, and the approval or disapproval of others all make one's actual choices different from one's preferences (Feingold, 1992). Thus, the literature on ideal partner choices does not provide much information about actual interpersonal choices. And research has not yet examined the actual degree of homophily in adolescent romantic relationships.

Given the seeming universality of homophily in relationships (McPherson et al., 2001), it would be easy to suggest that such findings would apply to adolescent romantic relationships, and, in fact, we expected to find such homophily in the two studies reported subsequently. Yet there are reasons to believe that selection, socialization, and deselection processes may or may not be the same as in older relationships. Romantic relationships are new in adolescence, and youth are just learning what these relationships are like and may be more likely to experiment with them. Adolescence is the time for developing an identity and establishing autonomy from one's family. Having different kinds of partners could serve as a means of learning who you are and what you like in a relationship. It could also show that your choices and decisions are distinct from those of your parents. As a 12th-grade girl in one of our studies put it:

"He was 2 years older and so they didn't like the fact that he was more experienced than I was, and um. They don't know that I had a sexual relationship with him, but I think in a way that, that was me in a way, not, I mean I really didn't have much to rebel against. But I almost see it that way because you know a lot of my friends were dating and that you know, typically stereotypical nice guy you know the guy you wanna bring home to mom and. He wasn't really that and so it was kinda like my, my little rebel."

Adolescents may also select romantic partners on a different basis than adults would select partners as the relationships and their functions are different. In fact, adolescents report that they value different characteristics in a marital partner, romantic relationship, and casual sex partner (Hansen, 1977; Regan & Joshi, 2003).

With regard to socialization effects, one might expect them to have relatively little influence as adolescent romantic relationships are relatively short lived and do not entail the level of dedication or obligation that can develop in committed adult relationships. On the other hand, they are central features of adolescents' social worlds. Having such a relationship is quite desirable to most adolescents, and they may be more willing to do things or make changes to attract someone or keep a partner. Moreover, adolescents may be more likely to be influenced by a partner, because these are a new form of relationship in which they have less guidance or experience about what is and is not expected or reasonable. A romantic partner is the fourth most likely person to offer drugs but is second only to a family member in terms of being difficult to refuse; approximately one-half of the offers from romantic partners are accepted (Trost, Langan, & Kellar-Guenther, 1999).

Finally, the deselection process for adolescents may also differ from that of adults. Most adolescent relationships are not expected to endure; and in fact, adolescents may not want them to last forever. After all, most youth see adolescence as a time for affiliation, not a time for finding a marital partner. The factors determining dissolution may differ in relationships involving less commitment or obligation from those involving more commitment (Laursen & Jensen-Campbell, 1999).

All of these considerations underscore the importance of examining homophily in adolescent romantic relationships. In effect, the nature of homophily may not be the same as romantic relationships later in development.

A Study of Homophily in Middle-Adolescent Romantic Relationships

In one study, we examined the degree of homophily in middle-adolescent romantic relationship using data from Project STAR, a longitudinal study of romantic relationships, other close relationships, and adjustment. The participants in the overall project are 100 girls and 100 boys who were recruited when they were in the tenth grade (14 to 16 years old). By design, the sample's ethnicity sample closely approximated that of the United States; specifically, the sample was 70% European American, 12.5% African American, 12% Hispanic, 2.5% Asian, and 3% Other/Biracial. We recruited the participants from a range of schools and neighborhoods to obtain a diverse community sample. Consistent with our goals, the mean scores on most measures of adjustment, substance use, and sexual activity closely approximated the means of normative samples or large surveys.

The participants in Project STAR were not selected on the basis of their dating experience or relationship status. However, when they were seen for their yearly appointment or contacted by telephone at the 4- and 8-month interval between appointments, they were asked if they were in a romantic relationship of 3 months duration or longer. If so, the participant and partner were invited to come into a session to be observed interacting with each other.

During the first three waves of data collection, we collected observations from 83 participants. Some participants were observed more than once; in these cases, we used the questionnaire data about the participant and the partner he or she was first observed interacting with. The length of relationships averaged 10.79 months ($SD = 9.26$). The ethnic distribution resembled that of the larger sample.

We examined the degree of homophily in demographic characteristics, peer networks, and symptomatology. All were heterosexual relationships, and thus we examined the association between the girls' and boys' scores. We controlled for the influence of time of data collection as the data were collected over the course of the 3 years the participants were in high school.

Consistent with prior work on older couples, statistically significant homophily was found on several demographic scores (see Table 10.1). In particular, the girls and boys who were dating each other were significantly more likely to be from the same specific ethnic group and more likely to be the same in terms of ethnic majority/minority status. The girls and boys who were dating were also similar in socioeconomic status (SES), as measured by maternal education. Finally, they were similar in their own academic success as measured by self-reported grade point average (GPA).

Next we examined the degree of similarity in perceptions of peer relations (see Table 10.1). Their self-reported number of same gender friends and the number of other gender friends were significantly related.

TABLE 10.1. Homophily in Middle-Adolescent Romantic Relationships

Variable	Degree of correspondence
Demographic characteristics	
Ethnicity	.29**
Dichotomized Ethnicity	.40**
Maternal Education	.41**
Grade Point Average	.41**
Peer networks	
Number of Same Gender Friends	.42**
Number of Other Gender Friends	.45**
Symptoms	
Externalizing Scale	.23*
Internalizing Scale	.06

Note. Numbers are correlations between adolescent boy and girl scores, except for ethnicity which are kappas.
$*p < .05; **p < .01$.

Finally, we examined the degree of similarity in externalizing symptoms (delinquency and aggressive behaviors) and internalizing symptoms (depression, anxiety, and somatization) as assessed by the Youth Self Report (Achenbach, 1991). The externalizing scores of those dating each other were significantly correlated, but not their internalizing scores.

The significant relations in the couple's ethnicity and SES suggested that the homophily on the other characteristics could stem from demographic homophily. We reran the correlations controlling for the ethnicity of the boy and girl (dichotomized as majority/minority status). The correspondence in maternal education was still significant, but seemingly a little lower than when ethnicity was not controlled for ($r = .35$ vs. .40, respectively). The correlations, however, for GPA, peer network characteristics and symptoms were virtually identical to what they were when ethnicity was not controlled ($M r = 30$ vs. $M r = .29$, respectively). Similarly, when the maternal education of the two was controlled for, the correspondence in ethnicity was a little lower than when maternal education was not controlled for ($r = .33$ vs. $r = .40$, respectively), but the correlations for the other variables were essentially the same as they had been ($M r = .29$ and $M r = .29$, respectively). Thus, the homophily in these characteristics does not appear to be a result of demographic homophily.

The fact that homophily was found in the number of same and other gender friends suggested that the adolescent romantic homophily that was observed could stem from peer group or friend homophily. After all, adolescent romantic relationships are embedded in the general peer group context (Brown, 1999). Interactions with the other gender first occur in mixed-gender groups (Connolly, Craig, Goldberg, & Pepler, 2004); then dating begins, often in the company of other peers. Adolescents' peers monitor choices of partners, serving as messengers and matchmakers. A desirable choice may increase one's popularity, whereas an undesirable one may be sanctioned. Peers may promote romantic partner similarity along dimensions important to friendships and the peer group.

We were able to control for friend homophily because a close friend of the participant had also completed these questionnaires. Accordingly, we partialed out the corresponding characteristics of the participant's friends, when examining romantic homophily. The correlations on the demographic, network, and symptom variables were similar in magnitude to those when the friend characteristics were not controlled for ($M\ r$ = .32 vs. $M\ r$ = .34, respectively). In effect we found clear evidence of romantic homophily, and it cannot be attributed to demographic or friend homophily.

Homophily in Early-Adolescent Romantic Relationships

In a separate longitudinal study, V. A. Simon, Wargo Aikins, and Prinstein (2007) were able to distinguish selection and socialization effects in a sample of young adolescents. Using a longitudinal follow-back design, adolescents and their romantic partners were traced back to a prior data collection to examine prerelationship similarities. This strategy allowed for a relatively pure examination of selection effects, as neither adolescents nor partners identified themselves as being romantically involved at that time. Prerelationship similarities were then used to estimate the socialization effects of romantic partner characteristics on adolescents' psychosocial functioning after relationships were established.

The 78 young adolescents in this study were participants in Project ADAPT, a larger longitudinal study designed to examine developmental trajectories of psychosocial functioning during early and middle adolescence. To examine romantic partner selection and socialization, participants were selected from the larger school-based sample using three criteria: (1) all target participants were not in a romantic relationship at Time 1 (T1); (2) all target participants were in a romantic relationship between the first and second data collections; and (3) the romantic partners of target participants were also study participants. Only one partner within any romantic dyad was included as a target participant to avoid dependency in the data. This resulted in a data set in which each adolescent served as only target participant or as a romantic partner. At T1, romantic partners had not yet started dating each other, and all romantic relationships were initiated sometime before T2, with reported durations averaging 3.41 months (SD = 4.78).

At the beginning of the study, adolescents (48% female) were in the sixth (32%), seventh (35%), and eighth (33%) grades of a public school within a town of fairly homogeneous middle-class socioeconomic status. Per capital income of the town was $32,301, and school records indicated that 11% of students were eligible for free/reduced lunch. The ethnic composition of the sample also reflected that of the school district and included 87% European American, 2% African American, 4% Asian American, 2% Latino American, and 6% mixed ethnic background.

Data were collected in the school at two time points, 11 months apart. Sociometric ratings of popularity, physical attraction, body appeal, depressive symptoms, anxiety, peer aggression (relational and physical), and peer victimization (relational and physical) were obtained for participants and romantic partners at both time points using unlimited peer nomination procedures (Cillessen & Mayeux, 2004). Participants and partners also provided self-reports of depressive symptoms and anxiety at both time points.

To assess for the presence of romantic homophily, intraclass correlations between adolescents and prospective partners were calculated at T1. Significant prerelationship similarities were found between adolescents and their future romantic partners on peer popularity, attractiveness, body appeal, and depressive symptoms (self- and peer-rated). Intraclass correlations ranged from .25 for physical attractiveness to .59 for popularity and for self-reported depressive symptoms (all ps < .01). No prerelationship similarities were found for anxiety, peer aggression (physical or relational), or peer victimization (physical or relational).

Next, the influence of romantic partners was assessed by examining the influence of partners' prerelationship characteristics on participants' characteristics over time. A series of regression analyses were used to predict participants' functioning after relationships had begun (T2) from partners' functioning prior to the relationship (T1) after controlling for adolescents' own prerelationship functioning. This strategy is commonly used in studies of peer influence, where peer characteristics are typically examined as an additive effect. Significant partner effects are interpreted to reflect change in adolescents' functioning that is predicted by partner characteristics (i.e., partner influence). Lack of significant partner effects typically reflects the stability of adolescent functioning and a lack of peer influence. In this model, peers are presumed to influence all adolescents in a roughly equivalent manner. However, more recent conceptualizations characterize peer socialization as an interaction between characteristics of the socializing agent and the socialized individual (Dishion & Dodge, 2005; Duncan, Boisjoly, Kremer, Levey, & Eccles, 2005; Hartup, 1999, 2005). Accordingly, we examined romantic partner characteristics as a conditional influence that depended upon adolescents' and partners' prerelationship levels of functioning.

The additive and conditional influence of romantic partner characteristics were examined in a series of hierarchical regressions in which adolescents' T2 functioning was predicted from their own prerelationship functioning, romantic partners' prerelationship functioning, and the interaction of adolescents' and partners' prerelationship functioning. Dependent variables included adolescents' T2 popularity, physical attraction, peer aggression, peer victimization, depressive symptoms, and anxiety. The results of the analyses are presented in Table 10.2. Whereas selection effects were found for popularity, physical appearance, and depressive symptoms, socialization effects were found for all outcomes except physical appearance and self-reported anxiety. Hence, partner socialization effects may not be limited to characteristics on which partners are initially similar. Partners' prerelationship characteristics significantly influenced the stability of adolescents' functioning in all domains except physical appearance. Yet virtually all of the significant effects resulted from the interaction of partners' and adolescents' prerelationship functioning.

To understand the nature of the interactions, we conducted post-hoc analyses that examined the stability of adolescents' functioning from T1 to T2 when romantic partners were high $(M + SD)$ and low $(M - SD)$ on each of the dependent variables at T1 (Holmbeck, 2002; see also Aiken & West, 1991). For example, the post-hoc analysis for self-reported depression examined whether the association between adolescents' T1 and T2 depression scores varied by whether adolescents dated partners with high or low T1 depression scores. The results suggested that adolescents who were relatively low functioning prior to the relationship and who coupled with high-functioning partners tended to experience more change than their low-functioning peers who dated low-functioning partners. For example, adolescents who were low on popularity prior to the relationship and coupled with a partner high in popularity experienced more significant increases in popularity over time than their low-popular peers who dated low-popular partners. Similarly, adolescents who experienced high levels of psychosocial problems (i.e., depressive symptoms, anxiety, peer aggression, and peer victimization) prior to the relationship and who paired with partners with few problems tended to have fewer problems at T2 than similarly troubled adolescents who paired with high-problem partners. Figure 10.1 illustrates this pattern for the case of adolescents' self-rated depression. Ado-

TABLE 10.2. Summary of Hierarchical Regression Analyses Examining Main and Moderated Effects of Romantic Partner Characteristics on Target's Time 2 Outcomes

	PR attractive		PR popularity		SR depression		PR sadness		SR anxiety		PR anxiety		Physical aggression		Relational aggression		Physical victimization		Relational victimization	
	ΔR^2	β	ΔR^2	β	ΔR^2	β	ΔR^2	β	ΔR^2	β	ΔR^2	β	ΔR^2	β	ΔR^2	β	ΔR^2	β	ΔR^2	β
Step 1																				
T1 target participant (TP) functioning	.61***	.77***	.79***	.82***	.50***	.54***	.74***	.22*	.46***	.53**	.25***	.45***	.78***	.85***	.11**	.24*	.35***	.49***	.58***	.90***
Step 2																				
T1 romantic partner (RP) functioning	.00	.00	.01	.14	.01	.11	.03	.03	.00	.09	.02	-.16	.00	.10	.00	.77**	.01	.40**	.01	-.02
Step 3																				
T1 TP × RP Functioning	.01	-.08	.05*	-.22^	.04*	.24*	.14***	.74***	.01	-.11	.04*	.20*	.02*	.31*	.06**	.74**	.08***	.40***	.07**	.30**
Total R^2	.62***		.85***		.55***		.91***		.47***		.31***		.80***		.17***		.44***		.66***	

Note. At each step, ΔR^2 presented is for the step and β presented is for the final model. SR, self-rated; PR, peer rated; T1, Time 1 assessment.
*p < .05; **p < .01; ***p < .001.

214

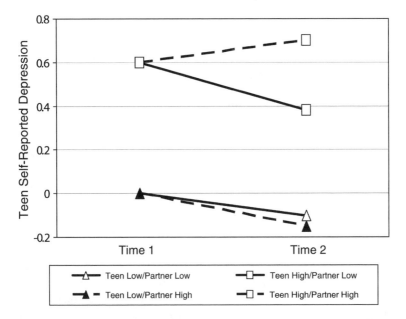

FIGURE 10.1. Graph of adolescents' self-reported depression at Times 1 and 2 by levels of adolescent and partner levels of depression at Time 1. Depression scores are reported as standardized scores. High depression at Time 1 $(M + SD)$ = .6. Low depression at Time 1 $(M - SD)$ = .0.

lescents' depression scores are plotted for T1 and T2 according to whether they and their partners were initially high $(M + SD)$ or low $(M - SD)$ on depression. Here it can be seen that adolescents who were initially high on self-rated depression and coupled with partners who were initially low on depression showed more significant changes in depressive symptoms over time than their equally depressed peers who dated high-depressed partners. These results suggest that high-functioning romantic partners appeared to exert greater influence on more poorly functioning youth.

Findings of positive change among youth who date high-functioning partners raise the interesting possibility that romantic partners may provide a mitigating influence on more poorly adjusted youth. Such consistent evidence of positive peer influence appears to be rare in the peer influence literature. Findings of stability among youth who date low-functioning partners could result from either symptom reinforcement or immunity to influence. Findings from studies of peer influence suggest that psychosocial problems thrive in dyads where both peers experience similar problems (symptom reinforcement), whereas high-functioning youth may be less susceptible to the influence of low-functioning peers (Adams, Bukowski, & Bagwell, 2005; Dishion & Dodge, 2005; Dishion, McCord, & Poulin, 1999). Although the current findings are consistent with this prediction, they do not assess the differential reasons for the stability findings. Uncovering the underlying processes for stability and instability will be an important task for future research.

INTEGRATING THE EMPIRICAL INVESTIGATIONS

Taken together, the two studies provide clear evidence of homophily in adolescent romantic relationships. Similarity was found on a range of different characteristics, including demographic characteristics, peer network characteristics, and psychosocial variables. The similarities in demographic characteristics, such as maternal education, ethnicity, and GPA are congruent with past work on adult romantic relationships and peer friendships (see McPherson et al., 2001). Such homophily could stem from either the social stratification of society or adolescents' preferences to associate with similar peers. The similarities in attractiveness and body appeal are consistent with the literature on matching of attractiveness in adult romantic relationships (see Feingold, 1988).

With regard to peer relationships, young-adolescent romantic couples were found to be similar in popularity, and middle-adolescent couples were similar in the size of their networks with same- and other-gender friends, which are also indicators of popularity. These findings support prior theoretical assertions that dating often occurs with those similar in social status (Brown, 1999).

Prior investigations have found evidence of homophily of aggressive and delinquent behaviors in friendships (Cairns, Cairns, Neckerman, Gest, & Gariepy, 1988; Haselager, Hartup, van Lieshout, & Riksen-Walraven, 1998). Just as adolescents may prefer peers who are similar in aggressive and delinquent behavior, they may prefer romantic partners who are similar on those features. Interestingly, homophily in romantic partners' aggressive and delinquent behaviors did not occur in the young-adolescent study. Physical and relational aggression are associated with perceived popularity in early adolescence (Cillessen & Mayeux, 2004; Rose, Swenson, & Waller, 2004). Similarly, bullies are also more likely to be dating in early adolescence (Connolly, Pepler, Craig, & Taradash, 2000). Being aggressive and engaging in mild levels of delinquent behavior (e.g. a "bad boy" or "bad girl") may make one an attractive romantic partner to most adolescents who are dating at an early age. If aggression were generally associated with attraction, matching on this characteristic may be less likely to occur. When more adolescents become actively involved in romantic relationships and aggressive and delinquent behaviors lose their general appeal, such behaviors may become differentially attractive as was found in the study of middle adolescents.

Homophily was also found in the internalizing symptoms in romantic relationships in early adolescence. Again, prior investigations have found evidence of homophily of depressive symptoms in friendships (Hogue & Steinberg, 1995; Stevens & Prinstein, 2005). Nondepressed individuals prefer to associate with other nondepressed individuals, whereas depressed individuals prefer other depressed individuals (Rosenblatt & Greenberg, 1988; Wenzlaff & Prohaska, 1989); apparently, this preference applies to romantic relationships as well as friendships. It is less apparent why this does not occur at both ages We believe that romantic partners are more likely to come from the immediate peer group during early adolescence than middle adolescence; if so, the peer group level effects on romantic partners may be stronger at the earlier ages.

It also appears that homophily in romantic relationships is somewhat distinct from homophily in friendships—at least by middle adolescence. One of the challenges for subsequent research will be to determine precisely what it is about romantic and peer experiences that lead each to have similar, yet distinct, associations with adolescents' psychosocial behavior. Moreover, it will be important for future research to take into account not only other peer relationships when examining romantic relationships, but also for studies of nonromantic peer relationships to take into account romantic relationships. Finally, it will be important to consider how particular instances of homophily may affect or be affected by other aspects of adolescents' social network

In the study of early adolescence we were able to between selection and socialization effects by examining the characteristics of adolescents before their romantic relationship had begun. In fact, we believe that this is the first naturalistic study to demonstrate that two adolescents in a romantic relationship resemble each other before the relationship has begun. As such, it provides an important extension of the experimental literature demonstrating that similarity is predictive of interpersonal attraction (e.g., Byrne, 1971).

As discussed previously, past research has used two strategies to find evidence of socialization effects. One approach has been to examine whether the degree of similarity is greater as the length of the relationship increases. The other strategy and the one used here has been to examine whether the interactions of partner and participant characteristics are predictive of change or stability in the participant. If the partner is different from the participant and is having a socializing effect, the participant should show greater change than if the partner were similar. Interestingly, when this later strategy has been used in investigations of committed relationships (e.g., Laub et al., 1998; Quinton et al., 1993; Werner & Smith, 2001), it seems to have been more successful than the typical study of examining changes in similarity as a function of length of relationship.

Moreover, studies of homophily may underestimate the socialization influences of romantic partners. Typically friends want their friends to behave in a similar manner as they do, but that is less the case in romantic relationships. For example, a boyfriend or girlfriend may want a partner to act more assertively in social contexts, because neither of them is particularly assertive, and the dyad would function better if at least one of them were. If the partner made such a change, the two would be less similar to each other. Even if the change were in the direction of making them more similar, the objective is typically not to make them similar per se. For example, one person may be careful about his or her appearance and may want a partner to be less slovenly, but the goal is usually not for the two to be similar in appearance per se. It is for the partner to be more careful about appearance. In fact, if the partner became even more careful about appearance than the one making the request, that may be even more desirable. In effect, we need to be aware that studies of homophily may underestimate the influence of a partner, and even when they do capture the effects (e.g. the two become similar), they don't necessarily depict the intent of the influence.

Although we are impressed by the influence such short-term romantic relationships may have, it is important to note that we do not know how long such influences last. In other words, some changes could reflect adaptations to a lifestyle that makes the romantic dyad function, but individuals may change back after a relationship has ended. Of course, such adaptations could have a significant impact on the course of their life; for example, being willing to engage in antisocial behavior for a partner could lead to incarceration. Sometimes changes may be lasting as well. In our romantic interviews, participants commonly discuss how they've changed as a consequence of relationship experiences. Work is needed to identify when changes endure and when they do not.

FUTURE DIRECTIONS

Multiple Influences of Romantic Relationships

In this chapter, we focused on how the characteristics of a romantic partner may influence an adolescent. Partner characteristics, however, are not the only way in which romantic experiences may have an impact on adolescents. The quality of the romantic relationship may affect the adolescent. For example, unsupportive relationships are linked to depression (Daley & Hammen, 2002). Similarly, specific events in romantic relationships may have an effect. For example, a romantic breakup is one of the strongest predictors of adolescent depression and suicide attempts

(Monroe, Rohde, Seeley, & Lewinsohn, 1999). Finally, the quantity of romantic experience may predict facets of social competence (Furman, Ho, & Low, 2007; Furman, Low, & Ho, 2007; Neeman, Hubbard, & Masten, 1995) and contribute to psychosocial development and adjustment (see Furman & Shaffer, 2003). At the same time, such romantic involvement, especially in early adolescence, is associated with poor academic performance, externalizing and internalizing symptoms, and substance use (see Furman, Ho, & Low, 2007).

Almost all of the work to date has focused on the effects of dating or romantic involvement, and we know virtually nothing about the effects of relationship quality, specific events, or partners. Not only does this void result in an underestimation of the influences of romantic experiences or facets of romantic experiences, but it may also lead us to misidentify the specific basis of the influence as these different facets are not likely to be independent of one another. For example, high-risk girls are more likely to date early, date older boys involved in problem behavior, have conflictual and unsupportive relationships, and become pregnant (Pawlby, Mills, & Quinton, 1997). Is their risk for pregnancy because of the timing of their dating, the characteristics of their partner, the nature of the relationships, or their own preexisting characteristics? Unless we simultaneously examine the role of all of these factors, we simply cannot determine which factors are primarily responsible.

In many respects, this point about romantic relationships is analogous to the idea that having a friendship, the quality of a friendship, and the characteristics of a friend may all be influential (Hartup, 1996). The point is particularly important for romantic experiences, however, as most (though not all) adolescents have friends and most friendships seem at least reasonably supportive, so understandably investigators studying friendships have focused on individual differences in the characteristics of the friend. In the case of romantic relationships, however, adolescents vary substantially in terms of whether they have a relationship and the quality of the relationship, as well as the characteristics of their partner. Thus, studying all facets of romantic experiences is particularly important.

Individual Differences in Selection and Social Influence

Work is needed on individual differences in selection, socialization, and deselection processes. For instance, simple main effects of partners were not found in the study of early adolescence. Instead, partner characteristics interacted with participant characteristics to predict stability. As an example, having a partner low in depressive symptoms made change more likely than having a partner who was high on depressive symptoms. Likewise, similarity, or certainly similarity on some characteristics, may be more important to some individuals than others. Some partners may be more influential than others, and some individuals may be more influenced. For example, rejection-sensitive individuals are more willing to engage in deviant behavior to keep their partner (Purdie & Downey, 2000). Boys are more likely to have an effect on girls' substance use than the reverse (Gaughan, 2006). The number of partners potentially available to an adolescent could also influence the selection or socialization processes.

In summary, this chapter presents some of the first evidence of homophily in adolescent romantic relationships. In some respects such evidence is not surprising in light of the seeming universality of homophily in relationships (McPherson et al., 2001). Yet the extension to adolescent romantic relationships is important given the typical nature of these relationships. They are new; they usually are short in length, and most adolescents would not want them to last them for a very long time. Yet similarity still seems to play an important role in these relationships. In fact, we found evidence of selection and socialization even in early adolescent relationships. And the homophily that does exist seems distinct from other homophily with friends. As intriguing as these findings are, they are just the initial step into a topic that may give us some clues into the factors that draw romantic partners together at different ages and their effects on people over time.

ACKNOWLEDGMENTS

Preparation of this chapter was supported by Grant 50106 from the National Institute of Mental Health (W. Furman, P.I.) and Grant HD049080 from the National Institute of Child Health and Human Development (W. Furman, P.I.). We thank Julie Wargo Aikins and Holly Escudero for their help with the data analyses. Appreciation is also expressed to Sarah Devine, Johanna Bick, Sharon Lewellyn, Lindsay Bannon, Alison Shainline, Annie Fairlie, Robin Carter, Daryn David, Carrie Hommel, Erica Foster, and the project staff for Project STAR and Project ADAPT for their assistance in the data collection of the projects. Thanks also go to the adolescents, families, and schools who are participating in Project STAR and Project ADAPT.

REFERENCES

Achenbach, T. M. (1991). *Integrative guide for the 1991 CBCL/4-18, YSR, and TRF Profiles.* Burlington: University of Vermont, Department of Psychiatry.
Acitelli, L. K., Kenny, D. A., & Weiner, D. (2001). The importance of similarity and understanding of partners' marital ideals to relationship satisfaction. *Personal Relationships, 8,* 167–185.

Adams R. E., Bukowski, W. M., & Bagwell, C. (2005). Stability of aggression during adolescence as moderated by reciprocated friendship status and friend's aggression. *International Journal of Behavioral Development, 29,* 139–145.

Aiken, L. S., & West, S. G. (1991). *Multiple regression: Testing and interpreting interactions.* Thousand Oaks, CA: Sage.

Anderson, C., Keltner, D., & John, O. P. (2003). Emotional convergence between people over time. *Journal of Personality and Social Psychology, 84,* 1054–1068.

Blackwell, D. L., & Lichter, D. T. (2004). Homogamy among dating, cohabiting, and married couples. *Social Quarterly, 45,* 719–737.

Brown, B. B. (1999). "You're going out with who?": Peer group influences on adolescent romantic relationships. In W. Furman, B. B. Brown, & C. Feiring (Eds.), *The development of romantic relationships in adolescence* (pp. 291–329). New York: Cambridge University Press.

Buss, D. M. (1985). Human mate selection. *American Scientist, 73,* 47–51.

Butterworth, P., & Rodgers, B. (2006). Concordance in the mental health of spouses: Analysis of a large national household panel survey. *Psychological Medicine, 36,* 685–697.

Byrne, D. (1971). *The attraction paradigm.* New York: Academic Press.

Cairns, R. B., Cairns, B. D., Neckerman, H. J., Gest, S. D., & Gariepy, J. (1988). Social networks and aggressive behavior: Peer support or peer rejection? *Developmental Psychology, 24,* 815–823.

Caspi, A., & Herbener, E. S. (1990). Continuity and change: Assortative marriage and the consistency of personality in adulthood. *Journal of Personality and Social Psychology, 58,* 250–258.

Cillessen, A. H., & Mayeux, L. (2004). From censure to reinforcement: Developmental changes in the association between aggression and social status. *Child Development, 75*(1), 147–163.

Connolly, J., Craig, W., Goldberg, A., & Pepler, D. (2004). Mixed-gender groups, dating, and romantic relationships in early adolescence. *Journal of Research on Adolescence, 14,* 185–207.

Connolly, J., Pepler, D., Craig, W., & Taradash, A. (2000). Dating experiences of bullies in early adolescence. *Child Maltreatment, 5,* 299–310.

Daley, S. E., & Hammen, C. (2002). Depressive symptoms and close relationships during the transition to adulthood: Perspectives from dysphoric women, their best friends, and their romantic partners. *Journal of Consulting and Clinical Psychology, 70,* 129–141.

Dishion, T., & Dodge, K. A. (2005). Peer contagion in interventions for children and adolescents: Moving towards an understanding of the ecology and dynamics of change. *Journal of Abnormal Child Psychology, 33,* 395–400.

Dishion, T., McCord, J., & Poulin, F. (1999). When interventions harm: Peer groups and problem behavior. *American Psychologist, 54,* 755–764.

Dowdy, B., & Kliewer, W. (1998). Dating, parent–adolescent conflict, and behavioral autonomy. *Journal of Youth and Adolescence, 27,* 473–492.

Duncan, G., Boisjoly, J., Kremer, M., Levy, D., & Eccles, J. (2005). Peer effects in drug use and sex among college students. *Journal of Abnormal Child Psychology, 33,* 375–385.

Eder, D. (1985). The cycle of popularity: Interpersonal relations among female adolescents. *Sociology of Education, 5,* 154–165.

Epstein, E., & Guttman, R. (1984). Mate selection in man: Evidence, theory, and outcome. *Social Biology, 31,* 243–278.

Erikson, E. H. (1968). *Identity: Youth and crisis*. New York: Norton.

Feingold, A. (1988). Matching for attractiveness in romantic partners and same-sex friends: A meta-analysis and theoretical critique. *Psychological Bulletin, 104,* 226–235.

Feingold, A. (1990). Gender differences in effects of physical attractiveness on romantic attraction: A comparison across five research paradigms. *Journal of Personality and Social Psychology, 59,* 981–993.

Feingold, A. (1992). Gender differences in mate selection preferences: A test of the parental investment model. *Psychological Bulletin, 112,* 125–139.

Feingold, A. (1998). Gender stereotyping for sociability, dominance, character, and mental health: A meta-analysis of findings from the bogus stranger paradigm. *Genetic, Social, and General Psychology Monographs, 124,* 253–270.

Furman, W., & Buhrmester, D. (1992). Age and sex differences in perceptions of networks of personal relationships. *Child Development, 63,* 103–115.

Furman, W., & Flanagan, A. (1997). The influence of earlier relationships on marriage: An attachment perspective. In W. K. Halford & H. J. Markman (Eds.), *Clinical handbook of marriage and couples interventions* (pp. 179–202). New York: Wiley.

Furman, W., Ho, M. H., & Low, S. M. (2007). The rocky road of adolescent romantic experience: Dating and adjustment. In R. C. Engels, M. Kerr, & H. Stattin (Eds.), *Friends, lovers, and groups: Key relationships in adolescence* (pp. 61–80). New York: Wiley.

Furman, W., Low, S. M., & Ho, M. H. (2007). *Romantic experience and psycho-social adjustment in middle adolescence*. Manuscript submitted for publication.

Furman, W., & Shaffer, L. (2003). The role of romantic relationships in adolescent development. In P. Florsheim (Ed.), *Adolescent romantic relations and sexual behavior: Theory, research, and practical implications* (pp. 3–22). Mahwah, NJ: Erlbaum.

Gaughan, M. (2006). The gender structure of adolescent peer influence on drinking. *Journal of Health and Social Behavior, 47,* 47–61.

Giordano, P. C., Manning, W. D., & Longmore, M. A. (2006). Adolescent romantic relationships: An emerging portrait of their nature and developmental significance. In A. C. Crouter & A. Booth (Eds.), *Romance and sex in adolescence and emerging adulthood: Risks and opportunities* (pp. 127–150). Mahwah, NJ: Erlbaum.

Gruber-Baldini, A. L., Schaie, K. W., & Willis, S. L. (1995). Similarity in married couples: A longitudinal study of mental abilities and rigidity flexibility. *Journal of Personality and Social Psychology, 69,* 191–203.

Hansen, S. L. (1977). Dating choices of high school students. *Family Coordinator, 27,* 133–138.

Hartup, W. W. (1996). The company they keep: Friendships and their developmental significance. *Child Development, 67,* 1–13.

Hartup, W. (1999). Constraints on peer socialization: Let me count the ways. *Merrill–Palmer Quarterly* [Special issue: Peer Influences in Childhood and Adolescence], *45,* 172–183.

Hartup, W. (2005). Peer interaction: What causes what? *Journal of Abnormal Child Psychology, 33,* 387–394.

Haselager, G. J., Hartup, W. W., van Lieshout, C. F., & Riksen-Walraven, J. M. (1998). Similarities between friends and nonfriends in middle childhood. *Child Development, 69,* 1198–1208.

Hill, C. T., Rubin, Z., & Peplau, L. A. (1976). Breakups before marriage: The end of 103 affairs. *Journal of Social Issues, 32,* 147–168.

Hogue, A., & Steinberg, L. (1995). Homophily of internalized distress in adolescent peer groups. *Developmental Psychology, 30,* 897–906.

Holmbeck, G. N. (2002). Post-hoc probing of significant moderational and mediational effects in studies of pediatric pupulations. *Journal of Pediatric Psychology, 27,* 87–96.

Houts, R. M., Robins, E., & Huston, T. L. (1996). Compatibility and the development of premarital relationships. *Journal of Marriage and the Family, 58,* 7–20.

Huston, T., & Levinger, G. (1978). Interpersonal attraction and relationships. *Annual Review of Psychology, 29,* 115–156.

Juhasz, A. M., Kaufman, B., & Meyer, H. (1986). Adolescent attitudes and beliefs about sexual behavior. *Child and Adolescent Social Work Journal, 3,* 177–193.

Kalmijn, M. (1998). Intermarriage and homogamy: Causes, patterns, trends. *Annual Review of Sociology, 24,* 395–421.

Kenrick, D. T., Gabrielidis, C., Keefe, R. C., & Cornelius, J. S. (1996). Adolescents' age preferences for dating partners: Support for an evolutionary model of life-history strategies. *Child Development, 67,* 1499–1511.

Klohnen, E., & Mendelsohn, G. (1998). Partner selection for personality characteristics: A couple-centered approach. *Personality and Social Psychology Bulletin, 24,* 268–278.

Larson, R. W., Clore, G. L., & Wood, G. A. (1999). The emotions of romantic relationships: Do they wreck havoc on adolescents? In W. Furman, B. B. Brown, & C. Feiring (Eds.), *The development of romantic relationships in adolescence* (pp. 19–49). Cambridge, UK: Cambridge University Press.

Laub, J. H., Nagin, D. S., & Sampson, R. J. (1998). Trajectories of change in criminal offending: Good marriages and the desistence process. *American Sociological Review, 63,* 225–238.

Laursen, B., & Jensen-Campbell, L. (1999). The nature and functions of social exchange in adolescent romantic relationships. In W. Furman, B. B. Brown, & C. Feiring (Eds.), *The development of romantic relationships in adolescence* (pp. 50–74). Cambridge, UK: Cambridge University Press.

Laursen, B., & Williams, V. A. (1997). Perceptions of interdependence and closeness in family and peer relationships among adolescents with and without romantic partners. In S. Shulman & W. A. Collins (Eds.), *Romantic relationships in adolescence: Developmental perspectives* (pp. 3–20). San Francisco: Jossey-Bass.

Lazarsfeld, P., & Merton, R. K. (1954). Friendship as a social process: A substantive and methodological analysis. In M. Berger, T. Abel, & C. H. Page (Eds.), *Freedom and control in modern society* (pp. 18–66). New York: Van Nostrand.

Levinger, G. (1976). A social psychological perspective on marital dissolution. *Journal of Social Issues, 32,* 21–47.

McPherson, M., Smith-Lovin, L., & Cook, J. M. (2001). Birds of a feather: Homophily in social networks. *Annual Review of Sociology, 27,* 415–444.

Monroe, S. M., Rohde, P., Seeley, J. R., & Lewinsohn, P. M. (1999). Life events and depression in adolescence: Relationship loss as a prospective risk factor for first onset of major depressive disorder. *Journal of Abnormal Psychology, 108,* 606–614.

Neeman, J., Hubbard, J., & Masten, A. S. (1995). The changing importance of romantic relationship involvement to competence from late childhood to late adolescence. *Development and Psychopathology, 7,* 727–750.

Newcomb, T. M. (1961). *The acquaintance process.* Oxford, UK: Holt, Rinehart & Winston.

Pawlby, S. J., Mills, A., & Quinton, D. (1997). Vulnerable adolescent girls: Opposite-sex relationships. *Journal of Child Psychology and Psychiatry, 38,* 909–920.

Purdie, V., & Downey, G. (2000). Rejection sensitivity and adolescent girls' vulnerability to relationship-centered difficulties. *Child Maltreatment: Journal of the American Professional Society on the Abuse of Children, 5,* 338–349.

Quinton, D., Pickles, A., Maughan, B., & Rutter, M. (1993). Partners, peers, and pathways: Assortative pairing and continuities in conduct disorder. *Development and Psychopathology, 5,* 763–783.

Regan, P. C., & Joshi, A. (2003). Ideal partner preferences among adolescents. *Social Behavior and Personality, 31,* 13–20.

Richards, M. H., Crowe, P. A., Larson, R., & Swarr, A. (1998). Developmental patterns and gender differences in the experience of peer companionship during adolescence. *Child Development, 69,* 154–163.

Roscoe, B., Diana, M. S., & Brooks, R. H. (1987). Early, middle, and late adolescents' views on dating and factors influencing partner selection. *Adoelscence, 22,* 59–68.

Rose, A. J., Swenson, L. P., & Waller, E. M. (2004). Overt and relational aggression and perceived popularity: Developmental differences in concurrent and prospective relations. *Developmental Psychology, 40*(3), 378–387.

Rosenblatt, A., & Greenberg, J. (1988). Depression and interpersonal attraction: The role of perceived similarity. *Journal of Personality and Social Psychology, 55,* 112–119.

Simon, R. W., Eder, D., & Evans, C. (1992). The development of feeling norms underlying romantic love among adolescent females. *Social Psychological Quarterly, 55,* 29–46.

Simon, V. A., Wargo Aikins, J., & Prinstein, M. (2007). *Romantic partner selection and socialization in early adolescence.* Manuscript submitted for publication.

Stevens, E. A., & Prinstein, M. J. (2005). Peer contagion of depressogenic attributional styles among adolescents: A longitudinal study. *Journal of Abnormal Child Psychology, 33,* 25–37.

Sullivan, H. S. (1953). *The interpersonal theory of psychiatry.* New York: Norton.

Thiessen, D. D., & Gregg, B. (1980). Human associative mating and genetic equilibrium: An evolutionary perspective. *Ethology and Sociobiology, 1,* 111–140.

Trost, M., Langan, E. J., & Kellar-Guenther, Y. (1999). Not everyone listens when you "just say no": Drug resistance in relational context. *Journal of Applied Communication Research, 27,* 120–138.

Wenzlaff, R. M., & Prohaska, M. L. (1989). When misery prefers company: Depression, attributions, and responses to others' moods. *Journal of Experimental Social Psychology, 25*(3), 220–233.

Werner, E. E., & Smith, R. S. (2001). *Journals from childhood to midlife: Risk, resilience, and recovery.* Ithaca, NY: Cornell University Press.

CHAPTER 11

Peer Influence in Involuntary Social Groups

Lessons from Research on Bullying

Jaana Juvonen *and* Adriana Galván

Youth associated with deviant or antisocial peers are likely to engage in disruptive or delinquent behavior (e.g., Berndt & Keefe, 1995; Fergusson & Horwood, 1996; Keenen, Loeber, Zhang, Stouthamer-Loeber, & Van Kammen, 1995; Lahey, Gordon, Loeber, Stouthamer-Loeber, & Farrington, 1999; Moffitt, 1993; Moffit & Caspi, 2001; Simons, Wu, Conger, & Lorenz, 1994). Although social influence processes are presumed to partly account for these robust findings, the specific mechanisms underlying the similarities between youth and their peers (i.e., homophily) are less well understood. Recent research on peer influence based on intervention studies (Dishion & Dodge, 2005; Dodge, Dishion, & Lansford, 2006) provides some insights into such processes (e.g., "deviance training"), but a number of questions remain regarding the ways in which antisocial behaviors become contagious within larger groups, such as classrooms.

In this chapter, we analyze within-group dynamics in involuntary social groups. By *involuntary social groups* we mean groups to which youth belong without having any choice over their membership. These include schools, classrooms, and most intervention settings. By focusing on involuntary, as opposed to self-selected groups (e.g., extracurricular clubs, friendships cliques), we are able to analyze emerging patterns of behavior that speak to what can be called "mere exposure effects," that is, how individuals are affected by the behaviors of some group members. Particularly relevant are questions about who is in the position to influence whom and which behaviors are most likely to become contagious.

Our analysis of the mechanisms of peer influence within involuntary social groups stems mainly from research on bullying or peer harassment (Graham & Juvonen, 2001). *Bullying* is defined as an imbalance of power between the perpetrator and the target: The bully abuses her or his power to intimidate the victim (Olweus, 1993) and the rest of the group. We propose that an imbalance of power within a group combined with unmet social needs of individuals wishing to belong to the group represent motivational "pulls" that can help us understand one set of mechanisms underlying peer influence.

Regardless of the form of bullying (name calling, physical aggression, gossiping), the very act of targeting a particular group member facilitates within-group conformity because of concerns and fears about one's own status within the group. Bystanders and witnesses rarely come to the aid of the victim but rather side with the bully to preserve their own status within the group (Salmivalli, 2002). This apparent tolerance of the bullying behavior therefore reinforces the actions of dominant perpetrators and supports the status hierarchy.

Attacks by dominant bullies combined with bystander concerns about their own status (and safety) give rise to social norms that do not reflect the private attitudes and feelings of most youth but nevertheless promote compliance within the group. Although little has been written about the social functions of bullying in this regard, research on related topics (i.e., teasing and gossip) is informative. Similarly to intimidating bullying tactics, teasing among friends (e.g., Eder, 1991, 1995) and gossip (Baumeister, Zhang, & Vohs, 2004; Eder & Enke, 1991) frequently involve commentary about what is not tolerated or accepted. For example, homophobic taunting and rumors about sexual behavior of peers guide the formation of norms for expressed sexuality. Gossip and teasing that focus on deviations or non-normative behaviors therefore help foster social norms. Similar dynamics are involved in bullying inasmuch as the bullying behavior targets specific stimuli (appearance, behavior) and threatens the targeted individuals' membership to the group. Unless other group members publicly challenge the bully, targeting of a particular person can promote false norms that then enhance the need for conformity or compliance within the group. Not all members of the group are similarly affected by norms promoted by bullying, however. As we discuss later, those who are not socially connected or who wish to gain in status are most likely to be influenced by within-group conformity pressures.

In sum, social dynamics involved in bullying can help us understand how social norms are formed and maintained within groups, and how perceptions of group norms, in turn, shape the behaviors of in-group members in ways that provide us at least one scaffold to understand mechanisms of negative peer influence. This approach represents a motivational analysis of peer influence that incorporates group- and individual-level processes.

Based on findings on bullying, three main theses help us understand which behaviors are likely to become contagious and who is in the position to influence whom.

1. To understand who is in the position to have influence over others, it is imperative to consider the social structure of the group. Particularly relevant is relative power or status of the group members and the behaviors associated with high status.
2. Identification of the within-group dynamics shaping the formation and maintenance of social norms is critical to gain insights about mechanisms underlying conformity pressures and increased homophily.
3. An examination of personal motives underlying peer modeling or emulation, in turn, can aid our comprehension of who is most influenced by whom.

These three main theses provide the structure for this chapter, which concludes with a discussion of further questions and prevention models.

SOCIAL STRUCTURE OF INVOLUNTARY PEER GROUPS

Some of the processes relevant to understanding bullying are similar to those established with research on nonhuman primates. Social groups (or troops) have social hierarchies established and maintained through demonstrations of power (e.g., Sapolsky, 2005). The maintenance of a dominance hierarchy not only serves the individual needs of the dominant leader but also protects the troop. By knowing everybody's place in the system, in-fighting is decreased and social order maintained (Savin-Williams, 1977); increased compliance fosters cohesiveness of the group and renders the troop stronger against potential enemies.

The social lives of young adolescents in schools are shaped by some of the same forces as other primates living in the wild. Youth are not born to a troop but are typically sent to a particular school based on where their families live. Adolescents rarely, if ever, have a say in their school or particular classroom. Smaller collectives (e.g., grade-levels or classrooms) within these institutions represent involuntary social groups, and the social hierarchies formed within such groups can help us understand who influences whom.

Organizations of Schools and Emergence of Social Hierarchies

Little is known about how the organizational features of schools affect the formation of peer groups, but it appears that lack of institutional or organizational structure facilitates the emergence and establishment of social structures and hierarchies. For example, the emergence of peer crowds, which are also hierarchically organized, is explained in part by high school students' need to master their social environment and their need to determine where they "fit in" (B. B. Brown, 1993). Hence, establishment of social hierarchies may become increasingly salient as youth transition from highly structured elementary schools (students are placed in self-contained classrooms with a fixed set of same age classmates and one primary teacher), to much larger and less structured middle schools where they have as many teachers and groups of classmates as they have subjects in their schedule (Juvonen, 2007).

Although middle schools are on average smaller than high schools and often rely more on organizational or instructional practices designed to help break down the anonymity and mass (e.g., teaming), social status hierarchies among students nevertheless emerge. Within the first few weeks of school, newcomers, that is, typically sixth-grade students, reach agreement about the dominance hierarchy within their grade. A consensus emerges concerning who are the "cool" or most popular kids and who are the ones with least status—the unpopular ones.

Consistent with primate research, those who abuse their power by intimidating others are perceived to be popular, whereas the submissive ones are unpopular in sixth grade (Juvonen, Graham, & Schuster, 2003). As shown in Figure 11.1, compared to students who are uninvolved (i.e., who do not have reputations of a bully or a victim), bullies are considered "cool" (cf. Gest, Graham-Bermann, & Hartup, 2001; La Fontana & Cillessen, 1998; Parkhurst & Hopmeyer, 1998), whereas victims are considered "uncool" (i.e., below the sample mean on peer nominations of "coolness"). Moreover, bully reputations are systematically associated with high social status over time. As shown in Figure 11.2, those identified as bullies based on peer nominations in the fall of sixth grade (Stable and Fall bullies) are concurrently considered cool. Whereas the coolness declines for the Fall bullies who no longer have such a reputation

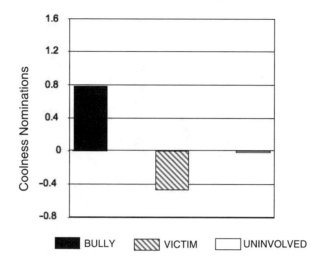

FIGURE 11.1. Perceived "coolness" in sixth grade.

during spring, the opposite is true for those identified as bullies during spring but not fall. Thus, status hierarchies are formed based on power or dominance, and one way to establish dominance is to resort to hostile means (Hawley, 1999).

Social Status and Power to Influence

Social ranking or status is associated with power to influence others. High-status individuals have social capital because they are looked up to and therefore are in the position to influence others (Prinstein & Cillessen, 2003; Prinstein, Meade, & Cohen, 2003). Cohen and Prinstein (2006), for example, showed that adolescent males emulated the risky responses (e.g., smoking marijuana) of high-status peers. Other work has also documented that engagement in risky behavior increases when individuals view the behaviors to typify high-status group members (Gibbons, Gerrard, Blanton, & Russell, 1998). Given the data on bullying and social status just presented, we presume that high-ranking bullies are also influential.

There are multiple reasons why high status individuals (whether they are bullies or not) possess power to influence others. By emulating the behaviors of dominant individuals, group members may increase their own social standing by appearing more like those in power (Moffitt, 1993). But when high status is associated with bullying, emulation may simply be self-protective. That is, by acting more like the domi-

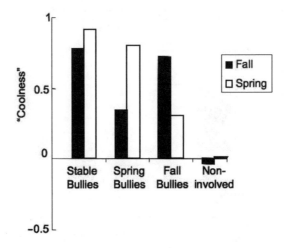

FIGURE 11.2. Changes in bullying status and "coolness."

nant individual, youth lower their risk of becoming the next victim and thereby protect (or even boost) their own social standing.

Recognition of the power structure of the group motivates group members to not only act like, or side with, the dominant individual, but also to avoid the lowest ranking members of the group. Adolescent males not only endorse the responses of the high-status peers, but they also distance themselves from the actions of their low-status peers (Cohen & Prinstein, 2006). Similar evidence is available from ethnographic research. For example, Kinney (1993) found that high school youth reject the attitudes and behaviors of low-status "nerds." Research on bullying, in turn, shows that peers deliberately distance themselves from victims of bullying, although these effects do vary by age and school context. When asked which classmate students "do not want to sit with during lunch at school," victim reputation was more strongly associated with social avoidance in middle school grades (i.e., sixth and eighth grade), whereas bully reputation become less strongly associated with avoidance to the point that the two were uncorrelated at eighth grade (see Figure 11.3). A desire to emulate high-status members and the need to avoid low-status individuals is socially adaptive for one's own status or ranking.

In sum, to understand who is in position to influence others, it is essential to consider the social structure of a group. Behaviors associated with high status are emulated, whereas characteristics linked with low status are avoided by those who wish to maintain their social status. Although high social ranking indicates the person's power to influence oth-

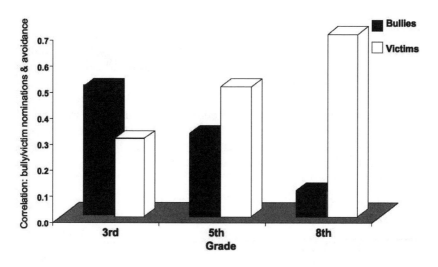

FIGURE 11.3. Bullies become less and victims more avoided by peers.

ers and bullying behavior is related to social status, it is not true that all influential group members engage in bullying. Bullying as a form of intimidation is simply one way to exert influence over others. Moreover, while behaviors of dominant individuals may be directly modeled by other group members, bullying also promotes perceptions of social norms that create compliance pressures.

FORMATION AND MAINTENANCE OF GROUP NORMS

The means that help someone gain and maintain high social status also shape group norms regarding acceptability of behaviors. The very characteristics targeted by bullying (clothing, body shape or size, demeanor, etc.) convey what is not tolerated by the members of this group. For example, Eder (1995) has demonstrated that in middle school norms about sexuality are enforced through the labeling of individuals as "sluts" and "fags." Even when the labels are incorrect, the process of gossip and ridicule reinforces notions about female and male sexuality. In other words, when someone calls a classmate a "fatso," the ridiculing signals the normativeness of body weight (i.e., "members of our group are not overweight"). Focusing on deviations or violations of social norms is an effective and informative way to foster conformity.

The mere witnessing of ridicule involving others heightens the observers' vulnerability, thereby increasing compliance to the perceived group norm, an effect labeled as "jeer pressure" (Janes & Olson, 2000). For instance, when witnessing someone else getting ridiculed for being gay, others are inhibited from displaying behaviors that maybe considered as signs of homosexuality. Thus, the potential threat that ridicule imposes on individual group members helps us understand the conformity pressures the intimidating behavior creates. The perceived reason or content of the derogatory remarks in turn conveys social norms, as suggested by research on teasing and gossip.

Teasing and Gossip as Methods to Reinforce Social Norms

Teasing and gossip are akin to bullying tactics: Teasing involves direct derogatory remarks about someone in the presence of others, whereas gossip entails spreading typically negative information about someone. These behaviors convey important information about what is not tolerated or accepted. By focusing on deviations from and violations of normative expectations, gossip and teasing help foster social norms that increase within-group conformity.

Although teasing can be conceptually distinguished from ridicule in terms of its intent (teasing with a friendly intent), the distinction can be made empirically mainly by the response of the target (Eder, 1995). If a comment "nice hair cut!" is met with a smile, the friendly intent presumably has worked. But if the target displays embarrassment or discomfort, the comment is construed as a derogatory remark about a bad hair cut. Thus, even the most well intended remark can be misconstrued as derogation. Therefore, the boundary between teasing and ridicule remains elusive.

Although bullying can serve similar functions as teasing, there are subtle differences in the ways the target is involved. Eder and Enke (1991) propose that teasing is an indirect method of enforcing social norms among group members by allowing marking of violations of norms without directly accusing someone. Hence, joking comments about the too-revealing nature of a shirt by one of the girls within a clique conveys not only to the target that she has "gone too far," but also reinforces the group's concern about its identity: "we don't wear clothes that are *that* revealing!" Hence, the content of the comments (teasing or more negatively intended bullying) provides insights into the group identity that bonds clique members together and possibly also separates them from other cliques. In bullying, the threat of exclusion is explicit and highly personal.

Gossip, like teasing, entails communication of valuable information about social norms (Baumeister et al., 2004). Moreover, participation in spreading of stories strengthens group members' social identity and sense of belonging within a group. Baumeister and colleagues (2004) demonstrated that those who spread rumors gain in social status because engaging in this activity conveys that the gossiper knows the rules that govern the collective. Hence, participation in gossip can strengthen and even elevate one's status within the group.

In sum, much like teasing and gossip, tactics used to bully peers often entail information about group norms. By targeting a specific individual within the collective, the perpetrator defines the "boundaries" of group membership and questions whether the target belongs to the group. Those observing such behavior are likely to modify their behavior out of the concern of becoming the next target. Bullying may therefore increase cohesiveness of the group—especially if no one challenges the bullying behavior.

Misperceived Acceptance of Norms Endorsed by Bullying

Bullying behavior rarely gets publicly challenged by peers and as a result, the apparent tolerance of this behavior reinforces what is unaccepted or "uncool" as well as supporting the impression that bullying is acceptable (Salmivalli & Voeten, 2004). When no one challenges the behavior of the bully, group norms that are not representative of, or necessarily even consistent with the private opinions and attitudes of its group members, are reinforced (Miller & Prentice, 1994a, 1994b). "Pluralistic ignorance" therefore arises when youth falsely assume that peers' behavior (i.e., noninterference with bullying) reflects their approval of bullying (Miller & Prentice, 1994b). Because of this misperception, the issue (e.g., being overweight) the bully attacks then comes to define the boundaries of group identity.

Some of the best evidence for pluralistic ignorance comes from research on college drinking. College students overestimate the level of alcohol consumption use among their peers (e.g., Baer, Stacy, & Larimer, 1991) and rate themselves as less comfortable with drinking on campus than the average student and other friends (Prentice & Miller, 1993). Individuals are more likely to engage in drinking because they think that is what it takes to belong to the group. When no one publicly questions the behavior, students behave in ways that strengthen their social identity and sense of belonging to the group.

Nonverbal cues also inadvertently enforce misperceived norms—that is, acceptance of negative behavior, such as bullying. When a student is being bullied, the witnesses might laugh or smile at the incident, as in the case of friendly teasing. (Indeed, the most frequently stated justification for bullying is "we didn't mean it, but just did it for fun.") The positive reactions on the part of the observers of bullying then further perpetuate misperceived norms of approval of the behavior. Similarly, if the target wants to hide or feign her embarrassment (e.g., not showing her vulnerability), the mere lack of negative response may prevent observers from intervening (cf. Salmivalli & Voeten, 2004). Recent data on sexual harassment of girls suggest that boys observing girls getting harassed by other boys do not come to the help of the girls because they do not want to appear overreacting to behaviors that seem not to bother the girls (C. S. Brown & Leaper, 2007). Hence, a false sense of acceptability of intimidation is fostered by the lack of negative reactions by the target and the subtle positive reactions by the observers.

Parents and teachers also contribute to the perceived acceptance of bullying by perpetuating the myth that youth need to develop a tougher skin and learn to defend themselves. Teachers convey this by not intervening with incidents (Juvonen et al., 2003). By not stopping the name calling or derogatory gesturing, the teacher conveys that the victim needs to learn to deal with such incidents by him- or herself. Student bystanders, in turn, can interpret the teachers' reluctance to intervene indicating that such behavior is not of concern. This interpretation further perpetuates misperceptions of the acceptability of bullying and the false social norms bullying promotes.

In sum, social norms conveyed through and about bullying are perpetuated by false assumptions. Peers witnessing bullying, victims, and nonintervening adults fail to communicate their private sentiments about bullying, subsequently encouraging bullying behaviors and enforcing conformity pressures based on partly arbitrary, if not false, group norms.

MOTIVES UNDERLYING PEER EMULATION OF BULLYING

Not all group members are affected by bullying and the norms that the behavior condones. Although humans have a need to belong (Baumeister & Leary, 1995), this need can be met in various ways. For example, some youth have less of a need to fit in within the parameters of the larger group (e.g., classroom) if they already possess high social standing within the larger group or if they are well connected to a smaller clique within the larger collective. In contrast, individuals whose social needs are not met (e.g., lower ranking individuals who do not have satisfying friendships) are particularly susceptible to the dynamics propelled by bullying. These are not necessarily friendless "losers" or socially inept youth (cf. Allen & Antonishak, Chapter 7). Anyone who is unsatisfied with existing social bonds or who strives to improve his or her status within group is more likely to conform to the group norms. If their skills are limited in enhancing their status, they may resort to bullying behaviors themselves. Unmet social needs therefore help us understand why bullying behavior increases especially at the times when reorganization of the social system is involved (e.g., when youth transfer to a new school).

Unmet Social Needs as an Impetus for Behavioral Changes

As mentioned previously, passive permission of bullying (e.g., not intervening) may be less about the endorsement of bullying and more about the need to protect one's social status. But it is also possible that those with unmet social needs emulate bullies as high-status members of a reference group with the hope of improving their social status (Cohen & Prinstein, 2006). This is not to suggest that adolescents want to become bullies per se, but perhaps they admire certain characteristics that bullies commonly possess: confidence, assertiveness, and dominance.

To test individual differences in the motivational "pull" that bullies have on changes in the antisocial behaviors of classmates, Juvonen and Ho (in press) examined peer nominations made by students in the fall of their first year in middle school. It was hypothesized that during this initial phase of social reorganization, students' sentiments toward bullies reveal their desire to emulate them. Two specific hypotheses related to the unmet social needs assumption were tested in contrast to the traditional peer socialization prediction. Consistent with the assumption that friends reinforce one another's behaviors, it was hypothesized that affiliation (indicated by reciprocal nominations of wanting to "hang out with") with a bully would increase antisocial behavior across grades six to eight. This prediction was compared with a prediction that unidirectional (unreciprocated) nominations would instead predict changes in antisocial behavior, inasmuch as youth are likely to modify their behavior to seek the company of someone who is not yet their friend. Additionally, it was predicted that students who consider bullies "cool" in the beginning of sixth grade are likely to increase their antisocial behavior as they try to fit in and behave according to the social norms conveyed by the dominant individuals of the group.

To test these hypotheses, co-nominations across particular pairs of questions were computed (cf. La Fontana & Cillessen, 2002). For example, the number of times the participants nominated the same classmate as engaging in bullying and as the one they wished to "hang out with" or considered "cool" or were summed to predict changes in antisocial behavior across middle school grades.

The findings revealed that the co-nominations of bullying and reciprocated nominations of wanting to "hang out with" (cf. mutual desire) did not predict increased antisocial behaviors, suggesting that if students already have a bully as a companion, they do not (need to) modify their own behaviors. In contrast, the unidirectional "want to hang out with" co-nominations with bullying predicted increased antisocial behaviors until the spring of eighth grade. That is, students who wanted to affiliate with peers who engaged in bullying in the fall of sixth grade became increasingly antisocial across the middle school grades. Also, the admiration of bullies (i.e., co-nominations of bullies and "cool kids") predicted increased teacher-rated antisocial behaviors by the end of seventh grade. In other words, students who considered bullies high in social status (i.e., "coolest") in the fall of sixth grade became more frequently engaged in antisocial behavior by the fall and spring of the following year. We suspect that those who believe that bullies have high social status are motivated to emulate the bullies as they seek to either establish or improve their own social standing during their second year in the new school.

In addition to modeling of high status or desired others, individuals with unmet social needs are more likely to explicitly do things that ought to help them be more included by peer groups (Willams, 2007). For instance, in one study, college students were either rejected or included by a social group and then asked to work on an idea-generation task with the same social group. They worked on the task either coactively, in which individual efforts could be easily assessed, or collectively, in which their efforts were unidentifiable and experimenters' evaluations would be spread across the group (Williams & Sommer, 1997). Individuals not rejected worked less hard collectively than coactively, the typical social loafing effect (Karau & Willams, 1993). Conversely, rejected females worked harder in the collective relative to the coactive condition, apparently to gain the group's approval. In another study, rejected participants were more likely to engage in nonconscious mimicry of a person with whom they spoke, especially if that person was an in-group member (Lakin & Chartrand, 2003).

But does emulation and modeling of high-status individuals earn a lower status individual social capital? Perhaps, as nonconscious mimicry has been shown to increase affiliation and rapport (Lakin & Chartrand, 2003). But this is not always the case; recent work has suggested that observed susceptibility to peer influence with a close friend decreases popularity over time (Allen, Porter, & McFarland, 2006). In other words, giving in to direct peer pressure is not valued by most adolescents (Allen & Antonishak, Chapter 7, this volume) and if done too frequently, one may be labeled a "pushover." This provides a paradox for the adolescent: how to convey "I think you're cool and want to be like you" to high-status peers without modeling everything they say and do.

In the case of bullying, by not objecting to or intervening with the behavior of the high-status bully, youth can have the best of both worlds: They do not risk their status by objecting to bullying, but they may not want to join in and engage in the activity either. Thus, there is a fine, but critical, line between overt conformity and skillful compliance. Research on self-presentation is relevant here inasmuch as it indicates how individuals manage others' impressions of themselves in a highly strategic manner.

Strategic Self-Presentation and Compliance

The focus of this section thus far has been on why adolescents with unmet social needs might emulate bullies. What about socially connected youth who do not necessarily have any unmet social needs? Socially connected youth, who possess skills to adjust their behavior according to the needs of the people they wish to get along with, are likely to resort to strategic self-presentation tactics to fit in (Baumeister, 1982; Leary & Kowalski, 1992). In other words, these youth can modify their behavior as needed (i.e., depending whom they try to impress or get along with) such that the way they behave in the presence of a bully is not necessarily consistent with their private beliefs. Interview data of middle school students reveal that although sixth-grade middle school students disapprove the ridiculing of "loners," they recognize that they themselves need to appear tough to fit in (Juvonen & Cadigan, 2002). Thus, some youth explicitly support or assist the bully to protect their public image and social status.

But how do they justify their negative behaviors? One reason accounting for the support of bullying concerns cognitive dissonance. *Cognitive dissonance* describes the uncomfortable tension that comes from holding two conflicting attitudes at the same time. For instance, an adolescent who privately disapproves bullying might not intervene with the ridicule her friend engages in. This tension between one's beliefs (e.g., bullying is not good) and positive sentiments toward the friend can undermine psychological balance (Schachter, 1951). This tension can be resolved by either explicitly criticizing or promoting the bullying behavior. When the need to belong is more critical than maintaining a private belief (e.g., sense of morality), youth are unlikely to challenge the friend's behavior. Going along with the friend is a strategic behavioral choice that enables youth to deal with conflicting demands. For these youth, behavioral strategies vary from one situation to the next. Hence, the bully has no long-lasting negative effects on the behaviors of socially connected youth.

Another reason teens passively encourage bullying is that they may not possess strategies for standing up for others in a manner that is socially acceptable among teenagers. In the previous example of a friend engaging in bullying, going against the friend jeopardizes the relationship. Not getting involved oneself but relying on others, in turn, would be considered threatening not only to the friendship but to one's public image. Reliance on others (e.g., informing a teacher about bullying) would be considered tattling—childish behavior that indicates dependency on adult authority (Juvonen & Cadigan, 2002). In light of these threats, it is easy to understand the "code of silence" that often is involved in long-term bullying incidents: No one wants to appear as a tattler. Hence, passive acceptance of bullying behavior does not necessarily mean that youth themselves come to initiate bullying. Rather, lack of "low-risk" strategies to challenge the behavior that one does not privately accept accounts for this apparent contradiction.

FURTHER QUESTIONS AND SOLUTIONS

In this chapter, we have analyzed negative peer influence in involuntary social groups. Specifically, we described research on bullying to exemplify how social structure, group norms, and personal motives influence emulation of antisocial behaviors. We have tried to respond to questions such as: Which behaviors are most likely to be modeled, and who is likely to influence whom and why? Unlike past writings on peer influence, we have proposed that these are motivational questions: Influence is a "pull" based on the imbalance of power within a group and unmet social needs at the level of an individual attempting to belong to the group. This motivational approach might help resolve some inconsistent findings on peer influence regarding the potential moderators of such influence (e.g., Hartup, 2005).

We began the chapter by arguing that considering the social structure of the group is critical to understanding who is in the position to influence others. Power or status of the bully is related to the amount of influence their behaviors have on others. We also contended that bullying (and the power associated with the bullies) serves a social function: by ridiculing those individuals who do not conform, bullying can shape and maintain group norms. Whereas most youth do not try to challenge the behavior of the perpetrator but rather passively encourage it, there are some who also more actively join in and emulate bullies. Preliminary evidence was provided supporting the notion that adolescents emulate high-status bullies because their social needs are not met. These findings suggest that emulation maybe motivated by the desire to improve one's own status or to connect with the "mighty." Finally, the apparent acceptance of bullying on the part of bystanders further promotes a norm that bullying is acceptable even when most youth privately condemn the behavior. These proposed mechanisms may therefore account for peer influence of bullying in involuntary social groups.

School Context and Imbalance of Power

Many questions remain. For example, how do the organizational features of schools (or lack of them) affect the formation of peer groups? In the first section of this chapter, we proposed that the relative lack of institutional or organizational structure (e.g., self-contained classrooms) in middle schools, compared to elementary schools, facilitate the emergence and establishment of the social hierarchy. The traditional developmental argument has been that peer group conformity peaks in early adolescence. Whether the conformity pressures depend on the developmental phase or on the structural or organization features of institutions in which youth reside at this phase (or both) deserve further examination.

One way to test such hypotheses is to compare adolescents in typical middle schools to those who reside in schools organizationally structured like elementary schools. Recent analyses comparing disciplinary records of sixth-grade students in elementary versus middle schools provide some indirect support for our prediction. Cook, MacCoun, Muschkin, and Vigdor (2007) found that sixth graders had higher rates of disciplinary infractions when the sixth grade was placed in middle as opposed to elementary school. Although the authors attribute the negative middle schools effects on the presence of older peers (who are more likely to engage in deviant behaviors), we postulate that in the case of incidents involving bullying, the need to establish a dominance hierarchy may account for at least part of the difference in disciplinary rates across the two settings. Hence, sixth graders in the new and expanding social environment misbehave more than sixth graders who remain in their elementary school, where there is no need to jockey for status.

But there surely are other features besides the size and classroom organization that are critical in determining whether disciplinary problems, including bullying, increase. Comparing middle schools and classrooms that vary in ethnic diversity, we find that African American and

Latino students feel safer, less bullied, and more connected in ethnically diverse schools (Juvonen, Nishina, & Graham, 2006). Given the heightened importance of ethnic identity, diversity is likely to promote multiple social norms (i.e., there is no one social hierarchy). Additionally, the numerical balance of power among groups (there is no one numerical majority group in diverse schools) may lessen to tensions related to power asymmetries.

The availability of multiple social norms offered through various groups and activities (e.g., specializations as part of a formal instructional plan or as part of extracurricular options) might be important in any school if the need to fit in within the *one* social hierarchy is diminished. Hence, bullying may serve less of a function—and therefore may not be as rampant—in schools that manage to promote multiple social norms such that all youth can find their niche and feel they belong.

Changing the Probullying Culture

Can anything be done in typical secondary schools that promote "the survival of the fittest" by remaining large, anonymous, and unstructured? Can the social dominance of bullies be decreased so that it does not promote false norms and compliance? We presume that bullying and its effect are pervasive when power matters, but in particular when bullies have an audience (Salmivalli & Voeten, 2004). Schoolwide antibullying interventions aim to change social norms that support bullying specifically by focusing on bystanders (Olweus & Limber, 1999). When bystanders are empowered to change the social dynamics, the acceptance of the behavior—and its negative ramifications on conformity—can be decreased (Salmivalli, Kaukiainen, & Voeten, 2005). By focusing on the entire social collective, school-wide antibullying programs empower students not only to defend themselves but also to stand up for others. Through the support of the behaviors that challenge bullying, the goal is to change the social norms that promote and maintain bullying. By changing the norms that support bullying, the compliance effects of bullying should then also decrease.

Most systemic antibullying programs start with consciousness-raising activities that help youth understand how subtle behaviors (e.g., standing around when someone is ridiculed, willingness to spread rumors, etc.) encourage bullying. Moreover, explicit teaching of strategies that help students deal with incidents is needed. Age-appropriate responses to bullying are often role-played and "face-saving one-liners" practiced with the guidance of teachers and other school staff (Juvonen & Graham, 2004). The shared awareness of a problem and collective support helps bystanders stick together. Thus, the socially uniting factor is no longer the concern for one's safety or status but the ability and confidence to object to the mean behaviors of peers.

Although programs based on these principles are promising (e.g., Olweus, 1993; Salmivalli et al., 2005), additional components are needed. For example, compared to younger children, adolescents are less frequently reminded by adults about the value placed on caring and kindness. Compared to students in elementary school, middle school students report it is less important to their parents that they do not make fun of peers or say mean things about others (Masten, Juvonen, & Spatzier, 2007). Compared to parents of elementary school-age students, parents of seventh and eighth graders are apt to talk less with their children about the need to get along with classmates. This lack of communication of values is interpreted by youth as indicating that these issues no longer matter. Yet parents (and teachers of older students) may simply not know how to convey their values in age-appropriate manner. Thus, communication of prosocial values in age-appropriate manner may enhance the effects of antibullying programs.

According to our analysis of bullying, the prosocial need to belong is met, paradoxically, by acting mean. Although this trend may be particularly salient during times of social reorganization as youth are acclimating to a new setting, the question is whether youth could be united by engaging in prosocial behaviors. Volunteer service programs (e.g., Teen Outreach Program) that enable youth to engage in helping others have been shown to be effective in decreasing problem behaviors and improving academic outcomes (Allen, Kuperminc, Philliber, & Herre, 1994; Allen, Philliber, Herrling, & Kuperminc, 1997). According to evaluations of middle school programs, relationships with peers (and site facilitators) are most effective in reducing problem behaviors (Allen et al., 1994). Unfortunately, these alternative means to meeting social needs of young adolescents are underutilized in today's large secondary schools. Hence, the needs of the most vulnerable continue to be met by resorting to antisocial behaviors.

REFERENCES

Allen, J. P., Kuperminc, G., Philliber, S., & Herre, K. (1994). Programmatic prevention of adolescent problem behaviors: The role of autonomy, relatedness, and volunteer service in the Teen Outreach Program. *American Journal of Community Psychology, 22*, 617–638.

Allen, J. P., Philliber, S. P., Herrling, S., & Kuperminc, G. P. (1997). Preventing teen pregnancy and academic failure: Experimental evaluation of a developmentally-based approach. *Child Development, 64*, 729–742.

Allen, J. P., Porter, M. R., & McFarland, F. C. (2006). Leaders and followers in adolescent close friendships: Susceptibility to peer influence as a predictor of risky behavior, friendship instability, and depression. *Development and Psychopathology, 18*, 155–172.

Baer, J., Stacy, A., & Larimer, M. (1991). Biases in the perception of drinking norms among college students. *Journal of Studies in Alcohol, 52*, 580–586.

Baumeister, R. F. (1982). A self-presentational view of social phenomena. *Psychological Bulletin, 91*, 3–26.

Baumeister, R. F., & Leary, M. R. (1995). The need to belong: Desire for interpersonal attachments as a fundamental human motivation. *Psychological Bulletin, 117*, 497–529.

Baumeister, R. F., Zhang, L., & Vohs, K. D. (2004). Gossip as cultural learning. *Review of General Psychology, 8*, 111–121.

Berndt, T. J., & Keefe, K. (1995). Friends' influence of adolescents' adjustment to school. *Child Development, 66*, 1312–1329.

Brown, B. B. (1993). Peer groups and peer cultures. In S. S. Feldman & G. R. Elliott (Eds.), *At the threshold: The developing adolescent* (pp. 171–196). Cambridge, MA: Harvard University Press.

Brown, C. S., & Leaper, C. (2007). *Sexual harassment among adolescent girls.* Manuscript submitted for publication.

Cohen, G. L., & Prinstein, M. J. (2006). Peer contagion of aggression and health-risk behavior among adolescent males: An experimental investigation of effects on public conduct and private attitudes. *Child Development, 77*, 967–983.

Cook, P. J., MacCoun, R., Muschkin, C., & Vigdor, J. (2007). *Should sixth grade be in elementary or middle school?: An analysis of grade configuration and students behavior* (Working papers series: SAN07-01). Durham, NC: Duke University, Terry Sanford Institute of Public Policy.

Dishion, T. J., & Dodge, K. A. (2005). Peer contagion in interventions for children and adolescents: Moving towards an understanding of the ecology and dynamics of change. *Journal of Abnormal Child Psychology, 33*, 395–400.

Dodge, K. A., Dishion, T. J., & Lansford, J. E. (Eds.). (2006). *Deviant peer influences in programs for youth: Problems and solutions.* New York: Guilford Press.

Eder, D. (1991). The role of teasing in adolescent peer culture. *Sociological Studies of Child Development, 4*, 181–197.

Eder, D. (1995). *School talk: Gender and adolescent school culture.* Mahwah, NJ: Erlbaum.

Eder, D., & Enke, J. L. (1991). The structure of gossip: Opportunities and constraints on collective expression among adolescents. *American Sociological Review, 56*, 494–508.

Fergusson, D. M., & Horwood, L. J. (1996). The role of adolescent peer affiliations in the continuity between childhood behavioral adjustment and juvenile offending. *Journal of Abnormal Child Psychology, 24*, 205–221.

Gest, S. D., Graham-Bermann, S. A., & Hartup, W. W. (2001). Peer experience: Common and unique features of friendships, network centrality, and sociometric status. *Social Development, 10*, 23–40.

Gibbons, F. X., Gerrard, M., Blanton, H., & Russell, D. W. (1998). Reasoned action and social reaction: Willingness and intention as independent predictors of health risk. *Journal of Personality and Social Psychology, 74*, 1164–1181.

Graham, S., & Juvonen, J. (2001). An attributional approach to peer victimization. In J.

Juvonen & S. Graham (Eds.), *Peer harassment in school: The plight of the vulnerable and victimized* (pp. 44–72). New York: Guilford Press.

Hawley, P. (1999). The ontogenesis of social dominance: A strategy-based evolutionary perspective. *Developmental Review, 19,* 97–132.

Hartup, W. W. (2005). Peer interaction: What causes what? *Journal of Abnormal Child Psychology, 33,* 387–394.

Janes, L. M., & Olson, J. M. (2000). Jeer pressure: the behavioral effects of observing ridicule of others. *Personality and Social Psychology Bulletin, 26,* 474–485.

Juvonen, J. (2007). Reforming middle schools: Focus on continuity, social connectedness, and engagement. *Educational Psychologist, 42,* 197–208.

Juvonen, J., & Cadigan, J. (2002). Social determinants of public behavior of middle school youth: Perceived peer norms and need to be accepted. In F. Pajares & T. Urdan (Eds.), *Adolescence and education: Vol. 2. Academic motivation of adolescents* (pp. 277–297). Greenwich, CT: Information Age.

Juvonen, J., & Graham, S. (2004). Research-based interventions on bullying. In C. E. Sanders & G. D. Phye (Eds.), *Bullying: Implications for the classroom* (pp. 229–255). San Diego, CA: Academic Press.

Juvonen, J., Graham, S., & Schuster, M. (2003). Bullying among young adolescents: The strong, weak, and troubled. *Pediatrics, 112,* 1231–1237.

Juvonen, J., & Ho, A. (in press). The motivating "pull" of bullies increasing antisocial behaviors across middle school grades. *Journal of Youth and Adolescence.*

Juvonen, J., & Murdock, T. B. (1997). *A cross-sectional analysis of peer reactions to bullying and victimization in school.* Unpublished manuscript.

Juvonen, J., Nishina, A., & Graham, S. (2006). Ethnic diversity and perceptions of safety in urban middle schools. *Psychological Science, 17,* 393–400.

Karau, S. J., & Williams, K. D. (1993). Social loafing: A meta-analytic review and theoretical integration. *Journal of Personality and Social Psychology, 65,* 681–706.

Keenen, K., Loeber, R., Zhang, Q., Stouthamer-Loeber, M., & Van Kammen, W. B. (1995). The influence of deviant peers on the development of boy's disruptive and delinquent behavior: A temporal analysis. *Development and Psychopathology, 7,* 715–726.

Kinney, D. A. (1993). From nerds to normals: The recovery of identity among adolescents from middle school to high school. *Sociology of Education, 66,* 21–40.

La Fontana, K. M., & Cillessen, A. H. N. (1998). The nature of children's stereotypes of popularity. *Social Development, 7,* 301–320.

LaFontana, K. M., & Cillessen, A. H. N. (2002). Children's perceptions of popular and unpopular peers: A multi-method assessment. *Developmental Psychology, 38,* 635–647.

Lahey, B. B., Gordon, R. A., Loeber, R., Stouthamer-Loeber, M., & Farrington, D. P. (1999). Boys who join gangs: A prospective study of predictors of gang entry. *Journal of Abnormal Child Psychology, 27,* 261–276.

Lakin, J. L., & Chartrand, T. L. (2003). Using nonconscious mimicry to create affiliation and rapport. *Psychological Science, 14,* 334–339.

Leary, M. R., & Kowalski, R. M. (1992). Impression management: A literature review and a two-component model. *Psychological Bulletin, 107,* 34–47.

Masten, C. L., Juvonen, J., & Spatzier, A. (2007). *Relative importance of parents and peers: Differences in academic and social behaviors during early adolescence.* Manuscript submitted for publication.

Miller, D. T., & Prentice, D. A. (1994a). Collective errors and errors about the collective. *Personality and Social Psychology Bulletin, 20,* 541–550.

Miller, D. T., & Prentice, D. A. (1994b). The self and the collective. *Personality and Social Psychology Bulletin, 20,* 451–453.

Moffitt, T. E. (1993). Adolescence-limited and life-course-persistent antisocial behavior: A developmental taxonomy. *Psychological Review, 100,* 674–701.

Moffitt, T. E., & Caspi, A. (2001). Childhood predictors differentiate life-course persistent and adolescence-limited antisocial pathways among males and females. *Developmental Psychopathology, 13,* 355–375.

Olweus, D. (1993). *Bullying at school: What we know and what we can do.* Cambridge, MA: Blackwell.

Olweus, D., & Limber, S. (1999). The bullying prevention program. In D. S. Elliott (Series Ed.), *Blueprints for violence prevention.* Boulder: University of Colorado, Center for the Study and Prevention of Violence, Institute of Behavioral Science. Available at *http://www.colorado.edu/cspv/blueprints/model/programs/BPP.html*

Parkhurst, J. T., & Hopmeyer, A. (1998). Sociometric popularity and peer-perceived popularity: Two distinct dimensions of peer status. *Journal of Early Adolescence, 18,* 125–144.

Prentice, D. A., & Miller, D. T. (1993). Pluralistic ignorance and alcohol use on campus: Some consequences of misperceiving the norm. *Journal of Personality and Social Psychology, 64,* 243–256.

Prinstein, M. J., & Cillessen, A. H. N. (2003). Forms and functions of adolescent peer aggression associated with high levels of peer status. *Merrill–Palmer Quarterly, 49,* 310–342.

Prinstein, M. J., Meade, C. S., & Cohen, G. L. (2003). Adolescent oral sex, peer popularity, and perceptions of best friends' sexual behavior. *Journal of Pediatric Psychology, 28,* 243–249.

Salmivalli, C. (2002). Group view of victimization: Empirical findings and their implications. In J. Juvonen & S. Graham (Eds.), *Peer harassment in school: The plight of the vulnerable and victimized* (pp. 398–419). New York: Guilford Press.

Salmivalli, C., Kaukiainen, A., & Voeten, M. (2005). Anti-bullying intervention: Implementation and outcome. *British Journal of Educational Psychology, 75,* 465–487.

Salmivalli, C., & Voeten, M. (2004). Connections between attitudes, group norms, and behaviour in bullying situations. *International Journal of Behavioral Development, 28,* 246–258.

Sapolsky, R. M. (2005). The influence of social hierarchy on primate health. *Science, 308,* 648–652.

Savin-Williams, R. C. (1977). Dominance in a human adolescent group. *Animal Behaviour, 25,* 400–406.

Schachter, S. (1951). Deviation, rejection, and communication. *Journal of Abnormal and Social Psychology, 46,* 190–207.

Simons, R. L., Wu, C., Conger, R. D., & Lorenz, F. O. (1994). Two routes to delinquency: Differences in the impact of parenting and deviant peers for early versus late starters. *Criminology, 32,* 247–275.

Williams, K. D. (2007). Ostracism. *Annual Review of Psychology, 58,* 425–452.

Williams, K. D., & Sommer, K. L. (1997). Social ostracism by one's coworkers: Does rejection lead to loafing or compensation? *Personality and Social Psychology Bulletin, 23,* 693–706.

Index

Page numbers followed by *f* indicate figure, *t* indicate table